Alfred Bishop Mason

The Constitutional Law of the United States of America

Alfred Bishop Mason

The Constitutional Law of the United States of America

ISBN/EAN: 9783337233181

Printed in Europe, USA, Canada, Australia, Japan

Cover: Foto ©Suzi / pixelio.de

More available books at **www.hansebooks.com**

THE CONSTITUTIONAL LAW

OF THE

UNITED STATES OF AMERICA.

BY
Dr. H. von HOLST,
PRIVY COUNCILOR AND PROFESSOR IN THE UNIVERSITY OF FREIBURG.

AUTHORIZED EDITION.

TRANSLATED BY
ALFRED BISHOP MASON.

CHICAGO, ILL.:
CALLAGHAN & COMPANY.
1887.

PREFACE.

This treatise on the constitution of the United States is but a sketch. I, this time, could not attempt to write a more pretentious work, for it was to form part of Marquardsen's "Handbuch des Oeffentlichen Rechts." Editor and publisher had to insist upon it that I, like all the other contributors, consented to being bound by contract not to exceed a certain number of pages. Though they afterwards kindly allowed me nearly double the space originally agreed upon, yet no sooner had I dipped my pen into the inkstand than it became evident that even the most essential questions had to be treated with a brevity which more than once sorely tried my temper. Questions of less importance, though, too, of considerable interest, had to be compressed into a still smaller compass, and many a point which had found a place in my preparatory notes had to be thrown out entirely.

The difficulty in deciding what to retain and what to let go by the board, how much space to allow to each question and — last, not least — how to treat them, was greatly increased by the consideration that I was to write for European readers. Even the foremost American authors could serve me but to a very limited extent as models, because they have all written for Americans, while my task was not to be the instructor of those who are to the manor born, but the *cicerone* of strangers. These having but little time to spare, and their interest in the subject being but limited and quite unconnected with any practical purposes, they expect to be shown what from their standpoint merits the most attention. Besides, everything has to be presented in such a manner that they can really understand what they see — in this case by no means an easy task, for even educated Europeans frequently show an astonishing talent for misunderstanding the most lucid expositions of American institutions and their working.

It is not necessary further to enlarge upon these points, for what I have said is sufficient to show why the first inquiries with regard to a translation of the treatise were not received by me with a feeling of unmixed satisfaction. I not only could have dived deeper, and would have done so, if I had intended to write for Americans, but even if I had confined myself to a mere sketch, the perspective would have been somewhat different. Besides, the treatise had to be written at a time when I could not go either to England or the United States. My only literary resources were my private library and the notes previously taken in the British Museum and American libraries.

These statements I have had to make in justice to myself as a scholar and an author. To clear the way for a new book by explanations which have a rather strong flavor of excuses will, however, never be exactly to the liking of an author who thinks that he has any reputation to lose. Nevertheless I have concluded, upon more mature reflection, to give my formal assent to having the treatise translated, trusting that the American public will deal with it not only fairly but with the same kindness with which they have received my other and more pretentious writings. I, of course, do not expect to see it in the hands of lawyers arguing constitutional questions before court, or of statesmen busying themselves in congress to manufacture new constitutional nuts for judges, counselors and publicists to crack. But the juniors and seniors of the colleges, and perhaps even the students of the law schools, may find it quite a handy guide in the pursuit of their studies on the public law of their country. Nay, I am bold enough to hope that, as a convenient book of reference, if as nothing else, it will render some good services in the hands of men who have in no professional way anything to do with constitutional law, but are fully conscious how important it is that the citizen of a democratic republic stands on his own legs with regard to the public law of his country, instead of having implicitly to rely upon the wisdom of his daily paper and any stump speaker whom he may chance to hear.

H. VON HOLST.

FREIBURG, i. B., June 4, 1886.

[The translator has been aided in his work by Mr. O. J. Heyne.]

CONTENTS.

	Page.
PART I. GENESIS OF THE CONSTITUTION....	1
PART II. THE FEDERAL CONSTITUTION	36
PART III. CONSTITUTIONAL AND GENERAL LAW OF THE SEPARATE STATES.................................	263
APPENDIX: THE CONSTITUTION, WITH NOTES...................	337
INDEX......................	361

THE CONSTITUTIONAL LAW

OF

THE UNITED STATES OF AMERICA.

PART FIRST.

GENESIS OF THE FEDERAL CONSTITUTION.

AUTHORITIES. Peter Force: *American Archives*, 9 vols., Wash., 1833-37. *The Journals of Congress from 1774 to 1788*, 13 vols., Phila., 1777-88 (4 vols., Wash., 1823). *Secret Journals of the Acts and Proceedings of Congress from the First Meeting thereof to the Dissolution of the Confederation by the Adoption of the Constitution of the United States*, 4 vols., Boston, 1821. J. Elliot: *The Debates in the several State Conventions on the Adoption of the Federal Constitution as Recommended by the General Convention at Philadelphia in 1787, together with the Journal of the Federal Convention, Luther Martin's Letter, Gates's Minutes, Congressional Opinions, Virginia and Kentucky Resolutions of '98 and '99, and other Illustrations*, 5 vols., Phila., 1861. *Journals, Acts and Proceedings of the Convention assembled at Philadelphia which framed the Constitution of the United States*, Boston, 1819. *The Federalist* (H. B. Dawson's edition, 2 vols., Morrisania, 1864).

The Works of Benjamin Franklin, 10 vols., Phila., 1840. *The Works of John Adams*, 10 vols., Boston, 1856. *The Writings of George Washington*, 12 vols., New York, 1852. *The Writings of Thomas Jefferson*, 9 vols., Wash., 1853. *Letters and other Writings of James Madison*, 4 vols., Phila., 1865. *The Works of Alexander Hamilton*, 7 vols., New York, 1851. *The Works of Fisher Ames*, 2 vols., New York, 1869.

Sherman: *The Governmental History of the United States of America from the Earliest Settlement to the Adoption of the Consti-*

tution, Phila., 1860. R. Frothingham: *The Rise of the Republic of the United States*, Boston, 1872. G. Bancroft: *History of the United States, from the Discovery of the American Continent to the Close of the Revolutionary War*, 10 vols., Boston, 1834-74. G. Bancroft: *History of the Formation of the Constitution of the United States of America*, 2 vols., New York, 1882. R. Hildreth: *History of the United States from the Discovery of America to the End of the Sixteenth Congress*, 6 vols., New York, 1879 (new edition). G. Tucker: *The History of the United States from their Colonization to the End of the Twenty-Sixth Congress in 1841*. J. Grahame: *The History of the Rise and Progress of the United States of North America from their Colonization till the Declaration of Independence*, 4 vols., Phila., 1845. T. Pitkin: *A Political and Civil History of the United States of America from their Commencement to the Close of the Administration of Washington, including a Summary of the Political and Civil State of the New England Colonies Prior to that Period*, 2 vols., New Haven, 1828. H. Von Holst: *Verfassung und Demokratie der Vereinigten Staaten von America*, I. Theil, Düsseldorf, 1873 (*Von Holst's Constitutional History of the United States of America*. Vol. I., translated by John J. Lalor and Alfred Bishop Mason, Callaghan & Co., Chicago, 1877). G. T. Curtis: *History of the Constitution*, 2 vols., New York, 1863.[1]

§ 1. IN GENERAL. Like every constitution which has or can have a real life, that of the United States of America is a result of actual circumstances of the past and the present, and not a product of abstract political theorizing. It can therefore be understood and rightly judged only from the standpoint of the history of the development of the country. A knowledge of the facts of its origin is not, however, sufficient to understand and to judge it.

[1] For lack of space, I cannot enumerate many important biographies. Unfortunately, I must abandon the idea of specifying the books (their number is by no means small) which lay claim to scientific treatment of their subjects, which, while of service on this or that point, are in general either worthless or are crammed full of stupid blunders. Books once named are not repeated in subsequent lists of authorities. In the case of current official publications (laws, stenographic reports of the debates of congress, etc.) I do not give the number of volumes.

For, since the life of the people is the basis of the constitution, and undergoes a steady development, the constitution itself, quite apart from any formal alterations, must have a certain capacity for change, and this not the less real because there is no formal statement of it in the instrument itself. A constitution which resembles a Chinese shoe can suit only a nation that has sunk into Chinese inertia. The fundamental law of a state must have, without hurt to its firmness, enough elasticity to be able to meet fully every new development of national needs, without, however, either breaking loose from its general framework, or subjecting this to sudden change. The real essence of the constitution, as it takes concrete shape in legislation, must grow and change with the advancing public and private life of the people. Thus it is always in a steady process of development. This is an absolutely essential element in forming a judgment upon it, but is wholly ignored when it is interpreted simply by the rules which are binding upon judges in the application of ordinary statutory law to cases before them. These rules, indeed, are of full force in regard to the fundamental law, but the latter must nevertheless always be read, considered and criticised by the light of history.[1] If the statesman is bound to be, in the practical discharge of his duties, a conscientious jurist, the jurist must, in his work of examination and testing, always keep in mind the point of view of the statesman.

§ 2. History of the Origin of the Union.— The Articles of Confederation. The English colonies which changed themselves, July 4, 1776, into the United States of America had always — with the exception of the Dutch period of New Amsterdam (New York) — had an indi-

[1] Pomeroy: *An Introduction to the Constitutional Law of the United States*, §§ 18-21.

rect legal relation to each other, because they were all subject to the political control of the same mother-country. But quite apart from this, some among them very early established closer ties with one another. The contiguous territory of the colonies and the equality in outward conditions of life among the colonists developed a community of interests which grew steadily both broad and deep, and at last necessarily became stronger than the bonds of law which knit the separate colonies to the mother-land. On the other hand, the political and social organization of the different colonies took such different shapes, and the sparseness of the population and insufficient means of communication did so much to promote separate development, that from the very beginning of these gropings after union a tendency to limit the union at any rate to what was absolutely necessary showed itself clearly. The wishes and struggles of the people for political union did not hurry ahead of the development of actual circumstances. At the most they kept step with this development. Often they hobbled behind it slowly and unwillingly. The league of the united colonies of New England,— Massachusetts, Plymouth, Connecticut and New Haven,— in 1643 against the Indians and the Dutch, lost all significance with the occasion which had called it into life. After its unwept death decades passed by before there were any noteworthy signs of the existence of a wish to frame a new, broader and closer alliance. Outside enemies again gave the impulse, and the mother-country took the initiative. On account of the threatened war with France a congress was called at Albany in 1754, at which New Hampshire, Massachusetts, Rhode Island, Connecticut, New York, Pennsylvania and Maryland were represented. But while England expected to gain by this only more assurance of the safety of the colonies, and desired especially the establishment of a good understanding with the Indians, the representatives of the colonies were excited by thoughts of a permanent league with correspondingly wide aims.[1] Their suggestions, however, not only were received with no favor by the English government, but were rejected by all the colonial legislatures, without exception. The strife with the mother-country over the right of parliament to lay taxes on the colonies first made the latter see that their deepest interests made their firm alliance an imperative necessity. Nine colonies were represented at the congress at New York in October, 1765, which was answered by the repeal of the Stamp-act. The more the conflict took the shape of a revolution, the more overwhelming became the conviction that there was no longer a struggle between a number of like-minded colonists and the mother-country over a greater or less share of political rights, but that in fact against European England an America was arrayed. The more the colonies adapted their acts to this fact, the more they were impressed with the other fact, that just so far as they were conscious of belonging to each other, they were forced into a position apart from the rest of the world. They could not make simply *ad hoc* an offensive and defensive alliance, if the common weal was to be victoriously won, but at this time, long before the swing of mind and spirit had reached its highest point, every suggestion of a complete fusion was rejected decisively and with increasing emphasis. The congress which met at Philadelphia early in September, 1774, was attended by delegates from all the colonies except Georgia, was called a "continental congress," and spoke in the name

[1] See Kent: *Commentaries on American Law*, I., pp. 204-5.

of "the good people of these colonies," but it immediately voted that each colony should have an equal voice. This remained the rule in the second continental congress, which began its session May 10, 1775, at Philadelphia. In this, Georgia also was finally represented. The strife was now transferred from the forum to the tented field. Congress did not limit itself to trying to do what a general war demanded, such as the equipment of a continental army, the creation of a common treasury, etc., but it set itself up — without being regarded on this account as stepping beyond its powers — as an authorized leader of the colonies in their separate affairs, since it exhorted them to give themselves governments such as their needs and the common welfare demanded, and expressed the belief "that the exercise of every kind of authority under the crown of Great Britain should be totally suppressed." Not in pursuance of resolutions of the legislatures or of any extraordinary representative assemblies of the people of the different colonies, which might have given instructions binding upon the respective delegates, but by virtue of its own revolutionary authority, which, because it was revolutionary, had, and could have, no legal limits, congress stepped forth as the sole representative of the commonwealth to act for the common weal in accordance with this conviction. June 10, 1776, it voted to appoint a committee to draw a declaration "that these united colonies are, and of right ought to be, free and independent states."

As congress acted as a revolutionary representative of the entire commonwealth, so from the beginning it claimed full political independence and sovereignty only for the colonies as a united whole. The resolution passed on the following day to appoint a committee to draft a plan of confederation was, therefore, not only a direct result of, but was already contained in, the resolution of the 10th. Since the decision of congress was ratified by the acts of the colonies, its formal ratification by the governments or people of the different colonies was thought unnecessary and did not take place.[1] The declaration of independence, a formulization on the 4th of July of the resolution of the 10th of June, did not concern itself as to whether the colonies as states should enter into a political league of some kind or other, but simply as to how the Union, made as a matter of fact long before and now declared to exist as matter of law, should be shaped in detail. The constituent members of the Union have never legally or actually been "free and independent states" in the full and proper sense of the term.[2] As Lincoln said, the Union is older than the states, and the states became "states" only as constituent members of the Union; and the word "state" has, therefore, always had in America, legally and actually, only a limited meaning, which excludes the idea of "sovereignty" in the full and proper sense of the word.

It was more than a year (November 15, 1777) before congress finally decided how its own revolutionary authority, which so far had been limited only by its own

[1] The next resolution, which has been much too little considered in the conflict over questions of constitutional law, as to the political nature of the Union, cannot be harmonized with any other view than that here expressed. It reads: "Resolved, that copies of the declaration be sent to the several assemblies, conventions and committees, our councils of safety, and to the several commanding officers of the continental troops; that it be proclaimed in each of the United States and at the head of the army."

[2] Rüttimann, in his *Das Nordamerikanische Bundesstaatsrecht* (I., 23), affirms the contrary, but bases his opinion too closely upon the assumption that each colony had "its own constitution and a full political organization complete for all public purposes." Moreover, there are weighty arguments easy to cite against this latter assertion.

ideas and by public opinion, should be brought under and within fixed legal forms. The conclusions reached placed the Union upon a wholly new basis. The very title of the proposed paper showed this clearly. It was not a constitution, but "articles of confederation." The change was even more apparent in the opening sentence. In the declaration of independence the separate colonies are not once named. At the end, it says: "The foregoing declaration was, by order of congress, engrossed and signed by the following members." Under the signature of the presiding officer followed those of his colleagues in the order of their states. The name of the state was prefixed to the names of its representatives, without the addition of a single word. Now, on the contrary, there was an enumeration of the separate states whose "delegates" had, according to the next article, agreed upon a "confederation and perpetual union," but nothing more was said of the "people," of whom the first sentence of the declaration of independence had spoken. So, too, the articles of confederation did not begin with a recital of the rights and powers of the Union.

The second article — the first relates only to the name — declares that "each state *retains* its sovereignty, freedom and independence," as well as every power and every right not "expressly" delegated to congress. The third article takes a still more significant step forward, for it declares that "the said states hereby severally enter into a firm league of friendship with each other" for the purposes enumerated. Thus, in boldest opposition to facts, the Union appears, in the articles of confederation, as being first called into life by them, and the character of a simple league of states, now really given it for the first time, is put forward as one in full conformity with the actual and legal facts of the past. Congress transformed itself, so far as the nature of the mandates of its members was concerned, from a (revolutionary) government into a congress of delegates, for the right of recalling the members was reserved to the states. It is not expressly declared that this right belongs to the legislature, but the method of electing their delegates is wholly remitted to them. The people are mentioned only here and there as an object of the Union. As the source of power and as self-governing they never appear. So far as the Union is concerned, the legislatures are treated as the sole and unlimited bearers of sovereignty. They were to ratify the articles of confederation, and give them, by this ratification, the force of law, although they had been authorized to form a constitution for the Union, neither by the constitutions of their respective states, nor in any way whatever. Moreover, changes in the articles were made dependent upon their approval, and the consent of all the legislatures was required for the slightest change. Congress exhorted the legislatures, by an act of public usurpation against the legal consequences of historical facts, to transform the Union into a league of states, and the legislatures recklessly responded to this demand. The circumstance that some of them delayed, and for so long a time refused, their ratification was in no way connected with their legal incompetence, and did not result from any wish to keep for the Union the political nature given it by the course of the Revolution. They considered it as self-evident that congress, during this whole time, regarded the articles of confederation as having the force of law, and they would have offered the most stubborn opposition if it had sought once more, as in the beginning of the Revolution, to fix the boundaries of its own power. While it was recognized that the decisive steps of the continental congress had created a legal *status* for the

United States, not only as against England and the rest of the world, but also in relation to the different states, yet it cannot be questioned that, with the adoption of the articles of confederation, a revolution was accomplished. This revolution met with no opposition among the people. Its entire correspondence with their whole political thought and impulse was generally fully recognized, and another advance on the part of congress would unquestionably have met with an opposition not to be overcome.

The legal consequences of the decisive steps taken by the continental congress in regard to the relation of the colonies, i. e., the states, to each other, went far beyond the actual facts of the case, and in a conflict between law and fact it goes without saying that the latter must triumph. The population of the states was so little one people, and felt so little as one people, that they wished to be one, in the most essential matters, only far enough to conquer independence, and to assert their right to self-government.[1] It was supposed that the articles of confederation had preserved the powers which the central authority needed for the accomplishment of this first and most important end of the Revolution, but long before they had been ratified by the last legislature (that of Maryland, March 1, 1781), the bitterest experience had made it a question of the highest importance as to whether this view was sustained by hard facts. The weightiest rights of sovereignty essential to political life were, of course, granted to congress, and either wholly withdrawn from the separate states or given them only within very deeply cut limits. But it was soon evident that a wholly useless

---

[1] The fourth article contains provisions in regard to purely internal relations, and especially in regard to the interests and rights of individuals, which paved the way for a national fusion.

piece of political machinery had been created, which, under the best management, could turn out only quite useless work, and finally could not have been kept in order at all, if a number of distinguished men, with extraordinary patriotic abandonment and unselfishness, had not constantly put their shoulders to the wheel, and, by their great example, drawn the rest of the people so far after them that the worst was always happily avoided, until, with the help of France, the recognition of independence had been won. The question early pressed itself upon the most far-sighted patriots where the fault lay. Experience made them more and more of the opinion that the fault was one of principle, based not only upon the selfish wish of the states to remain just as far as possible the sole masters of their own fates, but partly also upon the fact that during the colonial period no experience had been gained as to the nature and proper conditions of existence of a great and entirely independent political commonwealth. The provisions which gave all the states the same legal weight, although their actual importance was so very different — for the weightiest decisions the approval of at least nine states was necessary,— were responsible for much, but the real evil evidently lay deeper. Matters were not in a bad shape because congress failed in passing the necessary resolutions and laws, but because its resolutions and laws had no result. The articles of confederation failed to recognize not only the fact that a free commonwealth may be no less endangered by a government too weak than by one too strong, but also that a grant of rights in itself confers no power. Right first becomes might when means are given it to make itself so, and these means had been denied to congress completely and on principle. It could resolve on everything necessary, but it could not do the most necessary thing. The execution of its resolutions depended wholly upon the thirteen state governments, to whose short-sightedness, laxity, distrust and separatism it could oppose only arguments and an appeal to patriotism, which, in the nature of things, under the most favorable circumstances, could have only a partial result. Congress wished to be a government, and yet could only give advice, because it had a legal will, not in reference to individuals, but only as regards the states. This was no omission in the articles of confederation, but a logical consequence of their fundamental principle. They left no room for organs of government. The United States were a confederation with a federal authority, but without a federal government; and they had a federal law, but needed no federal courts, because the states were almost exclusively the subjects of federal law; and behind the federal courts no federal power was created to give effect to their judgments.[1]

[1] Article IX. gives congress the power to establish prize courts and "courts for the trial of piracy and felonies committed on the high seas." Moreover, "all controversies concerning the private right of soil claimed under different grants of two or more states," and "all disputes and differences now subsisting, or that hereafter may arise between two or more states, concerning boundary, jurisdiction, or any other cause whatever," were to be decided by federal courts, in case one of the parties applied to congress. But these courts were not permanent. They were created by congress *ad hoc*, and that in a highly complicated and cumbrous way. The view expressed in the text finds its direct proof in the provision that, "if any of the parties shall refuse to submit to the authority of such court, or to appear or defend the claim or cause, the court shall nevertheless proceed to pronounce sentence or judgment, which shall in like manner be final and decisive." But nothing was said as to what should happen in case of a stubborn refusal to obey the judgment. Reporting the decision to congress is the only "security" given the parties. See T. Sergeant: *On the National Judiciary Powers Prior to the Adoption of the Constitution*, appendix to P. S. Duponceau: *Jurisdiction of United States Courts*, Phila., 1824.

§ 3. EFFORTS FOR REFORM. During the war, and even before the articles of confederation had received the formal sanction of the last state, the knowledge of the fact that the Union could not endure under its then organization had so far progressed that complaints and sorrows had given way to earnest attempts at reform. In November, 1780, delegates of the four New England states and of New York met at Hartford. Their immediate object was to place the finances of the Union upon a firmer basis, and especially to ensure the payment of interest on the federal debt through federal taxes or customs, but they were entirely conscious that this alone would be of no use. "All government supposes the power of coercion," they said in their address to the states. Of course, this had no immediate result. One could scarcely have been expected. It gave, however, a strong push in the right direction, and the work of moulding public opinion never ceased thereafter until the goal had been reached. A growing necessity forced men to lay their hands to the work again and again. The uselessness of all half-way measures showed more clearly, day by day, the only road to safety. Destruction often seemed unavoidable, unless, at least, the worst evils could be removed. The failure of the attempts to accomplish even this constantly drove home the conviction that the evil must be grappled with at the roots. The necessity of obtaining the approval of nine states for the more weighty decisions of congress, and of getting the consent of all of the legislatures for any constitutional change, made the application of palliatives impossible. Since this was impossible, a radical cure had to be found. But the struggle of many years over the palliatives did this further great good, that, day by day, it became more clear upon what points attention was to be concentrated, if the people were to be made ripe by necessity for the adoption of a reorganization of the Union upon the basis of another principle. Later, it was recognized as a piece of good fortune that the revolutionary war had been fought out under the articles of confederation, and the reorganization of the Union first undertaken after independence had been won. Under the pressure of the needs of war single improvements might have been more easily carried through, but the deeper and the more important these partial improvements were, so much the more difficult would have become a reorganization of the Union, complete and based upon principle. This could not possibly have been sought with success during war, at least during one which was, to a certain extent, a civil war. Peace alone could fully show where and how far the articles of confederation failed to ensure a permanent Union. Such a government must be equal, not only to the exceptional circumstances of a war, but, before everything else, to the accomplishment of the aims of the Union in the normal condition of peace. If the demands which congress had to meet in time of war were not only different from, but also many times greater than, those of peace, yet upon the other side patriotism and the overwhelming necessity of the attainment of the immediate end of the Revolution insured more willing and careful attention to the needs of the commonwealth than when, in the sober selfishness of times of peace, the necessity for this attention no longer forced itself, day by day, upon even the smallest understanding. As the pressure of war grew weaker, the evils of an unworkable government first fully developed. The prophetic phrase of the Hartford convention of November, 1780, that, after the acquisition of independence, peace and freedom could be won only by the legal consolidation of the Union, now found its fulfillment in a fashion which opened a darker outlook into the future than in the blackest days of the war. Now the most far-sighted felt their courage sink, while the short-sighted were blind, and the self-seekers and ignorant recklessly sought to use for their own advantage the evils which preyed on the life-blood of the Union. The political thought, feeling and will of the people in regard to the Union threatened to fall into a process of dry rot. The best men, who had done the best in time of war, therefore drew very close together in the knowledge that danger lay in delay and that they must not relax their efforts until they had wrung from selfishness, from doctrinaire confusion, and from the narrow pride and patriotism of the separate states, the salvation of the commonwealth which had been called into life at such a terrible cost.

§ 4. HISTORY OF THE DEVELOPMENT OF THE CONSTITUTION. In January, 1786, the legislature of Virginia invited the other states to send delegates to a convention at Annapolis, in order to consider how far a uniform system was necessary for the regulation of commerce, and to make proposals on this point. At the convention, which met in September, only five states were represented. Partly on account of this scanty representation, and partly because they saw nothing to be gained from the consideration of only one of so many weighty questions, the delegates resolved to leave their task undone and to call, instead, a general convention " to take into consideration the situation of the United States," and to ascertain what must be done " to render the constitution of the federal government adequate to the exigencies of the Union." The legislature of New York adopted this proposal as its own. On the motion of its delegates, congress voted in February, 1787, to call a convention at Philadelphia, " for the purpose of revising the articles of confederation, and reporting to congress and the several legislatures such alterations and provisions therein as shall, when agreed to in congress and confirmed by the states, render the federal constitution adequate to the exigencies of government and the preservation of the Union." All of the legislatures, with the exception of that of Rhode Island, responded to this call by naming delegates. The convention met at Philadelphia, May 14. It was the 25th of May before a sufficient number of states (seven) were represented to complete the formal organization of the convention by the choice of Washington as presiding officer, and to begin work. Meanwhile, the time had not been suffered to slip by unused. The delegates from Virginia, whose official head was Edmund Randolph, but whose brain was James Madison, had agreed among themselves that a simple modification of the articles of confederation would not do, but that, as Washington had written to Madison on the 31st of March, it was their duty "to probe the defects of the constitution to the bottom and provide a radical cure." The main points as to the way in which this was to happen had been reduced to writing, and they were laid before the convention by Randolph, in order to give a firm basis for its deliberations. This was of great importance, for Virginia was the strongest and most influential state of the Union. The tardiness of the delegates of most of the states (Rhode Island never sent delegates to the convention) was not adapted to strengthen the hopes of the patriots. The instructions given by Delaware to her delegates, to insist upon it that, as heretofore, every state should have an equal voice in the Union, of necessity strengthened the fear that now again no result would be reached. Nevertheless, the convention adopted Washington's view that it must turn out a finished piece of work, even if, as a result, its proposals were rejected. Its success was, of course, from the beginning greatly endangered, because the resolution of congress, literally read, imposed upon it a much more limited task, and the instructions of its delegates, so far as these fundamental questions were concerned, were in part in harmony with the resolution of congress. But the great majority of delegates were of the opinion that the convention was not to be bound by this formal invitation, if, in its opinion, its aims could not be reached by keeping within the limits set by that resolution and by the instructions of its members. Wholly independent of the existing law, it went on with its task to work out a plan for the formation of a Union capable of life and of development. It considered the articles of confederation only so far as the experience gained under them showed the errors to be avoided, and always with a constant and comprehensive appreciation of the fact that a Union capable of life and of development could be formed only by adapting it to the facts of the past and the present, and not by doing violence to them for the sake of any theory. The articles of confederation also had not been a product of doctrine alone, and the actual facts which had found in them an adequate expression were still a strong factor, even if somewhat weaker than before and no longer with the same claim to attention, because far-reaching changes had been accomplished or at least begun in the political feeling, and especially in the political knowledge, of the people. The knowledge that all the faults of the articles of confederation must be finally referred to their fundamental principle therefore could not mislead the convention. By adopting exactly the opposite direction, it was sure not to wander from the right path. Although it was compelled by necessity to give the Union another principle as a basis, yet the great question still remained whether it would do this with the necessary completeness and follow out the main lines of thought to their necessary results. Even if it decided to do so, it was still doubtful whether enough of the spirit of statesmanship could be found to so fashion the details of its task that on the one side sufficient care was taken to fully satisfy all the great needs of the state, and yet, upon the other hand, this was not reached by a consolidation which was not adapted to the actual condition of affairs, either in fact, or, at any rate, in the opinion of the majority. Every page of the history of the Union up to that time testified to the fact that this was a task which made the highest demands upon the political insight, as well as upon the patriotic self-sacrifice, of the delegates. The greatest difficulties grew out of the special interests of the slave-holders in the southern states, and out of the enormous differences in the size and population of the separate states; differences which, so far as concerned the population, were sure to increase constantly. These special interests of the slave-holders were, for two generations, the central problem of the history of the United States. The solution was found in a civil war which lasted four years. Since in this book the history of the constitution needs to be touched upon only so far as required in order to understand the constitutional law of to-day, we must omit any discussion of the constitutional provisions concerning slavery, because, apart from some indirect consequences which will be mentioned by-and-by, slavery in the United States belongs as completely to the history of the past as serfdom in Germany. Only this much must be said, that the representatives of the northern states agreed upon a compromise because some of the delegates on the other side declared that their states would never adopt a constitution which did not respond to their demands in regard to this overshadowing interest. Concerning representation, it was agreed that every five slaves should be reckoned as three freemen. The slave states thought they obtained an equivalent for this in the provision that direct taxes should be levied according to representation. As a further concession to the slave-holder, it was agreed that fugitive slaves should be delivered up by the other states upon demand. Finally, the immediate suppression of the African slave trade was postponed, but congress was given the right to forbid the importation of slaves after twenty years, *i. e.*, in 1808. It was thought that this provision ensured the gradual dying out of slavery, something which was still generally considered, or at least declared, desirable. Inasmuch as there was still no opposition to the opinion that slavery was a curse laid upon the land by England, great care was taken not to give the words slave and slavery a place in the constitution. They were expressed by the circumlocution: "persons held to service or labor." The question as to what should be done with the slaves as far as representation was concerned had had, as its condition precedent, that the absolute equality of the states established by the articles of confederation could no longer endure, *i. e.*, that each state could no longer have an equal voice in the government of the Union. But with this change the Union ceased to be a league of states. Whatever arrangement was made, the Union was changed into a federal state. How thoroughly this was to be done, and how strongly the national tendency was to appear in this consolidation, naturally depended, however, in the first place, if by no means exclusively, upon the question how far and in what way the actual importance of the separate states was to be the basis of their lawful participation in the federal power. The smaller states wished to maintain, just as far as possible, the then condition of affairs, and the large ones wished to make the reform as thorough as possible. This was not on account of any national feeling. The position of each state was determined by its separate interests. The smaller states thought that in a short time they must sink to the position of mere hangers-on, simply the recipients of the laws dictated by the large states, if the constituent members of the Union were to find their representation amid the federal powers no more as such members, but according to their population. The large states, to whom the actual or at least the claimed extent of their territory and their natural riches promised a development of power scarcely to be reckoned, did not wish to endanger this, and to let their people sink, in a certain sense, into citizens of the second class, ten, twenty, or one hundred of whom would be counted in all federal affairs only for as much as each citizen of the small states. Since the latter based their demands upon the actual law, and the application of force could not be thought of, and since the former were not at all in favor of a complete national fusion, a compromise between the two opposing interests had to be found. It was found when the law-making power was shared between two co-ordinate houses — one of them organized, as the large states wished, upon the democratic principle of numbers, while in the other, the states, as such, were represented, although, as I shall show later, the character of a house of states was not given to it in other respects.

Jefferson, in his democratic doctrinairism, even after the constitution had come to life, complained bitterly of the adoption of the two-chamber system, but he forgot that this would not have happened in the first place if the choice had been simply between one and two houses.

It happened because this decision made possible the establishment of the Union in a way in which it could live. So far as this was concerned, the weightiest point was that now, for the first time, a real law-making power had been created. Congress was no longer obliged, upon the address of the states, to pass resolutions in the shape of laws, but it could now pass laws for the people of the United States, and could intrust the execution of federal laws affecting single citizens to the proper federal powers. The Union had obtained such an independent lawmaking power that it could no longer be deprived of its own permanent courts. The emancipation of the Union from the state governments depended directly upon its emancipation from the state courts, for it would have been absurd to give it a wider sphere of jurisdiction of its own, and yet to deny it the organs needed for existence within that sphere. The union of an independent law-making power, of an independent executive and administration and of independent courts was, however, a national government in the full sense of the word. So far as principles were concerned, Washington's wish had come to fulfillment. The convention had decided upon the adoption of a radical cure. It was not simply that the powers of the single federal authority (the old congress) were now shared between three co-ordinate factors, but these were actual national powers which together formed a national government, because they were endowed not only with rights, but with the power to enforce those rights. So far as everything within the domain of the national authority was concerned, the political will of the commonwealth, expressed in a constitutional way, was placed high above the political will of the constituent members of that commonwealth and of their political organs. The subordination of the latter was brought about by the use of those fixed forms in which the life of a modern constitutional and lawful state can pursue its steady and orderly course.

Opinions were sharply opposed, not only about the ground-plan of the constitution, but also about the details by which this plan was to be filled. The holders of all of these views were forced, now one and now another, to remember not to let the better become the enemy of the good, and not to fear the worst possible consequences, because in this or that state of affairs something either undesirable or utterly repugnant *might* happen. The convention could not possibly draw a constitution which, in the forum of theory, would appear as a blameless and perfectly harmonious work. But such a constitution would have been of scant use to the United States, for the real conditions could not be compressed into rigidly logical form. The convention, which brought its work to a close September 17, characterized it in its address to congress as "the result of a spirit of amity and of mutual deference and concession." Since its task had not been to draw a model constitution, this was the best recommendation of its work, for, as it said, many-sided concession was "rendered indispensable" by the "peculiarity of our political situation," and in the nature of things that could not happen which the welfare of all demanded unless all made sacrifices to that end. It laid claim to the highest grade of perfection for its work, gave it the highest praise possible, when it expressed the conviction that the constitution was "liable to as few exceptions as could reasonably have been expected." Whether this self-criticism was well founded only the actual trial of the constitution could show. And whether that actual trial would be had was still by no means certain. It was only too sure that the draft, as it is called in the address to congress, would not command universal acquiescence. Since the convention was convinced that the fate of the Union depended upon the adoption or rejection of the constitution, it had taken care not to leave the weal and woe of the commonwealth wholly in the hands of a lessening minority. Although the articles of confederation required the consent of all the states for the least change in the constitution, and the convention had only been authorized to consider a revision of these articles, it had yet ventured in its proposal for a radical reorganization of the Union to adopt the provision that the new constitution should come into force as soon as it had been adopted by nine states.[1] This did not involve any tyranny by a majority, because it was expressly provided that the ratification was to be good only for the ratifying states.[2] In case four states or less than four did not ratify, they thus *ipso facto* cut themselves out of the Union until they thought good to re-enter it, or the other states, perhaps by force of irresistible necessity, compelled them to do so. But such compulsion certainly could have been tried with success only against the smaller states, and in that case, as we shall later see more closely, the whole fundamental law of the new federal power would have been shattered and racked in a terrible way. This provision was therefore a two-edged sword. On the one hand it was made very difficult for political blindness and the lack of national feeling to hinder the reorganization

[1] Cooley, *The General Principles of Constitutional Law*, page 16, rightly says: "It was a revolutionary proceeding."

[2] Since Schlief, *Die Verfassung der Nordamerikanischen Union*, is often cited by German authors, I think it my duty to show by example how little trustworthy a guide he is. He says, p. 8: "The fundamental law, according to article 7, was to come into force for all the states represented in the convention at Philadelphia, when nine of them approved it."

of the Union, but on the other hand this might easily bring about such an explosion of these forces that the damage done could be repaired, if at all, only by doing violence to the fundamental principles of the Union. There was another scarcely less significant possibility. It might be that nine or even ten states would adopt the constitution, and yet, as a result of the opposition of one or two states, the Union, in its new organization, backed by force of law, and with a constitution containing within itself all the conditions of life and development, would yet be from the very beginning a torso, incapable of life. For an instant it seemed as if this mischance would happen.

June 21, 1788, New Hampshire ratified the constitution. She was the ninth state to do so. Among those which had not ratified it were Virginia and New York. The first had taken such a position in the Union since the days of the continental congress, that the nation, without Virginia, would have been like Hamlet without the *rôle* of Hamlet. Public opinion was so evenly divided in Virginia, that a very little would have sufficed to turn the balance in the wrong direction. From the beginning of the debates in the ratification convention it was easy to see that the simple rejection of the constitution was not to be feared, but up to the last instant it seemed not impossible that the ratification would be merely a conditional one. Many not only shared Patrick Henry's belief that Virginia was in a position to dictate her own conditions to the other states, but they also agreed with him in his wish to do so in such a way that her ratification should be made dependent upon the adoption of certain amendments by the other states. In the vote upon this main proposition, the opposition came within eight votes of a majority, and the simple ratification was then carried by eighty-nine to seventy-nine. In New York, the condition of affairs was somewhat different. New York was then far removed from being what she is now, the Empire State, but it could not be denied that she had a great future, and her geographical position from the ocean to Lake Erie made her an absolute necessity. If she did not come into the Union, it was torn asunder into two halves which could not possibly remain bound together; for the geographical continuity of the national territory was a condition precedent of that free exchange of opinions, customs and interests, the difference in which had been stigmatized by the Philadelphia convention in the address to congress as the main source of the difficulties with which it had had to fight. While in New York, Alexander Hamilton, with the aid of John Jay, and especially of Madison, wrote in the eighty-five numbers of the *Federalist* the classic argument against the articles of confederation, and in favor of the new constitution, yet here also the opposition was the most passionate and stubborn. Yates and Lansing, who, with Hamilton, represented the state in Philadelphia, had been sustained by public opinion when they withdrew from the convention, because it over-passed its powers. Now the opposition, led by Governor Clinton, was so obstinate that even Hamilton doubted for an instant whether it would not compel concessions to it. If Madison and his friends had not carried the day in Virginia, the friends of the constitution in New York would unquestionably have lost the victory. But even the example of Virginia weakened the opposition in the ratification convention at Poughkeepsie only so far that they were willing to agree to ratification if the state reserved the right of re-calling it in case the other states did not approve the amendments demanded by New York.

Madison, who was asked by Hamilton for his opinion upon this proposal, wrote: "My opinion is that a reservation of a right to withdraw, if amendment be not decided on, under the form of the constitution, within a certain time, is a *conditional* ratification; that it does not make New York a member of the new Union, and, consequently, that she could not be received on that plan. The constitution requires an adoption *in toto* and *forever*. It has been so adopted by the other states. An adoption for a limited time would be as defective as an adoption of some of the articles only. In short, any *condition* whatever must vitiate the ratification. The idea of reserving a right to withdraw was started at Richmond, and considered as a conditional ratification, which was itself abandoned as worse than a rejection." This letter, which expressed in an authoritative way the views of the father of the constitution upon the legal nature of the federal compact, is of the highest importance in view of the war fought for five and seventy years over this fundamental question,— a war the final history of which was written in blood. The letter gave the day to the friends of the constitution. On July 25, the ratification convention, by a majority of five votes, decided for an unconditional ratification. After this, it was unanimously voted to request the legislatures to call a new convention in order to pass upon the amendments proposed. March 4, 1789, the new federal powers came into existence, although North Carolina and Rhode Island had not yet adopted the constitution. The legal position which these two states occupied in regard to the Union was not sharply insisted upon, because their delay could not be of any especial importance, and no one doubted that they would soon overcome their scruples. North Carolina speedily ratified (November 21, 1789). Little Rhode Island waited until May 29, 1790, and then decided upon acquiescence only by a majority of three votes.

John Quincy Adams said in a speech at the fiftieth jubilee of the constitution that it was wrung from the people through "grinding necessity." This was true. Hamilton had written in the *Federalist:* "The establishment of a constitution, in time of profound peace, by the voluntary consent of a whole people, is a *prodigy*, to the completion of which I look forward with trembling anxiety." If this miracle now happened, it was due to the fact that the hard lessons of daily experience had finally given wide circles of the "reluctant people" a glimmering knowledge of the great truth that, as he had hitherto said: "A nation without a national government is, in my view, an awful spectacle." Gouverneur Morris had explained, in Philadelphia, his approval of the constitution by saying that the question was simply: "Shall there be a national government or a general anarchy?" In the same way Washington had written, December 14, 1787, that the choice lay only between the adoption of the constitution and anarchy, for, he had added, if another convention is tried, its members will be more at odds than in the first; they will agree upon no common plan; either this constitution must be adopted or the Union dissolved. Only the conviction that further experimenting had become impossible, and that a trial must be made of this constitution if the nation was to be rescued from the wretched stagnation of all interests under the articles of confederation, wrung the adoption of the constitution from political doctrinairism and from particularist selfishness. Moreover, it had been adopted by all of the states without the application of any outside force. This was the decisive fact for the future, and not the particular arguments which here and there had carried the day. No state could rightly deduce from the history of its development the right to cut loose from it. If the duties and the limits of self-government were found to be a heavy chain, yet each state had, by a full and free expression of its own will, fastened this fetter upon itself; had placed itself under the control of this fundamental law; and had done so in the most formal way. The Philadelphia convention had not submitted its work to the legislatures for ratification, but had demanded that the legislatures should leave the decision to conventions called for this particular purpose. In accordance with the recommendations of congress, this demand had been carried out in all the states. The states were not bound to the constitution through the state governments, but the people, the sole source of all political power in a republican government, had ratified the constitution through their representatives, chosen *ad hoc*. The United States had therefore ceased to be a confederation, and had become in truth a Union. The instrument under which they had decided henceforth to live, not only was no longer called articles of confederation, but it was no longer a confederation compact. It was a union compact. It was, in the full sense of the word, a constitution, a fundamental law of the state, a law which could be changed only in the manner provided by itself, could be done away with only by general and free consent, and could be overthrown only by revolution, but could never, and under no circumstances, be nullified by one or more states.[1]

§ 5. THE FIFTEEN AMENDMENTS. The friends of the constitution had believed that they must stand firm in their demand for its unconditional adoption, but they had not thereby committed themselves to the view that the

[1] *Texas vs. White*, Wallace, VII., 726.

work of the Philadelphia convention could not be improved. As soon as the constitution had come into effect, this question began to be discussed. It was brought to an issue in the manner provided by the constitution. The friends of the constitution would, of course, have been slow to consent to material changes as long as its provisions had not been subjected to the only sufficient proof, that of experience. Criticism, however, was not at first directed against what it provided, but against what it either did not provide, or, in the opinion of the opposition, left doubtful. They proposed for the most part not changes but additions, and the victors consented to this the more willingly, since from the beginning they had sought to weaken the opposition by the assertion that everything which they wished to see expressly set forth was implied in the silence of the constitution on the questions at issue. Ten amendments were proposed by the first congress and adopted by the necessary number of legislatures. The first eight additional articles take certain things out of the legislative control of congress, and guarantee to individuals certain rights and the maintenance of certain forms of law, thought to be sure safeguards against abuse of power and injustice. The ninth declares that the enumeration of certain rights is not to be construed to deprive the people of others not enumerated, "retained by" the people. The tenth provides that "the powers not delegated to the United States by the constitution, nor prohibited by it to the states, are reserved to the states respectively, or to the people." On account of the fundamental idea from which these ten additional articles sprang, they were and are often called the American Bill of Rights. This phrase, borrowed from well-known events in the history of England during the seventeenth century, and the contents of the first eight articles, clearly show how much the political thought of this generation found its point of departure in the internal struggles of the mother-land, and how far it was still removed from fully recognizing the essential differences in the actual conditions of the two countries. However, no one in the United States will to-day deny that experience has justified those who were not content with the legal results to be deduced from the silence of the constitution upon the questions at issue, but wished express provisions which should give the least possible occasion for a controversy.

The eleventh article, which was recommended by the third congress at its second session (1794) to the legislatures, bears quite a different character. It declares that no state can be brought before the federal courts by citizens of another state, or by subjects of a foreign state. This provision, which has given rise to much complaint, and has very recently been again vigorously discussed, was partly a new manifestation of the spirit which before the adoption of the constitution had been the dominant one, but was especially due to the feeling that it was derogatory to the dignity of a state to let itself be dragged into court by individuals as a party with the same standing before the court as themselves.

The twelfth article provided a new method of electing the president and vice-president. It was proposed at the first session of the eighth congress (1803) as a result of the discomforts and dangers which in the fourth presidential election had resulted from the original provisions.[1]

The thirteenth, fourteenth and fifteenth amendments, passed respectively at the second session of the thirty-eighth congress, the first of the thirty-ninth, and the third of the fortieth, were caused by the civil war, and relate

[1] See my *Constitutional History of the United States*, I, 168–176.

to the abolition of slavery, to different questions which arose from the reconstruction of the terribly shattered Union, and to the enfranchisement of the negroes and former slaves.[1]

[1] The proclamation issued by W. H. Seward, as secretary of state, in pursuance of a law of April 20, 1818, announcing that the thirteenth amendment had become a part of the constitution, was dated December 18, 1865. The seceded states had been notified by congress and the president, that the adoption of this amendment was a condition precedent to their re-admission into the Union. The reconstruction bill was sent to the president just before the close of the session. It was not signed by him, but in a proclamation dated July 8, 1864, Lincoln declared himself to be in substantial accord with its provisions. It may be said with considerable confidence that even without this compulsion the necessary number of states would have approved the amendment, but yet it is not to be questioned that the consent of part of the states was obtained under a certain compulsion. So, too, it must be recognized as an anomaly that states which were actually at the time neither full members of the Union, nor entitled to equal rights under it, voted upon an amendment to the constitution.

The definitive proclamation about the fourteenth amendment was dated July 28, 1868. A proclamation of July 20 had declared the amendment adopted if the ratifying resolutions of Ohio and New Jersey were to be considered as of full force and effect, although these states (in January and April respectively) had rescinded these resolutions. Congress was not content with the form of this proclamation. It passed a resolution July 21, which declared that the amendment had been adopted, and named Ohio and New Jersey among the ratifying states. Thereupon Seward issued his second proclamation with express reference to the resolution of congress. The question whether a state has a right to recall its consent as long as an amendment has not yet become an actual part of the constitution has not yet been fully decided. For judicial decisions "in a somewhat analogous case," holding that the approval once given remains binding, see Cooley, *The General Principles of Constitutional Law in the United States of America*, p. 204. In the fourth edition of Story's *Commentaries*, edited by Cooley, II., pp. 652, 653, the learned judge shows himself decidedly inclined to the opposite opinion. Oregon's recall of her approval was evidently of no effect.

Other amendments to the constitution have often been proposed, but these have failed to receive the necessary number of votes, either in congress or among the states. Experience has shown that the provisions of the constitution about amendments are sufficient on the one hand to meet the demands of development, and on the other to put so strong a curb upon a restless search after novelty that the democratic republic has been more conservative in its fundamental law than any state whatever of the European continent.

§ 6. THE TERRITORY OF THE UNION AND ITS CONSTITUENT MEMBERS. The original boundaries of the territory of the Union could not exactly be defined, because the provisions about them in the charters of a part of the colonies were decidedly vague. Even the treaty of peace was not entirely clear on this question. The United States have repeatedly been involved in disputes about boundaries with England. Part of these disputes were of a later origin. All of them, however, have been peaceably settled, which is equivalent to saying that the claims of the United States have not always been completely granted. This was especially so in the compromise which brought to an end the controversy of many years over the Oregon boundary. They accepted a very small part of their original claim.[1] But if they could not obtain everything which they believed might be claimed as their own, or might be got, yet their territory, by purchase, by the provisions of treaties of peace and other treaties, and by annexation, grew to an amazing extent. While the

because it did not take place until after the issue of Seward's proclamation.

The fifteenth amendment was declared adopted by a proclamation of March 30, 1870.

[1] See my *Constitutional History*, vol. III., chaps. 2, 6, 8 and 13.

GENESIS OF THE FEDERAL CONSTITUTION. 33

thirteen original states, New Hampshire, Massachusetts, Rhode Island, Connecticut, New York, New Jersey, Pennsylvania, Delaware, Maryland, Virginia, North Carolina, South Carolina and Georgia, have within their present boundaries only 325,065 square miles, the whole territory of the Union, according to the latest figures, now contains 3,602,990 square miles. The states which have been made out of the lands ceded to the Union by the original states, and out of the territory more lately acquired, contain 1,761,695 square miles. There are twenty-five of them, which have been admitted into the Union in the following order:[1] Kentucky, February 4, 1791 (June 1, 1792); Vermont, February 18, 1791 (March 4, 1791); Tennessee, June 1, 1796; Ohio, April 30, 1802 (November 29, 1802); Louisiana, April 8, 1812 (April 30, 1812); Indiana, December 11, 1816; Mississippi, December 10, 1817; Illinois, December 3, 1818; Alabama, December 14, 1819; Maine, March 3, 1820 (March 15, 1820); Missouri, March 2, 1821 (August 10, 1821); Arkansas, June 15, 1836; Michigan, January 26, 1837; Florida, March 3, 1845; Iowa, March 3, 1845 (December 28, 1846); Texas (resolutions of annexation were passed March 1, 1845), December 29, 1845; Wisconsin, March 3, 1847 (May 29, 1848); California, September 9, 1850; Minnesota, May 4, 1858 (May 11, 1858); Oregon, February 14, 1859; Kansas, January 29, 1861; West Virginia, December 31, 1862 (June 19, 1863); Nevada, March 21, 1864 (October 31, 1864); Nebraska, February 9, 1867 (March 1, 1867); Colorado, March 3, 1875 (August 1, 1876). The Union, therefore, consists, at the present time (1886), of thirty-eight states, with an area of 2,086,760 square miles. The remainder of the national territory contains nine organized

[1] I give the date of the act of admission, and, if the actual entry into the Union took place later, I give that date also in parenthesis.

territories, the Indian Territory, which has no territorial government, and the District of Columbia, the seat of the federal government. The territories were organized in the following order: New Mexico and Utah, September 9, 1850; Washington, March 2, 1853; Dakota, March 2, 1861; Arizona, February 24, 1863; Idaho, March 3, 1863; Montana, May 26, 1864; Wyoming, July 25, 1868; (Alaska, July 27, 1868).[1] The population of the United States, according to the census of 1790, was 3,929,827 souls. According to that of 1880 it was 50,155,783.[2] Alaska and the Indian Territory are not included. The

[1] Organized not as a territory but as a collection district. The object of the law, according to its title, is "to extend the laws of the United States relating to customs, commerce and navigation" over Alaska. *Statutes at Large*, XV., 240.

[2] Since, in the part of this work devoted to the constitutional law of the single states, they cannot be all separately treated, it seems proper to give here their area and population according to the census of 1880:

	Area in Square Miles.	Population.
New Hampshire	9,305	346,991
Massachusetts	8,315	1,783,085
Rhode Island	1,250	276,531
Connecticut	4,990	622,700
New York	49,170	5,082,871
New Jersey	7,815	1,131,116
Pennsylvania	45,215	4,282,801
Delaware	2,050	146,608
Maryland	12,210	934,943
Virginia	42,450	1,512,565
North Carolina	52,250	1,399,750
South Carolina	30,570	995,577
Georgia	59,475	1,542,180
Kentucky	40,400	1,648,690
Vermont	9,565	332,286
Tennessee	42,050	1,542,359
Ohio	41,060	3,198,162
Louisiana	48,720	939,946
Indiana	36,350	1,978,301
Mississippi	46,810	1,131,597
Illinois	56,650	3,077,871
Alabama	52,250	1,262,505
Maine	33,040	648,936
Missouri	69,415	2,168,380

view almost universally accepted by the founders of the republic, that the federal principle could last only as long as the federal state did not grow beyond certain bounds, has therefore been overthrown by experience. But without doubt this is mainly, if not exclusively, on account of the many-sided changes which the life of civilized people has undergone, through the development in modern times of means of communication. No one now doubts that the Union to-day is far stronger than if it counted only thirteen states, and that it grows stronger with each passing year.

	Area in Square Miles.	Population.
Arkansas	53,850	802,525
Michigan	58,915	1,636,937
Florida	58,680	269,493
Iowa	56,025	1,624,615
Texas	265,780	1,591,749
Wisconsin	56,040	1,315,497
California	158,360	864,694
Minnesota	83,365	780,773
Oregon	96,030	174,768
Kansas	82,080	996,096
West Virginia	24,780	618,457
Nevada	110,700	62,266
Nebraska	76,855	452,402
Colorado	103,925	194,327
Territories.		
New Mexico	122,580	10,844
Utah	84,970	143,963
Washington	69,180	75,116
Dakota	149,100	135,177
Arizona	113,020	5,280
Idaho	84,800	32,610
Montana	146,080	39,159
Wyoming	64,690	20,789

According to race, the population is divided into 43,402,970 whites, 6,580,793 negroes, 105,607 Chinese, and 66,407 Indians, exclusive of the wild tribes, and of the Indian population in the Indian Territory and in Alaska. About one-eighth of the population (6,679,973) are of foreign birth.

PART SECOND.

THE FEDERAL CONSTITUTION.

AUTHORITIES. *U. S. Supreme Court Reports* (Dallas, 4 vols. to 1804; Cranch, 8 vols. to 1815; Wheaton, 13 vols. to 1827; Peters, 16 vols. to 1842; Howard, 24 vols. to 1860; Black, 2 vols. to 1862; Wallace, 22 vols. to 1874; Otto, 17 vols. to 1882; since then, Davis. Otto's reports are usually cited in American books, not by his name, but as "U. S. Reports,"— the general name for the series of supreme court decisions. I shall follow this example. In my *Constitutional History of the United States* I have hitherto taken my references from Curtis's edition of the supreme court reports, so far as that goes. In 1882 the Lawyers Co-operative Publishing Company (Rochester, N. Y.) began, under the editorship of Stephen R. Williams, an edition which is more complete, more convenient, and in many respects more valuable. Up to April, 1885, 22 volumes appeared, coming down to the October term, 1884). *U. S. Statutes at Large.* (The student cannot dispense with them, although the *Revised Statutes*, 1875; 2d edition, 1878; Supplement, 1874-81, are more convenient, lighten the task of research by their topical arrangement, and derive an especial value from their references to the decisions of the supreme court. They contain only the laws at present in force.) *U. S. Digest*, B. V. Abbott, 15 vols., Boston, 1874-78; *New Series*, 9 vols., 1870-78; 10 vols. by J. E. Hudson and G. F. Williams, continuation by Williams alone. A. C. Freeman, *Digest of American Decisions*, vol. I, San Francisco, 1882. *Opinions of the Attorneys-General.* The stenographic reports of the proceedings in congress, which have appeared under different titles. *The Debates and Proceedings in the Congress of the United States* come down to the conclusion of the first session of the twenty-fifth congress (October 6, 1837), 28 vols., Wash., 1825-1837. The *Congressional Globe* begins in 1833 and extends to 1873. The *Congressional Record* covers the time since. Some of the official publications of the government, usually referred to as a whole as *Congressional Documents*, are an important source of information. Among these, the *Reports of Committees* are of especial value, and that, too, for constitutional history. Since both the inferior federal courts and the state courts have to pass upon the constitutionality of federal and state laws, and all the disputed questions of constitutional law cannot possibly be brought before the supreme court for adjudication, the decisions of these other courts often carry great weight. But the enormous number of these decisions makes an exhaustive review of them more and more of an impossibility, even to the most learned American jurists.

J. Wilson, *Works*, 3 vols., Phila., 1804. J. Taylor, *Construction Construed and Constitutions Vindicated*, 1820. Ibid., *New Views of the Constitution of the United States*, 1823. R. Mohl, *Das Bundesstaatsrecht der Vereinigten Staaten von Nord-Amerika*, Stuttg. and Tüb., 1824. J. Kent, *Commentaries on American Law*, 1st ed., 1826; 12th ed., 1873; 4 vols. Rawle, *A View of the Constitution of the United States of America*, 2d ed., Phila., 1829. Th. Sergeant, *Constitutional Law, being a Review of the Practice and Jurisdiction of the Courts of the United States and of Constitutional Points Decided*, 2d ed., Phila., 1830. J. Story, *Commentaries on the Constitution of the United States*, 2 vols., 1st ed., 1833; 4th ed., 1873. A. P. Upshur, *The Federal Government, its true Nature and Character, being a Review of Judge Story's Commentaries on the Constitution of the United States*, Petersburg, 1840. A. de Tocqueville, *De la Démocratie aux Etats-Unis*, 2 vols., Paris, 1835.

FUNDAMENTAL PRINCIPLES OF THE CONSTITUTION AND OF CONSTITUTIONAL LAW.

§ 7. THE SO-CALLED PREAMBLE. At the beginning of the constitution is the following sentence: "We, the people of the United States, in order to form a more perfect union, establish justice, insure domestic tranquillity, provide for the common defense, promote the general welfare, and secure the blessings of liberty to ourselves and our posterity, do ordain and establish this constitution for the United States of America." This sentence is ordinarily called the Preamble, a title which Farrar (pp. 85-89) rejects, because it must lead to entirely erroneous conclusions about its legal nature and scope. Farrar is right, because this is a technical expression, taken from English law;[1] and this expression does not cover

[1] Sedgwick, pp. 42-45.

the essential part of this introductory sentence of the constitution. It not only speaks, like a preamble, of the motives and aims of the law-giver, but it names the authority which here expresses its will; and it declares what this expression of will is, and upon whom it is to be binding. It is evident that this is not simply an outward and purely formal difference, but one of great material significance. This appears from a comparison of the introductory sentences of the articles of confederation with this; from the numerous changes which it had to undergo before it received its final form in the Philadelphia convention;[1] and from the long and earnest debates which it caused in some of the ratification conventions. It was almost universally recognized that the enumeration of certain objects did not make this clause an independent source of power to the federal authorities. Nevertheless, it did not by any means follow that no weight at all was to be given it because no legal consequences could be deduced from it. It had *not* "simply an historical significance," and the constitution did *not* "first begin with that which followed the preamble,"[2] but it is, in the proper sense of the word, a most essential part of the constitution itself, for it is to it what the enacting clause is to an ordinary law. The discussion of the aims enumerated in it, to which the American commentators for the most part devote much space, is unnecessary in a statement of existing constitutional law, because it is of a political rather than a legal nature. But the other parts of the preamble demand careful attention and would deserve it even if no independent legal significance were to be given to them, because they provide the natural start-

---

[1] Collected by Farrar, pp. 33-38.
[2] Schlief, p. 71.

ing point for a discussion of the principles which to a certain extent form the foundation of the whole constitution, as well as of the rules which control its interpretation and construction. The "people of the United States" name themselves as the framers of the constitution, that is, as the possessors of political omnipotence, of sovereignty. But who, then, are the people of the United States? This question was the formal beginning of the struggle between two political schools which culminated in the civil war, and is still carried on to-day with tongue and pen, though in a far milder way.

§ 8. THE DOCTRINE OF STATE SOVEREIGNTY. The premise of the argument of the so called state's-rights school is that there never has been, either in point of fact or in point of law, one people of the United States. The argument proceeds as follows. The people of each state, without being bound in any way by the action or the non-action of the other states, decided for themselves, through their authorized representatives, whether or not they would accept the draft of the Philadelphia convention. That the constitution is a work of states is therefore a fact which cannot be gotten rid of on the plea that the constitution begins with the words: " We, the people of the United States." If these words do not contain an evident falsehood, then must the phrase " United States " be read here as " states united; " but so read they say simply that the states, in order to better protect their interests, have entered into a new compact to regulate everything in regard to those matters as to which they wish to form one commonwealth. The political existence of the Union was not changed. The states were sovereign afterwards as well as before, and they alone were sovereign because a partition of sovereignty is impossible from its very meaning. It would be to turn nature upside down if the creator were made subordinate to the creature. There was no common judge standing above the federal powers and the states. If a conflict of authority broke out between them, the decisive judgment was left to the states, that is, to each of them for itself, as to what rights they had reserved for themselves and what powers they had given to the Union. If the federal government, in the opinion of a single state, exceeded its constitutional authority, that state was justified in declaring the particular law, so far as it came in question, to be null and void. John C. Calhoun,[1] of South Carolina, who with great logical acuteness developed into a complete system this so-called doctrine of nullification, declared that nullification was an "eminently conservative remedy," and affirmed that it, and it alone, could prevent the dissolution of the Union.[2] The younger school of the southern state's-rights men did not stand by him in this. The doctrine of nullification was constantly pushed into the background and often completely rejected, and on the

---

[1] See my book about him in the series of biographies edited by John T. Morse, under the general name of "American Statesmen."

[2] The doctrine in its beginnings goes back to the last years of the eighteenth century. The hated alien and sedition laws, whose unconstitutionality will scarcely be questioned by anyone to-day, gave the legislatures of Virginia and Kentucky the opportunity to proclaim the doctrine officially. When the anti-federalists in 1801 obtained the mastery, and the policy of the United States in the struggle with England seriously embarrassed the industrial interests, especially those of the New England states, the parties changed their standpoints. The federalists were now champions of state's rights. During the war with England they inserted in their political manifestoes the leading clauses of the Virginia and Kentucky resolutions, word for word. But it was under the pressure of the special interests of the slave-holders that the doctrine of state sovereignty was first fully framed, thought out to a logical end, and finally, with the most terrible zeal, transferred from theory to practice.

other hand, again and again and more unconditionally the last consequences were deduced from the premises of the state's-rights school. Since the constitution is a compact between sovereign states, they said, the states have the power to cut loose from the Union if the compact is broken, either by the national government or by the other states,— if it changes from a means of protection and of advancement into a source of destruction and certain ruin. Sovereignty is not only indivisible, but cannot be parted with, and the states, bound only through an act of their own free will, can be bound only as long as their will does not change; that is, as they wish to be bound. Secession is thus not a right *under* the constitution, that is, a constitutional right, but it is inherent in the nature of the states, and therefore could not possibly be given up by the adoption of the constitution. The attempt to prevent by force the secession of a state is not a suppression of a rebellion, but an international war. Others did not go as far, and thought they had found a middle course. They admitted that secession was a revolutionary act, but affirmed that the federal government was not empowered to use force against the sovereign states. This was the non-coercion theory. They claimed that the sovereign states had the right of neutrality; that is, that although they had not cut loose from the Union, they were justified in standing on one side as spectators during a conflict fought out with the sword between the federal government and the seceded states.

The result of the civil war made this one of the dead and gone doctrines of history. After its champions had appealed to the *ultima ratio* and had been completely conquered, it had no more political vitality. And it will never again have it. The victorious north did not even consider it necessary to guard itself against the possibility of the revival of this doctrine by inserting in the constitution a new express declaration against it. The opposite doctrine is thus unquestionably valid constitutional law to-day, whatever one may think on the question as to what *originally* was constitutional law. There is no need here of any further critical examination of the doctrine of state sovereignty. This is involved in the statement of the opposite doctrine, which is the constitutional law of to-day.

§ 9. THE PEOPLE OF THE UNITED STATES of course did not act as one uniform whole when they gave themselves this constitution. The people, that is, the part of the population of each state endowed with full political rights, acted for themselves, and had absolute freedom of decision. They could accept the draft of the Philadelphia convention through their authorized representatives, or they could reject it, and therewith cut loose from the Union, if the projected organization of the latter were accomplished. But their ratification did not make the draft a constitution. Their ratification was simply a declaration, binding in law, that if the people of at least eight other states came to the same conclusion, the organization of the Union should therewith become an accomplished fact; so that, for the states concerned, this draft should be good as a constitution given by the people of the United States to the United States. Only by and through the choice of its own people did each state become a constituent member of the Union. This, however, did not happen through an act of will of any single state, but the Philadelphia draft first became a constitution by the equal and co-operating consent of the people of nine states, and the states which ratified it afterwards evidently acquired by their ratification exactly the same legal *status* in the Union. Chief-justice Chase was unquestionably right when he said that "the Union of the states never was a purely artificial and arbitrary relation."[1] This fact, however, did not settle the matter at issue. Whether the states were or were not sovereign from the time of the declaration of independence, by common consent every one of them decided as a sovereign upon the adoption of the constitution, that is, upon its own entrance into the Union. On the other hand, whatever their legal *status* in the confederation and their political nature up to this time might have been, they were not sovereign by common consent, that is, according to the constitution, as members of the new Union. The Philadelphia convention began its labor by the adoption of a resolution which declared "that a *national* government ought to be established, consisting of a *supreme* legislative, executive and judiciary." If a state adopted the draft, its people thereby declared that they, as far and as widely as this draft provided, should be fused with the people of the other states into one people of the United States; and by the concurrent decision of all, this declaration, put in this way, was placed at the beginning of the constitution, so that this proclaimed itself as the work of this one people of the United States.

§ 10. THE CONSTITUTION is not a compact between the states, but it is, as it declares itself to be, a constitution, and in truth, *the* constitution of the United States, that is, of the Union, of the commonwealth formed out of the states. Therefore, it is unconditionally binding, as well for the whole people as for the states as such. No room for doubt is left, for the second section of the sixth article reads: "This constitution, and the laws of the United States which shall be made in pursuance thereof, and all

---

[1] *Texas vs. White*, Wallace, VII., 724.

treaties made or which shall be made under the authority of the United States, shall be the supreme law of the land, and the judges in every state shall be bound thereby, anything in the constitution or laws of any state to the contrary notwithstanding." The constitution is thus the law, and, moreover, the supreme law of the land. The constitutions of the separate states are their fundamental laws only in regard to those matters which are not submitted by the federal constitution to federal authority. This provision makes the constitution an integral part of the constitution of each state.[1] If there is a conflict between them, then the provision of the state constitution opposed to the federal constitution is *ipso facto* null and void. All judges, and therefore, evidently, all other state officers, and all citizens of the state, are absolutely bound down to this fundamental principle. He who seeks to overthrow it lays hands on the fundamental law of the land. The federal government, which is bound to give the constitution life and being by law, is therefore not only empowered but directed to break down any opposition;— if possible, by the ordinary and peaceful powers of the state as provided by the constitution, but in case of need, by force.

§ 11. THE RIGHT AND THE DUTY OF USING FORCE follow directly from the ideas of "law" and "government." They are, moreover, set forth in the constitution in a way quite beyond doubt. The third section of the second article provides that the president " shall take care that the laws be faithfully executed." The constitution is the supreme law of the land, and the president's highest duty is therefore to take care that it shall be executed everywhere and under all circumstances. It provides in the

[1] *Taylor vs. Taintor*, Wallace, XVI., 366.

seventh paragraph of the first section of the second article that he shall, upon entering office, take the following oath: "I do solemnly swear (or affirm) that I will faithfully execute the office of president of the United States, and will, to the best of my ability, preserve, protect and defend the constitution of the United States." If the constitution laid upon him this duty, it must also have intended that he should have, or should be able to obtain, the means by which to fulfill the duty in all cases. Whether and how far it is his privilege to decide for himself whether the application of force is necessary in a given case, and actually to use force, need not be discussed at this point, where only questions of general principles are at issue. Here it is sufficient to show that if, and so far as, he is not authorized to do this, the law-making power is. Article I., section 8, paragraph 18, says that congress shall have power "to make all laws which shall be necessary and proper for carrying into execution the foregoing powers and all other powers vested by this constitution in the government of the United States, or in any department or officer thereof." It is the president's duty, and therefore also within his power, to preserve, protect and defend the constitution, and congress is therefore bound to give him the means to use this power, that is, to come up to this duty. In case that not only individuals but states as such should rebel against the laws or the constitution, the right of the federal government to use force can be in no way questioned; and if other means are not sufficient, it is so much the more bound to use force because the political order or the very existence of the Union is endangered in so much higher a degree. If the federal government seeks by force to command obedience to the laws and the constitution, and the opposition becomes in substance and form a war, this war may be conducted for the sake of humanity and policy as a war with a foreign power under all the rules of international law, but legally the government has to do only with a rebellion.[1]

§ 12. THE SECESSION OF A STATE is simply a fact, not a legal proceeding. As long as the people of the United States, whose work the constitution is, did not themselves decide to destroy this work, that is, the Union,— in other words, as long as they wished to continue to be one people,— the constitution of the Union, despite any fact whatever, remained from the standpoint of law wholly unchanged.[2] On questions of this sort, single states have as little right of action as single individuals. An ordinance of secession is wholly null and void. Despite it, the state remains a member of the Union and its citizens remain citizens of the Union. Its and their duties under

---

[1] In the *Prize Cases* (Black, II., 635), the supreme court says that the rebels were at the same time a war-making power and traitors, and were therefore subject to the consequences to be deduced from either the one or the other character. The United States, on the other hand, bore the double character of a war-making power and of the sovereign, and had therefore the rights of both.

It seems to me strange to refer the right to suppress a rebellion to the right to declare war, as the supreme court does in *Texas vs. White* (Wallace, VII., 700). The Philadelphia convention certainly had no thought of civil war when it gave this right to congress. I think, therefore, that it is at least an unfortunate formulization of the idea I have already recognized as just, when the supreme court declares in the *Prize Cases* just quoted that congress alone has the right to declare war. In the case of a civil war, according to my judgment, formed from the standpoint of constitutional law, the lawful government has nothing whatever to do with declaring war. A war is a fact which has simply to be recognized. If congress merely recognizes the fact, the views expressed in the text and by the supreme court come into harmony.

[2] These fundamental principles are clearly and sharply formulated in *Cohens vs. Virginia,* Wheaton, VI., 264.

the constitution continue wholly unaltered.[1] No new act of admission is necessary, therefore, in order to allow a state which has been in rebellion to enter again into the full enjoyment of its constitutional rights. It is again an equal member of the Union when it has been recognized as such by the political powers of the Union, and its representatives and senators have been admitted by congress.[2]

§ 13. RECONSTRUCTION. It was thus not a legal, but a political question, how the so-called reconstruction was to be accomplished. The courts had to decide, upon a given case, what the political powers of the federal government had determined in regard to that case, and had to base their judgment upon this determination; but it did not appertain to them to decide, in addition to this, what these political powers *ought* to have decided.

These remarks have by no means exhausted the consequences which are to be deduced from the opening sentence of the constitution. It is only when this sentence is analyzed from exactly the opposite standpoint that its full influence upon the political nature of the Union is first recognized.

§ 14. THE UNITED STATES. The people of the United States name themselves as the possessors of sovereignty, and act throughout as such; so that they give to the United States the constitution. The people of the United States, however, is not exactly the same thing as the population of the North American republic. As the Union has never been a purely arbitrary and theoretical creation, so also the name United States is no arbitrary and casual phrase, but is due to the political facts of the

---

[1] *White vs. Cannon*, Wallace, VI., 443; *White vs. Hart*, Ibid., XIII., 646.
[2] *Texas vs. White*, Wallace, VII., 700.

Union. The United States is not only the name of a thing, but the thing itself. As the population of the Union, in giving itself a constitution, acted not as one simple whole but in and through its organization into states, an organization historic and existing by law, so it did not by the constitution organize or wish to organize a close national state. It changed the federation of states, a federation with the loosest powers, into a federal state, upon a deep-laid, national foundation. Out of the federation there came an actual Union, but the Union was not divided into provinces, which were still called states. Its constituent members were actually states and must always remain states. It was a mistaken use of the word "sovereign" (because it led to conclusions false from the standpoint of fact), if afterwards, as before, even in official utterances, men spoke of "sovereign" states; but the states had their own sphere of authority, and within this they were completely independent of the national government. The expression "people of the United States," it has been well said, does not on account of this become a shadow, without legal existence or incomprehensible. The possibility of misusing the word "people" in a demagogic way always remains, and this possibility will always be made use of from time to time; but if one has an honest wish to receive and understand the word in its constitutional sense, then there is less room for doubts than there would be if the Union were a single state.[1] The "people of the United States" are the

[1] Schlief (p. 10) affirms that even the mob can identify itself with this "we, the people of the United States." This is not to be questioned, but the constitution cannot be made answerable therefor. In his view the introductory words are "evidently an imitation of the introductory formula commonly used up to the present day in the constitutional monarchies of Europe in passing a law: 'We, king by the grace of God,'"—an assertion which is irreconcilable with

population of the United States, in the organization given them by the constitution and precisely fixed by it.¹ A condition precedent of this organization is the maintenance of their division into self-governing states. The states first came into existence with the Union and by means of it, but they are older than the constitution, and did not abandon their separate political existence by the adoption of the constitution, even if this gave them an essentially different character. If the states had no existence, from the standpoint of constitutional law, outside of the Union and independent of it, yet, on the other hand, the Union, from the same standpoint, had just as little an existence without the states. The supreme court says that "the constitution in all its provisions looks to an indestructible Union composed of indestructible states." ² The same authority declares in *Cohens vs. Virginia:* "America has chosen to be in many respects and in re-

---

even a superficial knowledge of the history of the development of the constitution. A constitution cannot be "critically developed from *one* underlying thought" (p. 6) if it is to be anything more than a worthless product of a doctrine of abstract logic. It is to be understood only from the historic standpoint. Schlief, for the most part, does not state, as he promises to do, what "the actual constitutional law of the Union" is. Instead of this he states what, in his opinion, the constitutional law should be, frequently what it should not be, and only what it is in accordance with his erroneous view.

¹ Story is therefore unquestionably wrong when he says (I., 249) that a majority of the whole people can unquestionably change the constitution at will. For in this case "people" seems to be used as synonymous with "population." Judge Jameson (*The Constitutional Convention*, pp. 19, 20) neatly sums up the whole constitutional doctrine in the sentence: "Sovereignty resides in the society or body politic; in the corporate unit resulting from the organization of many into one, and not in the individuals constituting such unit, nor in any number of them, except as organized into a body politic and acting as such." See also in the same work pp. 524–526.

² *Texas vs. White.*

gard to many purposes a nation, and for all these purposes her government is complete." The court proceeds to explain, however, that America wished to be a nation only in certain respects and for certain aims, and in regard to all others the federal government is without any authority whatever; it is as little sovereign as the states.

§ 15. SOVEREIGNTY, which in fact is indivisible, rests only in the people of the United States. The people have intrusted the federal government with the use of certain rights, while others, according to their will, as fixed in the constitution, remain in the states,— others, but not all others. The ninth amendment reads: "The enumeration in the constitution of certain rights shall not be construed to deny or disparage others retained by the people." This article is in direct connection with the preceding amendments which, as has been said, are ordinarily called the American Bill of Rights. Speaking generally, it rests upon the fundamental view that certain rights (among them those expressly named) belong to the people, *i. e.*, in this case to the individual citizens, and that these rights are to be completely withdrawn from the cognizance of the political powers.[1] On this point the

[1] While, by the first amendment, certain things were expressly withdrawn from the legislative authority of congress, congress is not named in the seven following amendments. Yet it has always been held by the courts that they relate only to the federal government and not to the state governments. But if the states, so far as the federal constitution is concerned, are in law perfectly free to act in regard to the matters to which the first eight amendments relate, yet the reason for these amendments was as a matter of fact the unanimous conviction of the population of all the states that these barriers must be erected against *every* government, if freedom was to be ensured. It is only in regard to some of the least important provisions that this is either untrue or true only in a limited degree. Farrar (pp. 59, 60) affirms that these rights are "held by every member of the nation, under and by virtue of the constitution of the United

tenth amendment is conclusive. It says: "The powers not delegated to the United States by the constitution, nor prohibited by it to the states, are reserved to the states respectively or to the people."[1] We are considering this tenth amendment here only in regard to the matter immediately before us. It is evident that among the rights which are neither given to the federal government nor reserved to the separate states is the weightiest of all; yes, the one which embraces all others, *i. e.*, the right to change the constitution and to partition power in whatever way is desired, between the federal government and the states.[2] The sovereign people

States, independent of any other earthly power, and, of course, cannot be destroyed or abridged by the laws of any particular state." There are numberless judicial decisions against this view, but, nevertheless, a state law which forbade the open carrying of arms has been declared unconstitutional.

[1] Cooley, *Principles*, 29, says that whatever is not granted to the federal government belongs to the states, or to the people thereof. The expression "people" in the tenth amendment is generally understood in this way. In maintenance of this view, it is ordinarily said that here the phrase is used that powers are "reserved to" the states and the people, while the ninth amendment speaks of powers "retained by" the people. I do not overlook the weight of this reasoning, but yet cannot persuade myself that here only the people of the separate states are meant. According to the context, certainly another meaning is possible, and the great care with which the constitution has been drawn throughout suffices to show that the "thereof" which would have excluded every doubt would have been added if only the people of the separate states had been spoken of. Be this as it may, the views expressed in the text would not be influenced thereby, because they need not be made dependent upon the tenth amendment. Jameson (p. 86) is of the opinion that this amendment relates "not to the people of the states but to the people of the Union."

[2] As long as the political nature of the United States is not subjected to a change which, in the essential sense of the word, is material, this can happen only by increasing, diminishing, or in some way

thus did not, in adopting the constitution, leave the stage, but they can at any instant use again, to the fullest extent, their sovereignty. But even so, only the sovereign people of the United States can do this. The population of the Union cannot. The least, as well as the most incisive and comprehensive, change can lawfully be made only in the way provided in the constitution, because the sovereign people has decided that it will make changes of the constitution only in these fixed ways. Naturally, it can change this decision as well as all others in a constitutional way.[1] In the United States, therefore, sovereignty is actually, as the idea demands, unlimited and undivided, but the exercise of the rights of sovereignty is given to the organs of the commonwealth only in part.

fashioning differently the powers of the federal government. The supreme court says, in *Sturgis vs. Crowninshield*, Wheaton, IV., 122, that there was no reason for setting forth in the constitution the powers which remained in the states, and it would have been improper to do so, because these had their origin, not in the American people, but in the people of the separate states, and were no further affected by the adoption of the constitution than was involved by the provisions of the constitution. The constitution not only withdraws from the states certain rights in order to give them to the federal government, but it also forbids them to do certain things without authorizing the federal government to do them. But while it says what the federal government can and cannot do, it can only say what the states cannot do; and it expressly sets forth that certain rights are reserved to them. So far as their relations to the Union do not come into question, it cannot, however, direct them to do anything whatever. We shall discuss later whether and how far powers were taken from the states in order to give them to the federal government.

[1] Only on one point can it be doubtful whether a constitutional change can be made without the consent of all the states. Article V., which relates to the amendment of the constitution, provides "that no state, without its consent, shall be deprived of its equal suffrage in the senate." If a change in the constitution on this point

§ 16. THE AUTHORITY OF THE FEDERAL GOVERNMENT AND OF THE STATES. The authority of the federal government, as well as of the states, is a limited one, and the boundary between the two is set forth in the constitution. From the "nature of the state," from the "reason of the state," from "public opinion," from political policy, and even from necessity, the federal government can deduce no powers whatever.[1] It has no inherent rights whatever. All its powers are delegated, and it has only the powers which are given it by the constitution. It is by no means necessary, however, that the delegation should be expressed in so many words. The provision of the articles of confederation on this point contains the word "expressly," and when the tenth amendment was discussed in congress, it was moved to incorporate this word in the constitution. Madison and others opposed it on the ground that general expressions must be used in the constitution, if it was not to descend into the most minute particulars. A stiff and literal interpretation of these clauses is not to be given, for the constitution was framed, not for the moment, and not in relation to one fixed state of facts, but with the idea of its

should be determined upon by a constitutional majority, and a state which did not consent should thereby be deprived of its equal representation in the senate, the danger against which the states were to be absolutely assured would be brought about in an indirect way.

[1] The supreme court says that the constitution "is a law for rulers and people, equally in war and in peace, and covers with the shield of its protection all classes of men, at all times, and under all circumstances." The doctrine that it can be thrust on one side in order to meet the pressing necessities of a great crisis has the most destructive consequences. It "leads directly to anarchy or despotism, but the theory of necessity on which it is based is false; for the government, within the constitution, has all the powers granted to it which are necessary to preserve its existence." *Ex parte Milligan*, Wallace, IV., 120, 121.

lasting for generations and meeting the demands of constantly changing conditions of affairs. Every power, therefore, of such a general character must include also all the powers which are naturally implied in it and are required for the attainment of the end sought by it (implied powers).[1] This argument, which the supreme court has since formulated most precisely in *Martin vs. Hunter* (Wheaton, I., 304), was convincing, and the proposal was not adopted. If it had been, a change in principle would have been made in the constitution by this tenth amendment. The nation would have gone back in part to the fundamental ideas of the confederation,— ideas which were purposely and decisively opposed by the constitution. If congress, in the paragraph already quoted, was authorized to "make all laws which shall be necessary and proper" to carry out any of the powers delegated it by the constitution, yet this "necessary" is not to be understood in the absolute sense of the word. The "proper" qualifies it. The assertion that congress can use only the means, without which it would be absolutely impossible to discharge the task imposed upon the different federal powers by the constitution, imputes an absurdity to the framers of the constitution. If the end is constitutional, congress has free choice of any and all means which in the nature of things correspond to the end to be reached, so far as their use is not forbidden it by the constitution. Whether they are proper, congress alone is to judge. This is a question, not of law, but of politics. The powers of the federal government are in exact relation with the tasks imposed upon it. Paragraph 18 of the eighth section of

[1] In a certain way, therefore, it is right to say that not only the powers of congress, but much more the matters in regard to which congress is empowered to act, are set forth in the constitution, but, in my opinion, Tiffany (p. 179) puts this too baldly.

the first article is just as little a source of new and independent powers for congress as the tenth amendment is a limitation of the sphere of authority provided by the constitution for the national government.

§ 17. INTERPRETATION AND CONSTRUCTION OF THE CONSTITUTION. The two provisions mentioned simply formulate and make precise the fundamental principles which control the interpretation and construction of the whole constitution. We must apply to them, as well as to the rest of the constitution, the further principle that words are to be understood in their natural and — when a technical expression of different meanings is used — in their ordinary sense. No violence must be done to them. Their scope must not be stretched by skillful interpretation. They must not, however, be too literally read. Moreover, the same word has by no means the same meaning in every part of the constitution, and as every single word must be interpreted by its context, so must every single clause be read and interpreted in unison with all the other clauses. The constitution is a whole. It is not to be made an arena for juristic hair-splitting. In every doubtful case, the point of view from which to ascertain the true intent of the framers of the constitution must be the general end which the provision was intended to serve. Judges as well as law-givers must recognize the absolute impossibility of any conflict between the different provisions of the constitution. Since the will of the people as expressed in the constitution is unconditionally supreme, the fact must be recognized that this will is never untrue to itself, and is always entirely conscious of itself. But the expression of this will cannot always be put with such absolute certainty as to leave no room for honorable differences of opinion. This is implied, indeed, in that general method of expression in the constitution which we have recognized as a necessity lying in the very nature of the thing. It is partly due, too, to the fact that the constitution was not, to the people who gave it, an end in itself, but a means to the end, and this end seemed to demand that, in regard to certain things, the establishment of an inviolable principle should be avoided.

§ 18. THE LIMITS OF AUTHORITY. This has especial reference to the dividing line between the authority of the federal powers and of the states. The all-pervading fundamental thought of the constitution is that certain interests are common to the whole people of the Union, and that therefore, in regard to these, political powers have been intrusted to a central government, and that other interests and needs must be left to the care of the states, because they vary according to locality. But the people have, in addition, rights, interests, and needs which are both national and local in their nature, and, in regard to these, both the federal and state governments must have duties and powers corresponding to these duties. It by no means follows from the delegation of a power to the federal government that the same power does not belong to the states. In every single case, the question must be put whether the delegation of authority to the one involves its withdrawal from the other. If this question cannot be answered affirmatively, one must further inquire what relation prevails in general between the concurrent powers of the national government and the states. When the constitution expressly withdraws something from the states, or gives it exclusively to the national government, of course no difficulty can arise. Even when neither of these contingencies happens, the exclusive power of the national government must be recognized, if the nature of things forbids the subjection of the citizens in regard to the question at issue to two different and independent legislative wills. Again, some powers are delegated to the federal government without any obligation to use them. Thus congress has a right to pass a general bankrupt law, but it need not do so. It has repeatedly done so, and repeatedly repealed the law at short intervals. In such a case, there is nothing to prevent the states from exercising a similar power, as long as the federal government does not exercise it, but as soon as the latter does so, the state laws will *ipso facto* become of no validity unless the nature of the matter permits two different legislative wills to act upon it at the same time. Here, in distinction from the case last mentioned, the exclusiveness of the federal authority does not depend upon the nature of the right in itself, but it comes into force for the first time by the use of the right. Finally, it often happens, as for example, in regard to the right of taxation, that it is either convenient or even necessary that the individual should be subject at the same time to different legislative wills. But the fact that this may happen without conflict between these wills does not exclude the possibility of conflict. If conflict comes, the state laws must yield to the national laws, but they yield to them only so far as they are irreconcilable with them. In principle, the authority of the states suffers no wrong, but they cannot exercise it in a particular way because the national government, in regard to the method of exercising the same power, has so far the preference that the accomplishment of its will cannot be interfered with, and of course not actually hindered. If a conflict *of* rights cannot happen, yet, from the manifold nature of these legal possibilities, conflicts *over* rights may easily arise. And even when the respective spheres of the federal and of the state governments do not intersect each other in this way, yet, of course, a question may arise between them under every provision of the constitution, as to whether each of them has acted within its constitutional powers. The framers of the constitution could not have overlooked this, and hence it is *a priori* evident that they must have taken care to bring about a legal decision of all such questions. If this were not so, the corner-stone of their whole building would have been wanting. But if this is so, then no ground is left for seeking such remedies as nullification, which can be based upon not a single word in the constitution. It is not by the spinning of a web of logic out of unproved and unprovable assertions that we can find what the constitutional law upon this point must be. The constitution shows what the constitutional law is.

§ 19. CONFLICTS OF AUTHORITY. If the rule that words are to be understood in their natural sense is followed, all difficulties which arise from the doctrine of state sovereignty in regard to the decision of unavoidable conflicts of authority disappear. The constitution is not a compact between the federal government and the states, and inasmuch as they do not stand in the relation of parties to each other or of parts of one another, there is no need of a common arbiter superior to them to decide questions between them. The non-existence of such an arbiter, therefore, does not imply that either of the alleged parties must ultimately decide for itself. The people of the United States and the population of the states are the same individuals. Federal government and state governments are their creatures, and have the same object — the welfare of the people. The co-ordination of the federal government and of the states, so far as the affairs of the commonwealth are concerned, is an absurdity just as it is an absurdity to claim that the federal government, the creature of the constitution, is one of the parties to the constitutional compact. It is an "agent," as the champions of the doctrine of state sovereignty, in opposition to their own theory of "parties," call it, but it is not, as they affirm, an agent of the states, but an agent of the people of the United States, and their exclusive agency for all their affairs as a commonwealth. It is as little master as it is servant of the states; but, as the general delegate of the master of the commonwealth for the commonwealth, it alone has authority within the sphere allotted to it. The Union is through the constitution a legal state. If the constituent members of a state had each for itself the power of ultimate decision as to what is law, this would be a negation in principle of the idea of a legal state. The commonwealth has given to the federal government its own sphere, and, therefore, the parts of the commonwealth cannot be judges as to whether it has overstepped its limits.[1] The opinion of the commonwealth can find lawful expression only in the manner provided by the constitution, *i. e.*, through the constitutional organs of the commonwealth in the discharge of their constitutional functions.

On the other hand, it has been claimed that the federal government could break through the paper barriers of the constitution at every point and make itself absolute master, if it alone must decide upon the constitutionality of its acts. In theory, this conclusion cannot be questioned, but in practice it is, in substance, an utterly false conclusion. The constitution avoids this danger in a practical way by the organization of that whole apparatus

[1] Story, I., p. 256, in his discussion of this question, recalls the fact that even under the articles of confederation, according to an unanimous vote of congress, the states were not authorized to put their own construction upon treaties, because treaties were made not by them but by congress.

of government which the Americans ordinarily call "a system of checks and balances." The law-making power of congress is under the direct control of the conditional veto right of the president. The members of both houses of congress are directly or indirectly elected by the people, and not at long intervals. The people are therefore always able to prevent an unconstitutional misuse of the law-making power by intrusting it to persons who will, with greater faith, fulfill their first duty of keeping the constitution in view, in their law-making, as the supreme and absolutely binding law of the land. Intentional and preconcerted usurpations are therefore possible only with the actual sanction of the people from the very beginning. This, however, does not give a sufficient protection against systematic oppression of minorities, and still less does it ensure to individuals that their constitutional rights shall not be interfered with and trenched upon in good faith through unconstitutional laws or acts of the federal powers. But the framers of the constitution intended to transform the old Union, not only into a state capable of life, but into such a state founded upon law, and they therefore could not forget to endow it expressly with the majesty of law, and that in such a way that the law should be as fully protected under all circumstances as it can be in the nature of man and of human institutions.

The third article relates to the "judicial power," *i. e.*, to the judicial majesty of the United States, creates the supreme court of the United States as the highest organ of this power, authorizes congress to create other federal courts, and declares that "the judicial power shall extend to all cases in law and equity arising under this constitution, the laws of the United States, and treaties made, or which shall be made, under their authority," that is, under that which it afterwards designates as the supreme law of the land. It could not be more clearly stated that nowhere and nohow outside of the federal government are single parts of the commonwealth and of the whole people to decide in the last instance, but that a factor of the federal government, created for this purpose, is to decide, in a way binding upon all, what the law is, according to the constitution and the federal laws, provided the questions in dispute come in form and substance within the scope of this provision. There is not the slightest support in the constitution for the assertion of the state's-rights school that this can never be the case in disputes about the respective authority of the federal government and the sovereign states. This assertion rests only upon a general abstract argument from the alleged nature of the Union as a league of states.[1] On the other hand, it has never been questioned that this clause does not cover all the disputed questions of constitutional law, and that even questions of the relative authority of the federal government and of the states cannot always be brought within it. In the first

---

[1] Even Madison could bring forward no other argument when he, well-called the father of the constitution, was driven by the stream of events into the front rank of the state's-rights school. He said, in 1800, in the Virginia report, "in relation to the rights of the parties to the constitutional compact," that the federal courts could not possibly decide in the last instance, because, "on any other hypothesis, the delegation of judicial power would annul the authority delegating it." The *Federalist*, No. 39, had expressly stated that the supreme court "in controversies between the two jurisdictions," that is, of the states and of the Union, "is ultimately to decide." In 1810, Pennsylvania proposed to create, by an amendment to the constitution, another tribunal for the decision of such questions. Nine states, among them six slave states, with Virginia at their head, rejected this upon the ground that the supreme court was already entrusted with this task. Not one state voted for the amendment.

place, the controversy must have assumed the form of an actual law-suit in order to come before the courts at all. If it has been brought before them in this form, yet they never sit as courts to decide directly upon the constitutionality of laws, or of other acts of the government. They decide constitutional questions in a given case only by stating the reasons for their judgment. Strictly speaking, it is only the case which is decided, and therefore their judgment is absolutely binding on all individuals and on all political powers only so far as this case is concerned. But since it is fair to assume that in all analogous cases the same decision would be given, the reasons for a judgment upon the constitutionality of the law usually amount to an actual decision of the question of constitutionality. But that these questions cannot be *decided*, in a proper sense of the word, is clear from the fact that the supreme court can change its opinion, and has changed it, in constitutional questions of the highest significance after the lapse of a comparatively short time.[1] It sometimes only needs the introduction of a single

[1] Thus, for example, in the so-called legal tender cases in 1870, by five to three votes, the court denied congress the power to make the paper money of the United States legal tender for debts contracted previously. In the following year, this decision was reversed. The reversal was brought about by adding one judge to the supreme court, and by notifying the president that the senate would make its approval of the nomination of the new judge, as well as of one to fill a vacancy which had meanwhile occurred, dependent upon the position of the candidates on this question. President Grant responded to the wish of his party and the previous majority became a minority. See the article entitled "The Session," in *The North American Review*, CXI., pp. 48, 49. The new decision based the power upon the war power. Now, in 1884, the authority has been again recognized, but inasmuch as, in this case, an appeal to the war power was not possible, it has been deduced from the right to borrow money. The majority of 1871 declared that this had nothing to do with the matter, and therefore based it upon the war power.

new judge to transform the minority into a majority. Moreover, the supreme court is not superior, but equal, to the two other factors of the federal government. Within the sphere of their authority, the latter are not only authorized but directed to judge with entire independence of the constitutionality of their acts. While the supreme court has always given its opinion in the last instance in regard to disputed questions of constitutional law which belonged to its forum, and were brought before it in a constitutional way,[1] it has also repeatedly declared that it was neither directed nor permitted to concern itself with the political duties of the president, and especially was not authorized to interfere with them upon the assumption that he was about to carry out an unconstitutional law.[2] And it is even more certain that it does not belong to the supreme court to make rules for the exercise by congress of its legislative powers. The task of the court is to say what *is* law under the constitution, the federal laws and treaties. The task of congress, on the other hand, is to decide what shall be law under the constitution.[3] Thus, for example, not the court, but congress

---

[1] See *Martin vs. Hunter*, Wheaton, I., 304; *McCulloch vs. Maryland*, Ibid., IV., 316; *Cohens vs. Virginia*, Ibid., VI., 264; *Gibbons vs. Ogden*, Ibid., IX., 210; *Bank of Hamilton vs. Dudley*, Peters, II., 524; *Chisholm vs. Georgia*, Dallas, II., 419; *Ware vs. Hilton*, Ibid., III., 199.

[2] See *Mississippi vs. Johnson*, Wallace, IV., 475, and *Georgia vs. Stanton*, Ibid., VI., 51.

[3] That the courts actually take part in the *formation* of law cannot be questioned. They cannot, however, on this account, lay claim, as Pomeroy (pp. 66, 67) would have them do, to a share of the law-making power. The constitution expressly entrusts congress with "all" the law-making powers delegated in it and by it, and there can be no constitutional law-making power which is not created by the constitution. The judges are never authorized, where they find a gap in constitutional law, in customary law, or in statute law,

alone, must decide whether the means chosen by congress for the exercise of a constitutional power are " necessary and proper." The court has simply to decide in a given case whether the power which is claimed is constitutional, and whether the choice of the means selected is not denied by the constitution. In a word, the domain of the court is not politics but law, and this must control it in deciding questions of law. The other federal powers must, as Lincoln said in his inaugural address, give great moral weight to the court's decisions upon the constitutionality of laws and other governmental acts, so far as these decisions are not *dicta*. But except in the particular case at issue, the decisions have no political control of the co-ordinate powers. If this were granted, the people would have abdicated and have placed their fate in the hands of the court.

This has two consequences of far-reaching significance. In the first place, sufficient time may elapse before disputed questions of constitutional law come before the supreme court in such a way that it can deliver a judgment upon them, so that, meanwhile, the action of the other factors of the national government may create such a state of facts as to make it, from a political, and often even from a legal, standpoint, a very serious matter to declare the laws or actions in question to be unconstitutional. The supreme court would, in such a case, come to such a conclusion with the more difficulty, because

to decide according to their own free will, *i. e.*, to decide, as lawmakers, what the law shall be. Wherever, in such a case, they do by their judgments aid in the formation of law, it happens only in this way: that they follow to their logical conclusion, and apply to the given case, provisions of constitutional, customary or statute law. The formation of law is therefore, in such a case, not to be considered as the creation of a new law. The law is already in existence, but it first assumes fixed form upon its application to a concrete case.

from the beginning it has made it a maxim that no law should be declared unconstitutional simply because there were arguments of a certain weight against its constitutionality, *i. e.*, that the presumption should always be for instead of against the constitutionality of the acts of the other factors of the government.[1] But besides this, there are other disputed constitutional questions which, in their nature, can never be brought before the supreme court or decided by it. Moreover, violations of the constitution may happen, and those who are injured by

[1] See Cooley, *Constitutional Limitations*, pp. 182–185, where the judicial decisions setting forth this principle are collected. The sentence quoted from a decision by Justice Washington is especially noteworthy. In the *Sinking Fund Cases* (99 U. S., Otto, IX., 7–18), it is said: "This declaration should never be made except in a clear case. Every possible presumption is in favor of the validity of a statute, and this continues until the contrary is shown beyond a rational doubt. One branch of the government cannot encroach on the domain of another without danger. The safety of our institutions depends in no small degree on a strict observance of this salutary rule." James B. Thayer thinks that the whole emphasis should be laid upon the word "rational," and goes on to say: "But in determining the constitutionality of legislative action, a court is called upon to consider what, under the constitution, is the admissible view, rather than what is the right view of legislative power." *The Nation*, April 10, 1884. Upon the question of the unconstitutionality of laws, the following statements are of great significance: "The same statute may be in part constitutional, and in part unconstitutional, and if the parts are wholly independent of each other, that which is constitutional may stand, while that which is unconstitutional will be rejected. But if they are so mutually connected with, and dependent upon, each other as conditions, considerations, or compensations for each other, as to warrant a belief that the legislature intended them as a whole, and that if all could not be carried into effect, the legislature would not pass the residue independently, and some parts are unconstitutional, all of the provisions which are thus dependent, conditional or connected, must fall with them." Hammond, I., 22, § 63, where the judicial decisions upon this question are cited.

5

them cannot, whether states or individuals, obtain justice through the courts.[1] When the wrongs suffered are political in their origin, the remedies must be sought in a political way. Of course, they can frequently be obtained only indirectly, and can simply prevent further injustice. They cannot give satisfaction for the wrong already done. Yet it does not by any means follow from this that the sovereign states are authorized "to interpose," as the state's-rights school phrases it. In these cases the different factors of the federal government must themselves decide ultimately upon the extent of their constitutional powers. If each state had the right, so far as its interests were in question, to decide on such a point, the federal government would cease to be a government, and anarchy would become the supreme law of the Union. And so the argument that the president, and especially congress, if withdrawn from judicial control, can bend the constitution to their usurping wills, is of no avail. It is a fundamental principle, not only of politics, but of constitutional law, that the possibility of the misuse of a power is not a proof of the non-existence of the power.

[1] So far as the supreme court is concerned, it is a significant fact that it can be appealed to only in certain cases specified in the constitution, but congress is to decide in which of these cases there shall be a right to appeal. In one case, in which the question of the constitutionality of the reconstruction laws could be raised only by an appeal, congress took away from the supreme court the right to take cognizance of the case, and this, too, after the appeal had already been taken. The reason for this was, of course, that congress thought it undesirable to have a decision of the supreme court. See *McCardle's Case*, Wallace, VII., 506.

ORGANIZATION OF THE FEDERAL GOVERNMENT.

§ 20. THE THREE DEPARTMENTS. The articles of confederation preserved the actual condition of affairs brought about by the Revolution, and entrusted the entire business of the federation to one single organ. On the other hand, the constitution established three departments. These together constitute the government. In spoken and written discussions of this change, Montesquieu's doctrine of the division of powers was mainly relied upon. But the type presented by the English constitution had already had much greater influence. Yet the lessons derived from the country's own sad experience were decisive. And therefore the authors of the constitution did not seek to copy the English pattern exactly. Much less did they pursue the principle they recognized with stubborn doctrinairism and short-sightedness to its logical consequences. The three governmental factors were congress, the president, and the supreme court. They were endowed with the legislative, executive and judicial powers. But while their respective jurisdictions are sufficiently defined as between themselves, these jurisdictions by no means completely coincide with these three forms of political action. They intersect each other in manifold ways, and often the authoritative will works its ends only by their co-operation. The three departments stand side by side, but are not, as is frequently asserted, independent of one another. This is so little the case that Pomeroy (p. 89) rightly says: "Each is so completely dependent on the others that without them it could do practically nothing." That this was so arranged with full intention appears from the *Federalist* (No. 48): "Unless these departments be so far connected and blended as to give to each a constitutional control over the others, the degree of separation which the maxim requires as essential to a free government can never, in practice, be duly maintained." In the organization of the government each department was given a constitutional control of the other two. Hence there can be no superiority or inferiority among them. It is, moreover, a fundamental principle of the constitution that the three factors of government are in complete co-ordination,—co-ordinate, but not of equal power. In this respect the constitution put them on an entirely different footing, and the actual development of circumstances has very considerably increased this original difference. For that difference has its only source in the nature of things, *i. e.*, in the nature of the functions with which they are entrusted. In the political contests of the past — sometimes impliedly, sometimes expressly — congress has repeatedly claimed, and at least once the president[1] has claimed, a certain superior authority. Both rested the claim upon being in a higher degree than the other the representative of the "people," the source of all power. Of such a difference the constitution knows naught. Even though it existed, the co-ordination of the governmental factors would be absolutely untouched, as each of them indubitably possesses only the powers delegated to it by the constitution. Apart from this, moreover, the claim would be untenable, because the condition precedent of the argument in support of the claim does not exist. The people of the United States, as a unified, organized body, never appear in the arena of political action. Even where the people act most directly, they always do so through their state organizations. None of the factors of government is, therefore, called into life in such a way as to justify it in designating itself as a direct representative

[1] Andrew Jackson.

of the people. There could be no claim of an order of rank among them, even if it were permitted to deduce the constitutional law of the land from "the democratic principle." In spite of the great *rôle* which appeals to "the democratic principle" have played in the constitutional history of the United States, there is not the least doubt of its absolute inapplicability, for these appeals substitute for the constitution this principle, or what is declared to be a consequence thereof. The sovereign people have made unto themselves the constitution as their supreme law. They have therein merely assigned a fixed place to each of the three factors of government, without regarding it as necessary either to the public dignity or interests to admeasure its respective authority in proportion to the participation of the people — the voters — in its organization. Had that been the intention of the authors of the constitution, they would not, on the one hand, have given that factor (the supreme court), to which its final interpretation as a rule belongs, the greatest possible stability, and, on the other, have withheld from the "people" every immediate influence upon the formation of this factor.

§ 21. THE TERM OF OFFICE. Just as the provision that the members of the supreme court shall be appointed by the president with the consent of the senate for life or during good behavior disregards "the democratic principle," so all the other provisions relating to the terms of office of the other possessors of the powers of government depend solely upon the demands of public policy. The president is elected for four years, and enters upon the duties of his office on the 4th day of March. Relative to eligibility for re-election, the constitution says nothing. A single re-election has frequently occurred, but a re-elected president has never even been renominated by his party, much less actually re-elected, for a third term.[1] The suggestion often made, to abolish the right of re-election, has thus far found so little approbation among the people that it has been somewhat vigorously agitated only during a few presidential campaigns. The vice-president is elected simultaneously with the president and for the same period of time. Congress consists of the house of representatives and of the senate. The members of the house of representatives are elected for two years. Their terms all end on every second 4th of March. Only in cases of vacancies does the governor of the state concerned order a special election to fill the vacancy (art. I., sec. 2, § 4).[2] This term of office is absolutely mandatory for the whole house. A dissolution of congress is not recognized by the constitution. The term of the house of representatives constitutes a legislative period and is the basis of political chronology. The count is by "congresses," and each new house of representatives brings a new "congress" into existence. The presidential term of office covers two legislative periods. The senators are elected by the different state legislatures for the term of six years. If a vacancy occurs, the governor of the state concerned is authorized to fill it provisionally by appointment, if the legislature is not in session at the time (art. I., sec. 3, § 2).[3] After the legislature is again in session, a new election of a senator takes place, not for a term of six years, but only for the unexpired part of the term. This is because the senate is not subject to an

[1] A portion of the republican party made very energetic but ultimately fruitless efforts in 1880 to break through this tradition in favor of General Grant.

[2] Vacancies occur through death, resignation, expulsion, and acceptance of an office incompatible with that of congressman.

[3] The governor is not authorized to make the appointment if the vacancy has not yet actually occurred, but is only prospective.

integral or total renewal, but yet at the expiration of each legislative period, one-third of the senators retire. On this account (according to art. I., sec. 3, § 2), at the foundation of the government, the senators were distributed into three classes by lot; but care was taken that both senators from one state did not fall into the same class. When a new state is admitted into the Union, its senators are likewise placed by lot in different classes. Thus the senatorial term of office, next to that of the federal judges, is not only the longest, but the senate itself is likewise, though not in the manner of the supreme court, a permanent body with perpetual succession. The government is on the one hand assured, by this systematic diversity of official terms, of the continual influx of new blood, which keeps it in immediate and active sympathy with the existing wishes of the people. On the other hand, the danger of the government's reflecting only the momentary popular humor is thus also obviated.

§ 22. MODE OF ELECTION.— THE ACTIVE RIGHT OF SUFFRAGE. A like amalgamation of a self-conscious democratic spirit and conservative forecast characterizes every provision concerning the formation of those two departments which, in the more limited sense of the word, are designated as the government.[1]

The members of the house of representatives must be elected " by the people of the several states " (art. I., sec. 2, § 1). Farrar (p. 150) thinks that by " people " is meant only citizens, and, in fact, only citizens of the United

---

[1] What is called the government in Europe is styled the administration in the United States. The difference of speech is well founded in fact. In these, as in all like cases where the ideas do not completely coincide, for the purpose of greater accuracy I shall always adhere to the American terminology, after the expression has once been explained.

States. This assertion is neither justified by the most famous commentators on the constitution, nor is it in accordance with practice. The provision is simply that the representatives shall receive their authority by a direct election, for further on it is set forth: "The electors in each state shall have the qualifications requisite for electors of the most numerous branch of the state legislature." The active right of voting for congressmen, it thus appears, is not established on the same basis for all of the United States, either by the constitution or laws of the Union. In each state it may be made dependent upon different conditions. Formerly the greatest diversities prevailed in this respect, and even now there is no complete uniformity. Yet from a constitutional standpoint it is not correct merely to state that the constitution left it entirely to the judgment of the states to determine the qualifications of the voter at elections to the house of representatives. It would be more correct to say that the states have never had any power whatever in the matter.[1] The states have only to decide who shall possess the franchise at elections to the most numerous branch of the state legislature. The constitution makes the possessors of this franchise the electors for the house of representatives. It may seem at first sight that this is only a logical distinction, without any practical difference. But this is not so. The states, in many instances, in framing their election laws, paid no attention to the elections for the house of representatives.

[1] Congress also has the right to protect voters in the exercise of the franchise; to punish election officials for unlawful practices; to direct the registration of voters, etc. How far it may exercise these rights is within its judgment, but so far as it does exercise them the conflicting provisions of the state laws will be of no avail. *Ex parte Siebold*, 100 U. S., 371; *Ex parte Clarke*, 100 U. S. (Otto, X.), 299.

They considered simply their own public affairs. This is why, for instance, many states have given the franchise to non-naturalized foreigners, who thereby were endowed under the constitution with the franchise at elections to the house of representatives. We have, then, this curious spectacle: that, in the democratic republic, male citizens of full age, of good character, and of sound mind, cannot vote for members of the people's house of the Union, while certain persons who are not citizens can do so. Having or not having the franchise depends, in the first place, upon the domicile. A change in that may give or may forfeit the franchise. In the United States, as such, universal suffrage (so called) does not exist. Moreover, citizenship is not a condition precedent of the franchise.[1]

The amendments adopted after the civil war have brought about a much greater uniformity with regard to the franchise, but the anomalies just noted have not been set aside. The second section of the fourteenth amendment declares that the states shall be represented in the house of representatives in proportion to the total number of their inhabitants, exclusive of the untaxed Indians.[2]

---

[1] See *Scott vs. Sanford* (better known as the Dred-Scott decision), Howard, XIX., 404-414.

[2] Art. I., sec. 2, § 3, provides that each five slaves (but this word was avoided) should be counted, in regard to representation, as three persons. The further declaration of this paragraph, that "direct taxes" should also be levied in proportion to the population of the states, is not touched by the fourteenth amendment, and is therefore still in full force. What is meant by "direct taxes" has evoked very divergent views, and there has been no authoritative decision of the question. I must therefore rely upon the simple statement of the clause, and can do this the more readily since before the civil war direct taxes were levied only thrice,— in 1798, 1813 and 1815. The nature of certain taxes levied during the war is a subject of controversy. Since its termination the controversy has again assumed a

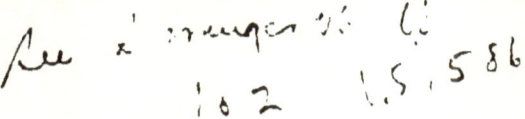

"But when the right to vote at any election for the choice of electors for president and vice-president of the United States, representatives in congress, the executive and judicial officers of a state, or the members of the legislature thereof, is denied to any of the male inhabitants of such state being twenty-one years of age and citizens of the United States, or in any way abridged, except for participation in rebellion or other crime, the basis of representation therein shall be reduced in the proportion which the number of such male citizens shall bear to the whole number of male citizens twenty-one years of age in such state." So far as this provision is concerned the right of the states to regulate the franchise according to their own opinions is not in the least abridged; but it puts a strong pressure on the states to introduce universal suffrage. Every considerable limitation of the right of suffrage henceforth would bring about a sensible diminution of a state's representation in the house of representatives. Pomeroy (p. 135) justly observes that this provision, directed mainly against the former slave states and intended to force them to grant full political equality to the freedmen, was the surrender of a fundamental principle of the constitution. It is not limited to the exercise of an influence upon the elections to the house of representatives. It subjects the states to the strongest pressure in framing their laws concerning the right of suffrage in state elections. Hitherto, on the contrary, the constitution had, as a matter of fundamental principle, left with

purely academic character, and the economic relations of the Union suggest that it will retain this character for generations to come. According to the decision of the supreme court in *Springer vs. The United States* (102 U. S., 586), the income tax is not a "direct tax" within the meaning of the constitution; only poll taxes and taxes on real estate are to be regarded as "direct."

the states the absolute right of self-government in all affairs peculiarly their own.

In one provision, the fifteenth amendment went far in advance of the fourteenth. It reads: "The right of citizens of the United States to vote shall not be denied or abridged by the United States or by any state on account of race, color or previous condition of servitude." In opposition to a widespread opinion, the courts have decided, in every case brought before them, that nobody obtained the right to vote by reason of this amendment. The United States, as well as the several states, can still withhold it forever from every colored man and former slave, but they cannot do so on account of his race, color or previous condition of servitude. The states' right of self-government relative to the franchise has now undoubtedly suffered a legal limitation, not because they have been obliged to grant the suffrage to certain persons, but because they are forbidden to refuse it on certain grounds.

The number of members of the house of representatives is not fixed by the constitution. It merely declares that every tenth year an enumeration of the people shall be made, that the number of representatives shall not exceed one for every 30,000 inhabitants, and that each state shall have at least one representative (art. I., sec. 2, § 3). The basis of representation has been repeatedly changed by law in accordance with the results of the decennial census. After the first census it was fixed at 33,000; now it is 154,325; and the number of members has grown from 65 and 105 to 325, to which a delegate from each of the eight territories is to be added.[1]

[1] There were 65 members according to the temporary provisions of the constitution, and 105 after March 4, 1793, upon the basis of the first census. Nevada had, according to the census of 1880, only a

Just as with reference to the membership of the house of representatives, so also in regard to the other regulations of elections — and that too for both houses — the constitution has guarded the possibility of letting experience shape matters in fullest accord with the changing demands of every new situation. Art. I., sec. 4, § 1, provides: "The times, places and manner of holding elections for senators and representatives shall be prescribed in each state by the legislature thereof, but the congress may at any time by law make or alter such regulations, except as to the places of choosing senators." This exception is evidently founded on the fact that the senators are elected by the legislatures, and it would not be in harmony with the federal character of the Union to grant to congress the right of determining the places for the meeting of the legislatures of the several states. For a long time congress made no use of the powers granted it by this clause. In 1842, for the first time, it declared that elections for the house of representatives should take place by districts.[1] But now, on the contrary, the constant and actual consolidation of the Union has found even in this respect a corresponding legal expression. An act of February 2, 1872, provides that from and after the year 1876 in every second year the election for members of the house of representatives shall take place on the Tuesday succeeding the first Monday of November in fixed geographical districts.[2]

population of 62,266, and would thus have probably had no representative, if the constitution had not provided in this way for such a case. So, too, the population of Delaware fell several hundreds below the established standard-number of 154,325. At this time four states have each but one representative.

[1] For a discussion of the disregard of this law on the part of several states and the approval of their action by the house of representatives, see my *Constitutional History*, II., 505 et seq.

[2] *Statutes at Large*, XVII., 28, secs. 2, 3. The fifth section of this law declares that in future no state shall be admitted into the Union

The votes cast must be on either written or printed ballots.[1] The elections of senators had already been, by an act of July 25, 1866, very precisely arranged and regulated. The election must take place on the second Tuesday after the assembling and organization of the legislature. In each house each member declares his vote *viva voce*. At noon of the day following both houses meet in joint convention, and if in each the same person has obtained a majority of all the votes cast, the election is completed. If this is not the case, or if one of the two houses has not entered upon the election in the manner prescribed, then the joint convention proceeds to *viva-voce* voting until a majority of the voters have united upon one person. The election is legal only when a majority of all the members elect are present and vote. For elections necessary on account of a vacancy substantially the same provisions obtain. The regular elections are held by the last legislature elected before the expiration of the term of office of a senator.

"without having the necessary population to entitle it to at least one representative according to the ratio of representation fixed by this bill." After the census of 1870, in accordance with the provisions of this act, there was one representative for every 131,425 inhabitants. As it is not intended to compel the states to headlong changes of their election districts, and the number thereof naturally often fails to agree with the number of representatives to which, on the basis of a new census, the states are entitled, they are permitted to elect the additional quota of representatives from the state at large,— congressmen at large.

[1] Act of February 28, 1871, sec. 19; *Statutes at Large*. XVII., 440. Formerly the states even in this respect could act as they deemed proper. It is left for them to determine whether an absolute majority is necessary to elect or a plurality shall suffice. In opposition to the law prevailing in England, the New England colonies adopted wholly or in part the principle of the absolute majority, but in the course of time the principle of plurality wins more and more the predominance in the United States, if indeed the former has not yet been completely displaced.

§ 23. THE RIGHT OF INSTRUCTION. No constitutional relation of any kind whatsoever exists between the senators and legislatures, after a valid and complete election. Legislatures have, indeed, very frequently, by passing resolutions, "instructed" the senators of their state — and that, too, without regard to whether they were elected by them or former legislatures — as to what attitude they should take upon certain questions. The senators — especially in early times those of the democratic party, as a rule — frequently acknowledged the right of "instruction." There is not, however, a particle of doubt that the claim of such a right, as has already been said, is not only extra-constitutional, but directly unconstitutional. The constitution does not once recognize the constituent's right of instruction. But the legislatures are as little the constituents of the senators as the presidential electors are the constituents of the president. Like the latter, they are merely entrusted with the election. If legislatures possessed the right of instruction, they would necessarily possess the power to enforce obedience. They would, therefore, have to be able to unseat a disobedient senator. But the constitution fixes the term at six years, and the legislatures cannot lengthen or shorten it by even one day. Since, moreover, in all the states, one house of the legislature is renewed at least every two years, the balance of parties during the senatorial term of office may be overthrown at least once, and quite likely twice. But even the most extreme state's-rights advocate never ventured the assertion that such an event imposed on a senator a moral obligation to resign. Nevertheless, if this happens, it is not simply on one certain question that he is out of accord with the will of the legislature: on all party questions he opposes it. A right of instruction that presupposes an identical partisan position is a manifest absurdity. And yet it must depend upon this presupposition, for the two senators of a state are elected by two different legislatures, and it is therefore a matter of common occurrence that they should belong to two different parties. Despite this, they are absolutely equal representatives of their state. The constitution (art. I., sec. 3, § 1) provides: "Each senator shall have one vote." It is therefore proper only in a very limited sense to call the senate the congressional house of states. The votes of the states are not cast there. Each senator votes according to his own convictions, and on his own personal responsibility. A legislature cannot assert that the state is practically deprived of its proper weight in the senate because the vote of a senator elected by a former legislature neutralizes the vote of one of an opposite party elected by a more recent legislature. The state has no right of complaint, moreover, even when — as may easily be the case — both senators belong to a party which, at the moment, is in a minority in the state.

There is no difference in the political existence of the house of representatives and of the senate, from the standpoint of constitutional law. Their functions are not quite the same; the mode of election, the voters, and the tenure of office are different; and in the senate the states as such have equal representation, whereas in the house of representatives representation is in proportion to the population. But the constitutional nature of the tenure of office is the same for both houses of congress. The mistake of the state's-rights conception of this question is, that it treats the legislatures and the states as identical. But according to the constitution, the latter, not the former, are represented in the senate.[1]

[1] It has happened that senators have resigned because obedience to instructions was irreconcilable with their consciences, and they recognized the right of the legislature to demand the representation of its views in the senate.

The conditions upon which the passive right of suffrage (the right to be voted for) depends are in substance the same for both houses of congress. For the senate they are simply somewhat more severe. To be eligible a person must be at least twenty-five (thirty) years of age, have been a citizen of the United States for at least seven (nine) years, and be an inhabitant of the state at the time of the election.[1] The third section of the fourteenth amendment moreover provides: " No person shall be a senator or representative in congress, or elector of president and vice-president, or hold any office, civil or military, under the United States or under any state, who, having previously taken an oath as a member of congress, or as an officer of the United States, or as a member of any state legislature, or as an executive or judicial officer of any state, to support the constitution of the United States, shall have engaged in insurrection or rebellion against the same, or given aid or comfort to the enemies thereof. But congress may, by a vote of two-thirds of each house, remove such disability." During the so-called period of reconstruction, these provisions were of great moment. Since its close, they are of importance only in so far as they tend to prevent the revival of doctrines which, in their ultimate consequences, led to the absurdity of constitutional rebellion.

§ 24. CONGRESS. As the elections to the house of representatives and to the senate in accordance with the provisions of the constitution and the laws proceed without the co-operation of the federal executive power, so in the regular course of affairs there is no need of its intervention to call the representatives and senators to assem-

[1] The tenure of office does not cease by reason of removal of the elected person to another state after his election. Diplomatic officials of the Union, even when at their posts in foreign countries, are recognized as "inhabitants" of their respective states and are eligible.

ble together in congress. Art. I., sec. 4, § 2, provides: "The congress shall assemble at least once in every year, and such meeting shall be on the first Monday in December, unless they shall by law appoint a different day."[1] The president can, however (art. II., sec. 3, § 2), "on extraordinary occasions convene both houses or either of them."[2]

In congress itself different views have been maintained with great vigor on the question as to whether the congress comes into life of and by itself by virtue of the meeting of the members of both houses, or whether the congress first exists when both houses have completed their organization.[3] The question, at bottom, however, has only an academic interest, as the co-operative action of both houses as a congress unquestionably is possible only after their formal organization is effected. Touching the senate, however, such an organization can be spoken of only in a very limited sense, since "the vice-president of the United States shall be president of the senate" (art. I., sec. 3, § 4). "The senate shall choose their other officers and also a president *pro tempore* in [case of] the absence of the vice-president, or when he shall exercise the office

---

[1] By virtue of the authority granted by the last clause, this provision was enlarged by the act of January 22, 1867, to the extent that congress should also meet upon the day its lawful existence begins, to wit, on March 4 of the odd-numbered years, and that every congress should thus have three regular sessions. This law, however, remained in force only for the three legislative periods of the 40th, 41st and 42d congresses.

[2] The clause proceeds: "And in case of disagreement between them, with respect to the time of adjournment, he may adjourn them to such time as he shall think proper." This power has never yet been used. It is, however, to be observed, that this right of adjournment by the president accrues only in the one particular case.

[3] See my *Constitutional History*, V., 212, 218.

of president of the United States."[1] The house of representatives, on the other hand, in addition to its other officers, has to elect its permanent chairman, who bears the title of speaker (art. I, sec. 2, § 5). As he has to appoint the standing committees which, so far as the house is concerned, as a rule practically shape all legislation, the election of the speaker is an act of pre-eminent political importance. In times of great political excitement, when neither party has an absolute majority, the organization of the house is apt to become a very serious question. The other factors of government have no power to enforce it.[2] In other words, the majority of the members-elect have the power to deprive the Union for the legislative two-year period of its law-making functions by preventing the organization of the house. On the other hand, neither of the two houses by itself can close a session after congress has once met either by virtue of the constitutional provisions or upon the call of the president. "Neither house, during the session of congress, shall, without the consent of the other, adjourn for more than three days, nor to any other place than that in which the two houses shall be sitting" (art. I., sec. 5, § 4).

§ 25. THE EXECUTIVE POWER. "The executive power shall be vested in a president of the United States of America" (art. II., sec. 1, § 1). The vice-president has no share in the executive power. His sole task, as long as the president acts as such, is that of presiding over the senate. Even though the executive authority is far removed from independence of the other factors of govern-

[1] Shortly before the close of each session, the vice-president gives the senate an opportunity to choose a president *pro tempore*, so that it shall not be without a presiding officer, if before the next session of congress the vice-president die or assume the office of president.

[2] See the sketch of the two-months campaign over the speakership in the 34th congress in my *Constitutional History*, V., 203-219. The house of representatives has no permanent vice-chairman.

ment, it is nevertheless singularly simple. The president is dependent in manifold ways upon the other factors, but he alone is the sole possessor of what the constitution describes as the executive power. The law may confer upon the so-called secretaries or members of the "cabinet," as well as upon other executive officers, independent functions, but the constitution recognizes no representative of the president, no one upon whom either the law or the free will of the president can temporarily confer even the slightest of the privileges and duties which the constitution grants to and imposes upon the bearer of the executive power. "In case of the removal of the president from office, or of his death, resignation, or inability to discharge the powers and duties of the said office, the same shall devolve on the vice-president, and the congress may by law provide for the case of removal, death, resignation or inability, both of the president and vice-president, declaring what officer shall then act as president, and such officer shall act accordingly, until the disability be removed or a president shall be elected." Art. II., sec. 1, § 5. The constitution thus creates in the person of the vice-president an official who in a given case is to take the place of the president. It commits to congress the task of providing for all cases in which he cannot discharge the duties of the office. But in every case the rights and duties of the place pass fully and wholly over to the designated person, either until the expiration of the term of office or temporarily. Any separation of these rights and duties, or of the responsibility imposed by them, is under all circumstances absolutely excluded.[1]

[1] By virtue of the authority conferred in the second clause of the paragraph cited above, congress has already provided, by the act of March 1, 1792, for the case of the inability of both the president and vice-president to act. After the vice-president, the president *pro*

As the president and vice-president are elected at and for the same time, the right to be chosen to both offices is dependent upon the same conditions (12th amendment). To be eligible, it is necessary to be a native-born citizen of the United States,[2] to be at least thirty-five years of age,

tempore of the senate, and after him the speaker of the house, takes the office. Whether these, like the vice-president, are to exercise the office of president until the expiration of the presidential term depends upon how near that is. As soon as the dual vacancy occurs, the secretary of state must notify the governor of every state. If this notification is issued less than two months before the first Wednesday in December, and the presidential term ends on the third day of March following, then the president *pro tempore* of the senate (or the speaker) performs the duties of the executive authority until the inauguration of the new president. If this be not the case, then the notification directs the choice or the appointment of electors. This is to take place thirty-four days before the first Wednesday in December, if at least two months intervene between this date and the proclamation. Otherwise it is to take place thirty-four days prior to the first Wednesday in December of the following year. The election by the electors is to take place on the first Wednesday of December. Neither the constitution nor the laws provide for vacancies occurring by reason of the impossibility of electing either a president or vice-president. If the house of representatives has to elect the president and does not do so before the 4th of March, when the new presidential term begins, then "the vice-president shall act as president" (12th amendment). Even so there is nothing determined as to who should act as president when, according to the act of March 1, 1792, the speaker ought to do so, and the vacancy occurs between the expiration of the legislative period and the organization of the new congress, so that there is no speaker. Hitherto by the death of the president the presidency has four times devolved upon the vice-president: John Tyler in place of W. H. Harrison, April 6, 1841; Millard Fillmore in place of Zachary Taylor, July 9, 1850; Andrew Johnson in place of Abraham Lincoln, April 15, 1865; Chester A. Arthur in place of James A. Garfield, September 20, 1881. A double vacancy has, however, never yet occurred.

[2] The exception in favor of those who at the time of the adoption of the constitution were citizens of the United States of course no longer applies.

and to have had a domicile in the United States for at least fourteen years. Art. II., sec. 1, § 4.[1] As to the eligibility of electors, the constitution contains only the negative provision that no senator, representative or official of the United States shall be an elector. Article II., § 1. The election is an indirect one. The constitution provides that every state shall have as many electors as it has senators and representatives in congress, but leaves it wholly to the legislatures to determine how they shall be chosen. Although they are elected at present in all the states by the people, yet so far as the federal constitution is concerned, this is solely a matter of fact. Every state is still authorized to do as South Carolina did for a long time,— have the electors appointed by the legislature. Or they can be chosen in any other manner whatsoever. The time when the election takes place is to be fixed by congress. By act of January 23, 1845, it fixed the first Tuesday after the first Monday in November of every fourth year. This law leaves it to the states to take proper legal measures to fill by substitutes any vacancies at the meeting of the electoral college.

The Mode of Election. The legislatures determine for their respective states the place of the election, but it is the duty of congress to fix the time, and it must be the same day for all of the states. By act of March 1, 1792, the election takes place on the first Wednesday in December. The electors must vote on separate ballots for one person for president, and for another as vice-president.[2]

[1] The constitution does not prohibit the selection of the president and vice-president from the same state, but the electors must vote, so far as one of the two offices is concerned, for a person who does not belong to their own state (12th amendment).

[2] According to the original scheme of the constitution, each elector simply placed two names on his ballot. Whoever received the greatest number of votes was to be president, and whoever had the next

The electors must prepare separate lists of all persons who receive any votes for either office, must subscribe and certify the lists, and having sealed them must send them, addressed to the president of the senate, to the seat of the federal government. "The president of the senate shall, in the presence of the senate and the house of representatives, open all the certificates and the votes shall then be counted." A majority of the votes of all the electors is necessary to an election. If none of the candidates for the presidency has received such a majority, then the house of representatives must elect one of the three candidates who received the greatest number of votes. In this case the house of representatives votes by states, and each state casts one vote. The ballot holds good if one or more members from two-thirds of the states be present. A majority of all the states is necessary to an election.¹ If no vice-president has been elected, the senate may choose one of the two candidates who received the greatest number of votes. Each senator casts one vote. To make a ballot valid, the presence of two-thirds of the senators is required. For an election the majority of all the senators is necessary.²

It is an undisputed fact that the twelfth amendment, which contains the provisions noted above, has become a mere empty form. The parties nominate their candidates in so-called national conventions, which have no legal ex-

highest number was to be vice-president, provided, in each case, that the candidate received a majority of all the votes cast. For the events of the election of 1800–1801, which led to the adoption of the twelfth amendment, see my *Constitutional History*, I., 168.

¹ See my *Constitutional History* (II., 4) as to the one presidential election (that of J. Q. Adams) which took place under this constitutional provision.

² Under this constitutional provision, R. M. Johnson was elected in 1837.

istence whatever, and the members of which are chosen without any legal control whatever. It has long been a subject of constant and loud complaint that not the mass of the people, but only the professional politicians, are represented in these conventions. In the interest of the managers, public opinion is often defied. The electors are mere ornamental figure-heads, without any will of their own. The people take not the least interest as to who are made electors, for the persons designated are held to be in honor bound to vote for the party candidates nominated by the national convention. Since the introduction of these conventions, no elector has ever ventured to act as the constitution intended, in accordance with his own judgment.[1] Not only in regard to the question as to which party shall carry the day, but also as to the persons chosen, the election of electors is the presidential election, and in ordinary conversation it is so called. The assembling and voting of the electoral college on the first Wednesday in December is an empty formality, for the decision was made in the preceding November. The development of actual facts has made the constitution a dead letter on this point.[2] The history of the presidential election of 1876–77 shows that even empty forms may become

[1] So, too, in former times, when the candidates were named by the party representatives in congress, the so-called "king caucus."

[2] Should accident so shape events that the presidential candidate of the victorious party should die immediately before the meeting of the electoral college, then the United States would again have a president who was, not only in form, but in truth, elected by the electors. The effects that such an accident might produce are incalculable. The most substantial result would probably be the final success of the efforts to bring the constitution again into accord with facts, and to have the president and vice-president elected directly by the people. If Horace Greeley had been, not the defeated, but the victorious, candidate, the constitution by his death in 1872 would have come to its rights.

of great significance. The after effects of the civil war came into play in a manner that threatened to be fatal. In some of the former slave states (Florida, South Carolina and Louisiana), both parties claimed the victory. If the electoral votes of all these states were given to the republicans, their candidate would be elected by a majority of one vote. But to whom did the constitution give the right to decide, if the legality of electoral votes was contested? — or if in one state two sets of electors should each claim to be legally chosen? The clause of the constitution already cited offered no such unquestionable solution of the problem that the most different doctrines might not have been advanced from the general standpoint of principle and of party interests. There were no precedents to indicate so precisely any particular path that congress would have been obliged to proceed therein. The position which congress took in regard to the electoral vote of Missouri in 1821, and of Michigan in 1837, had been generally understood hitherto as involving a claim on its part to the right to decide the validity of an electoral vote sent into it; and the twenty-second joint rule, concerning the counting of electoral votes (which was, however, no longer in force in 1876), was also based on this assumption. In 1857 the president of the senate declared, after he had announced the election of Buchanan, that he did not feel authorized to decide whether Wisconsin had voted for Fremont. And in 1873 congress refused to count the electoral vote of Louisiana, on account of fraud in the election. If the majority in both houses had now taken the same position, the minority would probably have been voted down by an appeal to precedent, and the affair would have been settled. But in the house of representatives the democrats, and in the senate the republicans, had a majority. It was therefore to be expected with certainty that they would take directly opposite grounds. The doctrine that both houses should be regarded as one composite body, and that the majority of all of the votes should decide, found not the slightest support in the constitution. Against the claim that congress was capable of deciding, the very important objection was raised, that the constitution provides only that the certificates shall be opened and counted " in the presence of the senate and house of representatives." All the other provisions indicate, however, an intention to assign to the states the right and responsibility of taking care that their electors shall be appointed in a constitutional and lawful manner, and their legal votes be properly conveyed to the president of the senate. The assertion of the republicans, that the decision belonged to this official, was equally untenable. Nowhere does the constitution empower him to count the votes. It declares simply that they "shall be counted,"—a formula which forces us to suppose that, according to the views of the framers of the constitution, the question was one simply of addition. The claim of the democrats that the decisive vote must be accorded to the house of representatives, because eventually the election of the president was incumbent upon it, was not a bit better founded. It was evident that no amicable adjustment would be attained, if the decision of the question were delayed until the official counting of the electoral votes. In harmony with public opinion, the most thoughtful leaders of both parties wished, however, to avoid the great commotions which would have been inevitable if the question were not decided before the beginning of the new presidential period. Refuge was therefore taken in an expedient which certainly cannot be called unconstitutional, but must be described as extra-constitutional. It could scarcely be resorted to again. A law was enacted, the essential provisions of which were as follows: If a state had sent in only one return of the electoral votes, it should not be rejected unless both houses should so decide; if two returns were sent in, these, together with all documents relating to them, should be referred to a commission of fifteen members; each house named five members of this commission: the law made four designated justices of the supreme court members, and these four were to select another justice of the supreme court as the fifteenth member; the decision of this commission was to be final, unless set aside by a concurrent resolution of both houses; an appeal to the courts was not forbidden. The republican candidate, Hayes, was installed in office under this law. The democrats accommodated themselves to circumstances, but adhered to the view that Tilden was the legally elected president. The manifold efforts to render the recurrence of such an event impossible, by amending the constitution or enacting proper laws, have not thus far as yet led to the desired result.

§ 26. THE "CABINET." The constitution knows nothing of a "cabinet." Even if the word has become as thoroughly naturalized in the language of America as in European states, it is nevertheless, from a constitutional standpoint, an abuse. The constitution speaks only of "executive departments." It does not call the heads of them ministers. It generally gives them no titles. By statute, the name "secretary" is given them. Collectively, the secretaries have no constitutional existence whatever. One of the two clauses of the constitution in which they are mentioned shows, however, that the framers intended to give the president, in the secretaries, not only executive organs of his will, but also counselors upon whose official counsel he might rest his acts and deeds — not legally, but morally and politically — when they were questioned by congress or the people. The president is authorized to "require the opinion in writing of the principal officer in each of the executive departments upon any subject relating to the duties of their respective offices." Art. II., sec. 2, § 1. The express grant of such a power in the fundamental law of the state means something only when thus interpreted. It is, therefore, certainly not in opposition to the spirit of the constitution if the secretaries have been more and more fused into a ministry which, as a whole, advises the president, so that his personal policy expands into the policy of the administration. But even if this is regarded not simply as permissible, but also as self-evident and necessary, still the president can never shield himself by an appeal to a resolution of his so-called cabinet. It is not opposed to the spirit of the constitution, and it is an irrepressible demand of modern government that, while the president resolves upon many things in his cabinet, he alone — not the cabinet — concludes, *i. e.*, decides. The political responsibility of each secretary extends beyond the limits of his own department, because he has voluntarily incurred a moral responsibility for the general character of the president's policy by sitting as a member of the cabinet. But, as the president possesses the sole right of decision, he cannot throw upon his cabinet his legal or political responsibility. As he can seek support in the opinion of each secretary about that official's own department, so he can seek it, by getting the opinion of all the secretaries together, about his general policy; but he cannot put his cabinet in the place which the constitution reserves for him. Because his position in relation to the cabinet is completely free, while as to the single minister it is limited by law, it is so much the more his duty to maintain with zealous care the constitutional relation — one which utterly excludes, according to its fundamental idea, a cabinet in the sense of those of the constitutional states of Europe. The constitution presupposes the existence of different "executive departments." These were, however, first created by law, and by law the duties and rights of all the secretaries have been accurately defined. The president decides for himself what he shall propose to his cabinet, how he shall count and weigh its votes, and to what degree he shall permit its counsels to influence his own decision. The secretaries are not (as executive officers) unconditionally subject to the will of the president. They are actual heads of departments, and that not because it has so pleased the president, or by force of circumstances, but because the law has made them such. The cabinet is, so to speak, only an inner chamber of the administration. Circumstances and the character of the president may permit it to attain great practical importance, but an official action of any kind whatever by the cabinet, as a body, seems impossible, as long as the whole political structure of the executive power is not subjected to a change in its principles such as could be effected only by a constitutional amendment. The fundamental character of the present relation between the president and congress is that they stand side by side. A cabinet, in the European sense of the term, would be justified, and its existence rendered possible, only when, in place of this relation, a far more intimate and organic union of the executive and legislature had been brought about. The introduction of a parliamentary government must not be thought of. That would put the entire constitution upon perfectly new bases. The administration could not be conducted *in* the name of a president and *under* the name of a cabinet by a committee of the law-making power. As before stated, the executive must be an independent and co-ordinate factor of government, and the bearer of this executive power must be president, not merely in form but in fact. The constitution grants the senate a right of control over the appointment of the secretaries, inasmuch as it requires the senate's confirmation of the president's nominations. But it would be a grievous sin against the spirit of the constitution if the senate were to misuse this right of confirmation so as to compel the president to appoint a particular person, or even a man in political accord with the majority of the senate. The provisions of the constitution as to the time of election, the method thereof, and the terms of office, of president, senators and representatives, leave no doubt that the framers of the constitution did not consider political harmony between the president and congress, or between the president and one of the two houses, as a matter of necessity. As the president is responsible for the administration, it is self-evident that, so far as political views do and must come into consideration in choosing the cabinet, those of the president must prevail. In theoretical discussions, as well as in political struggles between the executive and the legislative powers, the view has always obtained that the constitution gave the president full liberty to remove the secretaries.[1] The political school

---

[1] The conflict between Andrew Johnson and congress led to the enactment of the tenure-of-office act of March 2, 1867, which related to all the civil officials appointed by the president with the consent of the senate. But its main object was to compel the president to retain in office the secretaries who, in full accord with the majority of congress, were the bitterest opponents of his policy towards the rebel states. In my opinion, party passion alone dare dispute that congress, by the passage of this law, became guilty of the boldest usurpation and of gross violation of the true intent of the constitution. Barely

which treats constitutional and parliamentary government as identical ideas will not find, in the constitution of the greatest and freest republic of all time, the slightest support for its doctrine. But although a parliamentary government is absolutely excluded by the fundamental ideas of the constitution, yet for several years past the question has been discussed with increasing interest, whether the executive power, by law or constitutional amendment, should not be brought into closer communication with the legislative, so that its measures and views could be openly and directly represented in both houses of congress by the secretary of the department concerned. That the development of affairs is tending in this direction, congress has frequently been compelled to acknowledge, at least indirectly, for the secretaries furnish it the materials for many of its legislative labors. Its committees are not satisfied with the written information obtained, and so summon the secretaries, in order to obtain the desired information by oral discussions. Thus, finally,

had Grant become president than the most objectionable provisions were repealed by a new act of April 5, 1869. This is so framed that it can scarcely be declared to be unconstitutional. But the tendency to extend the constitutional authority of the senate glimmers even through this. Congress is unquestionably authorized to regulate by law the right of dismissal. Such a regulation in regard to administrative officials is urgently needed. An unqualified right of dismissal, conditioned only upon the senate's assent, should certainly not be accepted as such a legal regulation. As for the offices of a political character, the nature of things forbids bringing them into such a scheme. If the constitution had intended to confer on the senate a right of control over dismissals from them, it would have declared it as expressly as it does the senate's control over appointments. But, as to all other offices, the welfare of the state demands a limitation of the arbitrary power of dismissal exercised by the constantly changing political chiefs. The clause just mentioned of the act of April 5. 1869, simply couples the arbitrary will of the president and the arbitrary will of the senate.

many proposed laws, which officially have an entirely different paternity, are prepared in some bureau of the administration. But congress is too well aware of how very much the position of the executive would be strengthened, as against itself, if the secretaries received the right of debate in senate and house, and its tendency is too decided to elevate its own dignity and enlarge its own sphere of action at the cost of the executive, to permit those who perceive in such a change one of the most urgent and significant reforms to hope that their views may soon come to pass. But while the relation of the executive to the legislative power constitutes one of the greatest differences between the political institutions of the United States and those of all European constitutional nations, and probably will do so for a long time, the organization of the "administration" in America, and of the "government" in Europe, is in the main similar, and will become more so with the progressive development of the United States. Originally there were only four departments: that of state (foreign affairs), of the treasury (finances), of war, and of justice (attorney-general). In 1794 the postoffice department (postmaster-general) was added; in 1798 the navy department, and in 1849 the department of the interior.[1]

[1] By act of May 15, 1862, an agricultural department was also created. But its head is only a "commissioner." He is subject to none of the secretaries, but is not a member of the "cabinet."

By act of March 2, 1867, there was created within the department of the interior an "office of education," also administered by a "commissioner." The suggestion has already been made to change this bureau into an independent department, but there is no immediate prospect of this and possibly no necessity for it, since the school-system is a matter for the states.

Only the most important points of the organization and work of the departments can be sketched here.

The state department is not simply the ministry of foreign affairs. The secretary of state is also keeper of the great seal, and in the

§ 27. THE FEDERAL COURTS. The constitution establishes only the supreme court of the United States and makes it the duty of congress, according to the changing necessities of the times, to create and organize such inferior courts as it shall see proper. To be eligible for appointment to the office of justice in the United States

archives of this department the original records of the laws, of all resolutions of congress, etc., are preserved. The publication of the laws (in three newspapers), and the proclamation of an adoption of an amendment to the constitution, are among the secretary of state's functions. The fact deserves especial mention, that he is legally bound to present congress annually with a concise report of the changes made by other countries in their commercial and domestic policies. He has as aids a first and second assistant secretary of state, who are appointed by the president, subject to the consent of the senate.

The treasury department more than any of the others was from the beginning brought into a legal relation with congress, independent of the president. And as to this department it was admitted from the beginning that congress, in its legislation, could not do without executive co-operation. The very act of organization of September 2, 1789, provides: "That it shall be the duty of the secretary of the treasury to digest and prepare plans for the improvement and management of the revenue, and for the support of the public credit, . . . to make report, and give information, to either branch of the legislature in person or in writing (as he may be required) respecting all matters referred to him by the senate or house of representatives or which shall appertain to his office." *Stats. at Large*, I., 65, 66. An act of May 10, 1800, further provides: "That it shall be the duty of the secretary of the treasury to digest, prepare and lay before congress, at the commencement of every session, a report on the subject of finance, containing estimates of the public revenue and public expenditures, and plans for improving or increasing the revenues, from time to time, for the purpose of giving information to congress in adopting modes of raising the money requisite to meet the public expenditures." *Ibid.*, II., 79, 80. Among the reports which the secretary must annually lay before congress are particularly to be mentioned those prepared by the bureau of statistics "on the statistics of commerce and navigation" (act of February 10, 1820, *Ibid.*, III., 541), and "upon the condition of the agriculture, manufactures, domestic trade, currency and

supreme court requires no particular qualifications, according to the constitution. It provides only that the members of the supreme court shall be appointed by the president, with the advice and consent of the senate. In regard to the other federal judges, this is not expressly required, but the fact that congress has not reckoned

banks of the several states and territories" (June 15, 1844, *Ibid.*, V., 719), and a summary of the exports and imports of the past fiscal year (July 1 to June 30). Every three months a report of the expenditures and revenue, and once a month a report of the condition of the treasury during the last week of the month, must be published (June 17, 1844, *Ibid.*, V., 696). The accounts are examined by six auditors, above whom two comptrollers are placed in charge. The moneys are received and paid out by the treasurer. Payments are made on vouchers of the treasurer, countersigned by a comptroller and entered by the registrar. A commissioner of customs has charge of the revenue arising from custom duties. The system of internal taxation is managed by a commissioner of internal revenue. Among the other officials of the department, the director of the mint and the comptroller of the currency may be mentioned.

The most important officers of the war department are the adjutant-general, quartermaster-general, paymaster-general, commissary-general, surgeon-general, judge-advocate-general, chief of engineers and chief of ordnance. It is odd that the signal service also (chief signal officer) is placed under the war department, although its main object is to give information by telegram and by signals, for the benefit of agricultural and commercial interests, of the approach and force of storms, by means of observations taken at fixed meteorological stations.

The department of justice consists of an attorney-general, solicitor-general, two assistant-attorneys-general, solicitor of the treasury, solicitor of internal revenue, naval solicitor, and an examiner of claims for the state department. In the separate judicial districts, legal matters are attended to by a district attorney. The executive officers are called marshals. ("The marshals and their deputies shall have, in each state, the same powers, in executing the laws of the United States, as the sheriffs and their deputies in such state may have, by law, in executing the laws thereof." *Rev. Stat.*, sec. 788.)

In respect to the postoffice department, it need only be said that on account of the great number of postmasters necessarily appointed,

them among the "inferior officers," the appointment of which it may commit "to the president alone, to the courts, or to the heads of departments," is unquestionably in harmony with the intent of the constitution. This appears, too, from the fact that none of the federal judges, without exception, according to the constitution, can be removed from office during good behavior.[1] The

the department, under the "spoils" principle, has reached a commanding importance in party politics, with which, so far as its legitimate duties are concerned, it should have no connection.

The navy department is divided into eight "bureaus:" yards and docks; navigation (combined with a "hydrographic office"); ordnance; provisions and clothing; medicine and surgery; equipment and recruiting; construction and repair; and steam engineering. The heads of the bureaus must be chosen from particular ranks of the officers of the navy.

The duties of the interior department are the most extensive and comprise the most different objects: (1) census; (2) public lands; (3) Indian affairs; (4) patents; (5) bureau of education; (6) the geological surveys; (7) pensions, a branch which, since the civil war, and particularly of late years, has attained vast importance by reason of sweeping legislation; in the fiscal year 1883-84, $55,429,228 were paid out for pensions, more than one dollar *per capita* of the population; (8) preservation and distribution of the government's publications.

The business of the department of agriculture is "to acquire and diffuse among the people of the United States useful information on subjects connected with agriculture in the most general and comprehensive sense of that word, and to procure, propagate and distribute among the people new and valuable seeds and plants." *Rev. Stat.*, sec. 520. See W. Elmes, *Executive Departments of the U. S. Government*, Washington, 1879.

[1] Territorial judges are not federal judges within the meaning of article III., section 1. Although the inferior federal courts within the states are first created by law, they are nevertheless "constitutional" courts, *i. e.*, they are made by this article co-bearers of the judicial power of the United States. The territorial courts, on the other hand, are "legislative," *i. e.*, they were created by congress, not by virtue of this constitutional provision, but by virtue of its own general legislative power over the territories. *American Insurance Co. vs. Canter*, Peters, I., 546. I know of no judicial decision

constitution does not fix the number of members of the United States supreme court. The great act of September 24, 1789, which filled in the outline drawn by the constitution on this subject, provided that it should be composed of one chief justice and five associate justices. By the act of April 29, 1802, a sixth associate justice was created, and an act of March 3, 1837, increased their number to the present figure of eight.[1] To decide a case six justices must be present.[2] The act of 1789 created thirteen district courts with one judge each and three circuit courts. The latter form the courts of first appeal. Their organization has been modified in the course of years. There are now nine circuits. One is assigned to each justice of the supreme court. Every circuit has, besides, its own circuit judge, and finally every district judge, within certain limitations, can exercise the office of circuit judge.[3] Each one of these judges may, alone or in common with one of the two other judges, hold circuit court, and therefore in different parts of the same district there may be held simultaneously different circuit courts.

as to whether the removal of a federal judge by abolishing his office is constitutional. During the presidency of Jefferson, congress claimed this right, and some of the states have adopted the same course in regard to irremovable judges.

[1] It seems doubtful whether an attempt will be made to allay the increasing clamor concerning the extraordinary over-burdening of the supreme court, by a further increase of the number of associate justices. Manifold attempts have been made to find a good way out of the present wretched state of things, but more or less weighty objections have hitherto been made to each plan proposed.

[2] The term of the supreme court does not correspond with the calendar year. Its commencement has been repeatedly changed. By act of July 23, 1866, it was fixed for the second Monday in October. Originally the court was required to hold two sessions a year. This provision was repealed by act of April 29, 1802. These facts should be considered if mistakes in the year of a judicial decision are to be avoided.

[3] Act of April 10, 1869.

The number of district judges has increased to one hundred and sixteen. By act of February 24, 1855, the court of claims was created.[1]

RIGHTS, PRIVILEGES AND LIMITATIONS OF THE FEDERAL POWERS AND OF THE SEPARATE MEMBERS THEREOF.

§ 28. CONGRESS. The constitution expressly grants to both houses of congress the autonomy which in all constitutional states is deemed a necessary prerequisite of legislative bodies. Before all, "each house shall be the judge [of the validity] of the elections, returns and qualifications of its own members" (art. I., sec. 5, § 1).[2] It

---

[1] The organization of the court of claims was altered by act of March 3, 1863. It is at present composed of a chief justice and four associate judges, but only two are necessary to decide a case. The court sits in Washington. The annual session begins on the first Monday in December and continues till the cases before the court are disposed of. The following two provisions contain the most essential features in regard to its authority: It is empowered "to hear and determine all claims founded upon any law of congress, or upon any regulation of an executive department, or upon any contract, expressed or implied, with the government of the United States, and all claims which may be referred to it by either house of congress," and "all set-offs, counter-claims for damages, whether liquidated or unliquidated, or other demands whatsoever, on the part of the government of the United States against any person making claim against the government in said court." Although the court must in all these cases "decide," yet it has been claimed in the house of representatives that congress could set aside these decisions, inasmuch as it could refuse to make appropriations to pay the judgments against the United States. The house adopted the motion of Washburne, of Illinois, who supported this claim, but, neither from the motion itself, nor from the brief debates, does it appear whether the house pledged itself to this undoubtedly untenable view. See *Cong. Globe*, 2d sess. 38th Cong., 306. Appeals from the court of claims go to the supreme court. See W. A. Richardson, *History, Jurisdiction and Practice of the Court of Claims*, Washington, 1882.

[2] The "returns" or "certificates of election" are regarded as

is the province of each house to fix its own order of business, but the constitution makes a majority of all the members elected necessary to do any business. A less number may adjourn from day to day. In order that their labors may not be brought to a standstill, either by indifference or evil intent, the appearance of the absent members can be enforced in the manner provided and under penalty of the punishments imposed by the respective houses. The power to fix the order of business naturally implies the power to invest the chairman with the necessary disciplinary power to maintain order during the sessions. When it is further provided that each house may "punish its members for disorderly conduct," it is of course evident that something more is intended and a wider authority bestowed. This becomes entirely certain, when finally the right is expressly given them to

---

"*prima facie* evidence" of a legal election, and a further investigation takes place, as a rule, only when the opposing candidate contests the election. If a seat in the house of representatives be contested, the contestant must notify his opponent within a fixed period of time, and inform him in the way prescribed by law that, and upon what grounds, he intends to make the contest. The two parties must then themselves take measures to get the testimony. Ninety days are granted them within which to do so. The depositions of the witnesses are sent to the house. See, more fully, *Rev. Stat.*, secs. 105–130. See, also, F. C. Brightly, *A Collection of Leading Cases in the Law of Elections in the United States*, Phila., 1871; D. A. McKnight, *Electoral System of the United States*, Phila., 1878; D. C. McMillan, *Elective Franchise in the United States*, N. Y., 1878; G. W. McCrary, *American Law of Elections*, 2d ed., Chicago, 1880: F. Giauque, *United States Election and Naturalization Laws*, Cin., 1880.

The idea of "qualifications" was considerably enlarged by the civil war and by the third section of the fourteenth amendment, already cited. By the act of July 2, 1862, all federal officials were obliged to swear that they had in no manner whatever voluntarily taken part in the rebellion. This "test oath" was repealed in May, 1884.

"expel a member" by a two-thirds vote (art I., sec. 5, § 2). In times of very great excitement, it has nevertheless been asserted that all these provisions give each house only a power over its members which is disciplinary in the strict sense of the word, and therefore can be put in force only as to improper acts committed during the sessions.[1] Since there has been repeated occasion to take steps against members of each house under each of these two clauses, and since the majority has never taken this standpoint, it may now be regarded as finally settled that that interpretation is correct which is the broader, and at the same time, according to ordinary speech, unquestionably the more natural one. Both houses of congress must have been granted every power needed to guard themselves and their members against any impropriety on the part of a member and to preserve their dignity and reputation among the people. It is wholly for them to say what conduct they are to regard as dishonorable enough to require expulsion.[2] An appeal from their decision lies only to the court of public opinion, a court which brings in its verdict at the elections. What other punishments the houses may impose upon members is, on the other hand, a question which has never had an exact and unquestioned answer and never can have. Although the power is in form unconditional, it was certainly not intended to be unlimited. Custom has confined all punishments imposed to those not inconsistent with personal dignity, and this corresponds to the intention of the constitution.

[1] See my *Constitutional History*, V., 324.
[2] The misconduct need not be legally punishable. See the case of Senator W. Blount, in 1797. Story, § 838. Nor need it have been committed during the session of congress or at the seat of government.

The congressional power of punishment is not limited to members of the two houses, although the constitution contains no further provision on this point. The extension of the power rests upon the fact that both houses exercise judicial functions in certain cases, and by the common law every court has the power of punishment, in order to protect itself against insult, contempt and disobedience. The supreme court decided, in *Kilbourn vs. Thompson* (103 U. S., 168; Otto, XIII.), that the lower house may punish a contumacious witness whom it has summoned in reference to an impeachment or other matter which falls under one of the provisions of the constitution.[1] On the other hand, it has decided that the constitution granted neither house the right of punishment simply "for contempt." Whether the right existed in other cases than those enumerated, it did not care to decide on this occasion, but it laid down the general principle that it could never exist when, as in the case before it, the house had overstepped its constitutional jurisdiction.[2] The extensive disciplinary and penal powers of

---

[1] This, of course, applies also to the senate.
[2] Kilbourn had been committed to prison because he refused to produce his business account-books and correspondence.

As important as this decision is, it does not clear up all doubt on this question. And the question is of great importance in both principle and practice. Thus it leaves it doubtful whether the house of representatives of 1832 was authorized to have Samuel Houston arrested by its sergeant-at-arms, brought before its bar and censured, because he had beaten Stanbery, of Ohio, on the public street, on account of a speech delivered by Stanberry in the house. See Benton's *Abridgment of the Debates of Congress*, II., pp. 644–660 and 663–689. In a much older decision (1821), in *Anderson vs. Dunn* (Wheaton, VI., 204–235), the supreme court has undoubtedly recognized the right of the house of representatives to punish a "breach of its privileges" by arrest, censure and imprisonment, but not beyond the close of the session, and if the beating and unjustifiable imprisonment of the

both houses over their respective members are counterbalanced by the far-reaching immunity granted the members as to all other courts and public authorities by the next section, the sixth. The clauses in point are: The senators and representatives "shall in all cases be privileged from arrest"—treason, felony and breach of the peace excepted—"during their attendance at the session of their respective houses," and they shall not be called to account at any place whatsoever "for any speech or debate in either house." The word session is to be understood as meaning the whole session, and it includes the time "*eundo et ad propria redeundo.*"[1] So, too, the word arrest must not be interpreted here in its strictest sense. Summonses to appear as a witness or juror, under penalty, are not regarded as arrests. Again, the second clause is not, according to one view of it, to be interpreted in its strict verbal sense. The immunity is not limited to the speeches and debates. It extends also to the votes cast, the reports made, and in general to every official act as a member of one of the two houses.

In the case already cited of *Kilbourn vs. Thompson,* the supreme court dismissed the suit against the members of the committee which had issued the summons and declared the sergeant-at-arms alone liable. It is not, therefore, entirely without doubt how the clause is to be interpreted from the other standpoint. It is admitted that the privilege relates only to what is said or done

sergeant-at-arms is such a breach of its privileges, then the beating of a member is naturally much more so. But in the more recent decision the supreme court seems no longer to rely upon the reasoning on which it based its decision in the earlier case.

[1] "Except treason, felony and breach of the peace." This clause is so construed that all "indictable offenses," as well as constructive breaches of the peace, are included, and consequently the protection against arrest extends only to civil actions.

strictissime in the fulfillment of official duties. It is questionable, however, how this can be reconciled with the publication of speeches, reports, etc. The official publications, directed by either house or by the law, are now protected, even in England, against any claim for damages. But in the United States it is commonly assumed that a member of congress is at liberty to send to his constituents in printed form whatever he has said in congress, without exposing himself thereby to suit for slander, libel, etc. There are, nevertheless, older judicial decisions holding a directly opposite view. The question has not yet been brought to a definite issue by a decision of the supreme court.

Congressmen enjoy no further privileges. The constitution provides, however, that a seat in the federal legislature shall not be an unpaid honorary office, but that the senators and representatives shall receive compensation for their services. The amount is fixed by law, and it is paid out of the treasury of the United States. By the act of March 3, 1873, this salary of congressmen and territorial delegates was raised to $7,500 per annum, besides actual traveling expenses once each session on the most direct route to the seat of government. Public opinion condemned this law with such emphasis that it was repealed January 22, 1874, and the act of July 28, 1866, was again put in force. Under it the salary is $5,000 per annum, with mileage at twenty cents per mile for each journey to and from the regular sessions.

The privileges and rights granted congressmen, as well as the legal limitations to which they are subjected, have been regulated with a view to their office as law-makers. Their peculiar position is due to the fact that the interests of the state require that their independence be assured, so far as law can assure it. In fulfilling their duties to the best of their knowledge and conscience, they should not be influenced by fear of personal unpleasantness, injury or wrong resulting therefrom. Nor should they be exposed to the temptation of being turned away from the right path by the prospect of personal gain. Art. I., sec. 6, § 2, prohibits a senator or representative from being appointed to any federal office which was created, or the emoluments of which were increased, during his term of office. It is further provided, that no officer of the United States can be a member of either house of congress as long as he retains his office. A member of congress by accepting any other federal office thereby forfeits his seat, and although his re-election is not forbidden, he cannot take his seat again unless, prior thereto, he resigns his other office. As the members of congress fill a federal office in the broader sense of the word, they come under the provision in art. I., sec. 9, § 7, according to which no federal officer, without permission of congress, can accept from king, prince, or foreign state any "present, emolument, office or title of any kind whatever."

§ 29. THE PRESIDENT. In regard to his personal rights, the president occupies no peculiar position. The constitution (art. II., sec. 1, § 6) grants him a salary, with the proviso that it is not to be increased or diminished during his term of office. It also forbids his receiving any other income from the United States, or from any of the states. The salary, originally fixed at $25,000 per annum, was doubled by the act of March 3, 1873.

§ 30. THE JUDGES. The judges also at stated times draw salaries, which cannot be decreased as long as they are in office (art. III., sec. 1).[1] No personal privileges are

---

[1] The salary of the chief justice of the supreme court is $10,500; that of the associate justices is $10,000; that of the circuit judges $6,000; that of the district judges from $3,500 to $4,500; and that of

granted them by the constitution, and they are subject to no peculiar legal limitations.

THE FUNCTIONS OF THE GOVERNMENTAL FACTORS.

In order to avoid repetitions, otherwise inevitable, in a discussion of the powers of the governmental factors, their functions will be treated in this section principally on their *formal* side. Nothing will be said, therefore, about the judiciary, since the constitution contains no provisions of this sort in regard to it. A description of the entire judicial procedure is self-evidently out of place here. As for the executive functions, only those should and need be touched upon which present peculiarities of some kind or other.

§ 31. THE GENERAL LEGISLATIVE FUNCTIONS OF CONGRESS. The authority of either house of congress to establish its order of business is not unlimited. The constitution contains several provisions as to this, some of which have already been mentioned in another connec-

the judges of the court of claims $4,500. It is often said that these salaries are too low, because many lawyers are able to earn much more and there is therefore danger that the jurists best fitted by knowledge and character will no longer be willing to go upon the bench. It has, indeed, already happened that the enormous fees the large railroad corporations pay their attorneys have proved more attractive than the honors of the judiciary, but the latter are still prized so highly that finding fit men has, hitherto at least, been easy. It must, however, be admitted that in general the salaries of officials in the United States, especially of the higher grades, are too low. But raising them might have bad results as long as the principle of "rotation in office" is not given up. Only when an end is put to this folly can the most vigorous talents be expected to devote themselves gladly to the service of the state. Then they will not long be deterred by the low salary, especially if a system of pensions is introduced. Not only might this then be done without danger, but it would be an advantage from every point of view.

tion. There remains to be added that each house must keep a journal of its proceedings, in which the yeas and nays of a vote must be entered, whenever this is demanded by one-fifth of the members present. The journal must be published from time to time, but it is within the discretion of the two houses to suppress those parts which they think it necessary to keep secret (art. I., sec. 5, § 3). It is evident, therefore, that it is not an oversight that the constitution contains no express provisions as to whether the proceedings of congress shall be public or secret. Evidently publicity was intended to be the rule; but it was also intended to leave it wholly to the judgment of congress in what cases and upon what grounds an exception should be made. This corresponds, too, with actual custom. Till February 20, 1794, the senate, indeed, always met with closed doors, but since then the only permanent exceptions to the rule of publicity are the executive sessions, in which the senate performs no legislative duties, but acts as the adviser and controller of the executive. Moreover the obligation of secrecy as to occurrences in the executive sessions is frequently removed. The legislative functions, as far as the ordinary work of the two houses is concerned, are discharged *coram publico*. When the slavery question frequently brought passions to the boiling point, the "clearing of the galleries" was often demanded, but this was intended simply to secure protection against improper demonstrations of the spectators and was never regarded as a denial of publicity.

§ 32. THE PROCESS OF LEGISLATION. The legislative initiative, with a single exception (in favor of the house), which will be mentioned later on, belongs in an entirely equal degree to the two houses of congress. The constitution prescribes no forms which are to be observed in initiating legislation. Their establishment is entirely a matter of the rules adopted by either house. According to these, the preparation of a bill is mainly incumbent upon the standing committees, which, in the house of representatives, are appointed by the speaker, and in the senate are elected by the majority.[1] Special committees may

[1] In the 48th congress (1883-85), the senate had twenty-nine and the house forty-seven standing committees. For the introduction of a bill the committees require the permission of the respective house. This is, however, usually given either when the committee is appointed or by a permanent provision of the rules. The house must likewise be asked whether it will receive the report of the committee. As a rule the question is not actually put. An affirmative answer is assumed if no objection be made. Many of the customary formalities of the English parliament have been set aside. Minority reports are received as a matter of fact, although really, as a matter of parliamentary law, only the committee as such can report, and, of course, in a strict sense, only one report is possible — that of the majority. It is odd that the committees are bound by their decisions and cannot reconsider them. Cushing's *Law and Practice of Legislative Assemblies*, § 1915. The committees need an especial authorization in order "to send for persons, papers and records;" but the examination of voluntary witnesses may take place without such authority. In exceptional cases the committees are authorized, that is directed, to continue their labors after the close of the session. In the house of representatives, in the "morning hour" of Tuesday, Wednesday and Thursday, that is, after the reading of the journal, the standing committees are called upon by the speaker, in regular order, to present their reports and to make motions. An hour's time is given the maker of the report. He usually gives up a greater or less portion of this short time to general debate. The speaker, however, recognizes only those persons who have previously come to a private understanding with the maker of the report, and these only upon their promise to limit their remarks to a certain number of minutes. Immediately before the expiration of the hour the maker of the report demands the "previous question," that is, moves to close the debate, and this demand is generally granted, because it is to everybody's interest that the work of legislation be done in the speediest manner. For each one of them is particularly interested in some other bill, and the whole number of the bills is always so enormous that only a small

also be appointed, and each and every individual member, with the consent of his house, may introduce a bill.[1] What further treatment a bill once introduced experiences,—when it is taken up for discussion; whether a

fraction of them can ever be disposed of. The great majority are buried forever by reference to some committees, for the committees will not, or cannot, ever report upon them. When the previous question is carried no more amendments are in order, and the maker of the report has another hour for the discussion of the measure before the final vote takes place. An immense number of laws are thus passed in the house in the course of two hours. When a committee is called by the speaker, only the morning hours of two successive days belong to it. If, however, the morning hours of the second day have elapsed without arriving at a conclusion upon the bill in hand, then it becomes "unfinished business," and as such is at the head of the order of the day for the morning hours until it is disposed of. The four committees on printing, elections, ways and means and appropriations hold a privileged position. The remaining standing committees must be content with the time that is granted them by these four. Senator Hoar calculates that, on an average, not more than two hours is accorded each of them during an entire session. This fact is the more significant, since most of the bills are really discussed only in committee, and the committees have the right to meet with closed doors. To mention in the house any occurrence in the committee room, except upon the basis of the official report, makes the offender guilty of a "breach of privilege." It is, moreover, quite usual for the committees to examine experts, and as these are, for the most part, specially interested, the laws are based to a large extent upon *ex parte* testimony, while the whole body of legislation is far removed from anything like uniformity. It is only in regard to the appropriation bills that the house of representatives has retained the character of an advisory body. The appropriations are discussed in committee of the whole; the previous question cannot be moved; and the right to propose amendments is not only formally, but also actually, unlimited. See G. F. Hoar, *The Conduct of Business in Congress*, in the North American Review, February, 1879, p. 113 *et seq.*

[1] A standing opportunity to do so is presented in the morning hour of Monday. For then the states and territories are called in regular order for this purpose. It is also to be observed that on Mondays, after the morning hours, and on the last ten days of the session, the

committee is to pass upon it; whether it is subjected to preliminary consideration in the so-called committee of the whole, etc.,— all this is regulated by the general provisions of the rules or decided by resolution.[1] When a bill has passed, it is sent over to the other house with a message to that effect.[2] Whether the other house will consider and pass upon it is entirely at its pleasure. If it

"suspension of the rules" may be moved in order to take up and pass any bill. To pass the motion to suspend the rules a two-thirds majority is necessary. If passed, there can be no debate on the bill, and no amendment offered. Consequently, so far as the house of representatives is concerned, a bill may become a law by one vote, without any discussion and without the possibility of any changes whatever. At every session a vast number of bills are actually passed in this manner.

[1] The committee of the whole is actually the whole house (or senate). In the senate it is called the quasi-committee of the whole. In passing upon a measure it is subject to the same rules as prevail in the house. In truth the committee of the whole is not a committee at all, but the house itself transacting business in a peculiar, and in fact a simpler and freer, way. Its function corresponds with that of the committees in being simply a preparatory one. Its conclusions are only recommendations to the house, without any obligation whatever. The most significant advantage of the arrangement is the greater freedom and exhaustiveness of the discussions, as each member may speak as often as he chooses. The committee of the whole can consider only definite resolutions. In sessions of the "committee of the whole house on the state of the Union," every member may speak on any question he desires. The speaker does not preside over the committee of the whole. Any member whom the house may appoint takes the chair. In the house of representatives, since 1841, no speech is permitted to occupy more than one hour. At the expiration of the last minute the speaker's gavel stops the orator short, even in the middle of a sentence. By calling for the previous question, debate can not only be closed at any moment, but entirely prevented. Debate on the motion for the previous question is not allowed.

[2] That a simple majority of the members voting suffices to pass a bill is not expressly declared in the constitution, but it is regarded as self-evident, and it follows, too, from the exceptional provisions mentioned further on.

passes it without amendment, the bill goes to the president for his approval. If, on the contrary, it passes it with amendments, the bill is returned to the other house, which, when it again considers the matter, either concurs in the amendments or refuses to do so, or offers new amendments of its own. Thus, a bill may be bandied from one house to the other as long as there is any hope of its passage. If that cannot be directly attained and yet seems attainable, then one or the other house proposes the appointment of a conference committee. If the other house agrees to this and the conference committee arrives at any agreement, its report is, as a rule, concurred in by both houses, although, of course, neither is obliged to do so. If the conference committee does not come to an agreement, the usual process of bandying the bill back and forth can be taken up where it was interrupted, or a second or third conference committee may be appointed, until one of the houses in some way or other declares that it will no longer protract the discussion.

§ 33. THE CO-OPERATION OF THE PRESIDENT IN LEGISLATION. A bill passed by both houses of congress becomes law as a rule by the approval of the president. Yet this right of approval must not be considered as a part of the legislative power, for the constitution expressly declares that "all" the legislative authority granted shall vest in congress. The co-operation of the president in the matter of legislation is intended only as a control. Congress alone is the author of the laws. If the president has objections to raise against the legislative conclusions of congress, he is in duty bound to submit the latter for reconsideration. Then, in order to become laws, they must receive a two-thirds majority in each house.[1] It is.

---

[1] The phrase used in the constitution admits of various interpretations, as it is not very precise. Congress has adopted the view that a two-thirds majority of those voting, not of all the members elected.

therefore, unquestionably an abuse of language that the refusal to approve a bill should be called a veto, not only in ordinary speech, but also in official terminology. The word is not to be found in the constitution. It is borrowed from a state of affairs essentially different and does not harmonize with the constitutional nature of the president's co-operation in legislation. The president has no right to forbid congress to do anything. He can only state that he does not agree with it and declare his reasons therefor. Thereupon the constitution subjects the exercise of the legislative powers of congress in the particular case to more stringent conditions.[1]

is required. Since a simple majority is sufficient to transact business, under certain circumstances a bill may be made a law over the objections of the president by the majority of each house.

[1] On the other hand it is entirely within the discretion of the president as to what reasons he shall regard as sufficient in order to make use of this power. The exercise of it has led to many violent collisions between the executive and the legislative departments. In these conflicts the attempt has been made with much acumen to limit the president's freedom of action by invoking all sorts of doctrines. It is true that some of them have great political weight, but they lack a firm constitutional basis. During the "forties" the whigs agitated the entire repeal of the veto power, but only to their own hurt. Very recently an agitation has begun in the opposite direction. The president can refuse to approve only the whole bill, even if he takes exception to but one or two points in it. It is now proposed to give him, so far as the appropriation bills are concerned, the right to return individual appropriations for reconsideration and to give the others the force of law by approving them. It can scarcely be doubted that this decisive reform will surely be enacted sooner or later, but the battle for it will certainly be severe and probably be long. The president must state his objections in writing and return the bill to the house where it originated. The new vote upon it must be by roll-call. The vote of each member must be entered on the journal. The same rules apply in the other house, to which the bill and the president's objections are sent, if the first house has passed the bill again by a two-thirds majority. If the president does not

§ 34. THE PRESIDENT. The president's direct constitutional influence upon legislation is not limited to his co-operation and control, as sketched in the last paragraph. The constitution directs him from time to time to give congress "information of the state of the Union," and it is expressly made his duty to "recommend . . . such measures as he shall judge necessary and expedient" (art. II., sec. 3). In the legislative initiative, as well as in legislation, congress is subject in a certain way to the control of the president, but this control, so far as the initiative is concerned, is naturally positive, not negative. Even if he cannot himself submit any bills, he can nevertheless exert a pressure upon congress to prevent its being guilty of sins of omission, for in his messages he calls the attention of the whole people to those matters which require the enactment of laws, or at least make new laws seem desirable. His reports "of the state of the Union" appear in the form of the so-called messages. The annual messages are sent to congress at the beginning of the annual session. They discuss all important domestic and foreign relations pretty thoroughly, and are therefore always much more comprehensive than the ordinary crown speeches in the monarchies of Europe. Accompanying the messages are the exhaustive reports by the secretaries about their respective departments. The messages and reports are called the executive documents, and are cited

sign a bill or return it with his objections within ten days (Sundays excepted) after it has been sent to him, it becomes a law without his approval, unless congress has adjourned within the ten days (art. I., sec. 7, § 2). Thus a bill may become a law, even though the president has refrained from expressing any opinion about it, and it may also not become a law, because he has expressed no opinion. Every other order, resolution, or vote for which the concurrence of the two houses is necessary must likewise be presented to the president and is subject to the same provisions as the bills. The only exceptions are the resolutions to adjourn (art. I., sec. 7, § 3).

under this title in scientific and political literature. This designation embraces also the special messages, which, as their name implies, are issued on special occasions and relate to special business. The obligation to report to congress upon the state of the Union naturally does not exclude the president's right to express himself publicly in other ways and thus to address the whole people. But this happens very seldom, and — in accordance with unbroken custom — only in two distinct ways: by the inaugural address and by proclamations. The oath already mentioned which the president must take upon assuming his office is taken publicly upon the vast open portico of the capitol at Washington, and thereupon the president delivers his so-called inaugural address, in which he unfolds to the people the programme of his administration.[1] The occurrence of certain events, such as the admission of new states, is announced to the people, in accordance with legal precedents, by proclamation. The president also issues proclamations upon his own initiative. In these his character as the bearer of the executive power is more clearly and distinctly shown than in the messages or in the inaugural address. Many presidents have never had the opportunity of addressing the people in this most solemn and weighty manner, because the occasion must be highly significant and of a very special character to justify the use of this means or to make it appear necessary.[2]

[1] Washington, upon his retirement to private life, delivered a farewell address to the people, which to the present day is regarded by the American nation as among the greatest and most valuable records of its history. Jackson is the only president who followed this example. His opponents took bitter exception to his venturing in this way to range himself with the father of his country.

[2] By far the most important proclamations which the history of the United States has to show are Lincoln's emancipation proclamations of September 22, 1862, and January 1, 1863.

THE POWERS OF CONGRESS.

§ 35. GENERAL PRINCIPLES. To rightly understand not only the powers of congress, but also those of the other factors of government, it is necessary, in considering individual instances, to keep constantly in view the general principles concerned and the fundamental doctrines of constitutional law.

The constitution does not define the powers of the factors of the government. It simply enumerates them.[1] Since in their exercise they must necessarily be made definite, it devolves upon the governmental factors themselves to decide upon the limits of their own capacity. Thus the courts, and in the last instance the federal supreme court, under the principles and limitations already laid down, must be the controlling power in the decision. To define these powers correctly it must not be lost sight of that all the powers spring from one idea and are intended to reach one goal. They must therefore always be considered as a whole.[2] It follows from these premises, not only that besides the powers expressly granted there are others which are implied by those granted and result from them (implied and resulting powers), but that the second kind of powers is not distinguished in substance from the first. If the doctrine that the powers of the government are enumerated must be understood to mean that the expressly granted powers must be literally interpreted and that there can be no unenumerated power, then the federal government would be deprived of the possibility of existence.[3]

If the constitution can be interpreted in two ways, one of which assures the fulfillment of the object of its exist-

[1] *Gibbons vs. Ogden*, Wheaton, IX., 1.
[2] *The Legal Tender Cases*, Wallace, XII., 532.
[3] *Ibid.*, 546.

once, while the other tends to render it nugatory, there can be no doubt which is the right rendering.

§ 36. TAXATION, FINANCE AND THE PUBLIC DEBT. The financial distress which ever threatened more and more to be fatal to the republic, under the articles of confederation, deserves to be thanked, in the first instance, for the reorganization of the Union. The constitution therefore naturally takes ample care that the federal government shall not want the necessary material means to fulfill the object of the federation. Congress is empowered "to lay and collect taxes, duties, imposts and excises, to pay the debts and provide for the common defense and general welfare of the United States, but all duties, imposts and excises shall be uniform throughout the United States" (art. I., sec. 8, § 1). Congress may levy imposts of any kind, and as they are collected directly from the individual by organs of the federal government, without the mediation of the states, it can constantly satisfy the needs of the nation in their fullest range, for the amount of every impost, which congress is permitted to make, is left wholly to its own discretion. Political and economical considerations and regard for business interests set certain bounds to it in this respect, but its constitutional authority is unlimited.[1] But still the power of congress to levy taxes is not entirely unconditioned. In fact bounds are set to it in various directions by several express provisions of the consti-

---

[1] The Union is divided into collection districts. The president fixes their number and boundaries. In every district there is a collector who is allowed a number of assistants (deputy collectors). After a reduction earnestly undertaken, September 5, 1883, the number of revenue districts was eighty-four. The heads of the custom-houses are called collectors of customs.

See *McCulloch vs. Maryland*, Wheaton, IV., 316, 428. See, also, *Veazie Bank vs. Fenno*, Wallace, VIII., 548.

tution. "All duties, imposts and excises shall be uniform throughout the United States."[1] Moreover, direct taxes must be levied in proportion to the population of the states (art. I., sec. 2, § 3) and the census is made the basis (art. I., sec. 2, § 4).[2] Finally, "no tax or duty shall be laid on articles exported from any state."[3]

Further restrictions of the right of taxation result from the fact that congress can exercise it only for the fulfillment of the objects enumerated. The expression "general welfare" is indeed so comprehensive and vague that the discretion of congress is given the widest play. But however much this expression may be stretched, the mention of the three general purposes makes it certain that, for other purposes, no federal taxes can be levied. There are certain bounds, more or less clearly marked, within which the right of taxation unquestionably can-

[1] In *Loughborough vs. Blake*, Wheaton, V., 317, the federal supreme court decided that this means not only the states, but the entire domain of the Union. The provision thus extends also to the District of Columbia and to the territories.

[2] The words used are "capitation or other direct tax." In a recent decision (*Springer vs. United States*, 102 U. S., 586; Otto, XII.), the supreme court has affirmed the already dominant view, that only poll-taxes and taxes on real estate are direct taxes within the meaning of the constitution. An income tax thus comes under neither of the constitutional provisions cited.

[3] Schlief's view (pp. 233, 234), that this refers only to articles exported from one state of the Union into another, has never found a champion in the United States and never can find one. The debates of the Philadelphia convention over this paragraph were a struggle between the northern and southern states. The latter resisted with all their might the attempt to impose an export duty on their staple products, the result of slave labor, which were sent mainly to Europe. (See Elliot's *Debates*, V., 302, 357, 391, 432, 454, 538, 539.) The fact that the confederate states imposed a heavy tax on the exportation of cotton shows that the fear that congress for fiscal reasons would seize this means of raising money might easily have been justified, at least in times of distress.

not be exercised. Above all, everything which comes exclusively within the jurisdiction of the states must be left alone by congress.¹ Every tax which is confessedly laid for a private purpose is unconstitutional.² But the tax laws of congress never specify an object to which the funds yielded by the tax shall be applied. The courts are therefore not in a position to guard against the burdens imposed by a law upon the ground that an unconstitutional application of the resulting funds is intended. The constitutionality of federal taxes and of the use made of the federal funds are wholly distinct questions, which must be kept far apart. So far as appropriations are concerned, the courts evidently should decide against the power assumed by congress only in perfectly clear cases. For, in the nature of things, the legislative and not the judicial power has to discover what the "general welfare" demands and what may promote it. In congress, however, the very comprehensiveness and vagueness of the expression make it possible to raise the constitutional question continually, but the decision is usually made from a political rather than a legal standpoint, however much legal arguments may have been formally pushed into the foreground during the debate. The legislative history of the Union, especially until the outbreak of the rebellion, forms a continuous chain of illustrations of this fact. Protective taxes and those levied for the so-called "internal improvements," *i. e.*, building roads, improving rivers, etc., have been claimed to be unconstitutional. Theoretically the contest is not entirely at an end at the present day, but the actual development of affairs has been so great that the one set

---

¹ *Gibbons vs. Ogden*, Wheaton, IX., 199.
² See a number of instances and the judicial decisions upon them in Cooley, *Principles*, 58.

of contestants carry on the conflict on politico-economical grounds exclusively, and the others make their defense on the basis of the industrial and political interests concerned in the particular case, unless, indeed, no national importance can be given to the interest in dispute.

Finally, the states' concurrent right of taxation puts certain limitations upon the congressional right. Both are alike limited by several express provisions of the constitution. Without the consent of congress, the states can burden imports and exports with imposts of any kind whatever, only so far as is absolutely necessary for the execution of their inspection laws (art. I., sec. 10, § 2).[1] The states cannot levy a tonnage tax without the consent of congress (art. I., sec. 10, § 3). If, however, the conclusion were drawn from these express prohibitions that the states' right of taxation were subject to no further limitations, they might exert it in such a way that the federal government would be unable, except under great disadvantages, and perhaps not able at all, to carry out what it had found best to do in the discharge of its constitutional functions. And if the congressional power of taxation were subject only to the restrictions thus far noted, congress could so use it that the states would be hindered and crippled, even when they were acting within the constitutional limits of their authority. In either event, violence would be done to the fundamental idea of the constitution, that the federal government and the state governments have the same aim — the welfare of the people. The concurrent right, therefore, is subject in each case to those limitations which are necessary for the security of the interests entrusted by

---

[1] The net proceeds of such imposts must be paid over to the United States, and all such laws are subject to the revision and control of congress.

the people to the protection of the other political factor. It is impossible to point out every single consequence of this general principle. A few instances will make the matter sufficiently clear. The states cannot tax a bank created by the United States and acting as their fiscal agent, or the salary or other emoluments of federal officials, or federal bonds, etc.[1] Congress cannot tax state property, such as a railroad, salaries of state officials, municipalities and their property, etc.[2]

Among the debts of the United States for the payment of which congress could levy taxes are to be understood

[1] The fact that a corporation created by the United States renders its creator some service does not entitle it to exemption from all taxation by the states. *Railroad Co. vs. Peniston*, Wallace, XVIII., 5.
[2] See on this point, *McCulloch vs. Maryland*, Wheaton, IV., 816; *Veazie Bank vs. Fenno*, Wallace, VIII., 533; and *Collector vs. Day*, Wallace, XI., 113. The principal sources of income of the Union are the customs and the internal revenue taxes. The latter are sufficiently characterized by giving the principal heads of the income derived from them. The nation received in 1884 from distilled liquors, $76,905,385; from tobacco, $26,092,400; from malt liquors, $18,084,954. In 1883, it received from the sale of stamps, with which various articles had to be provided, $7,053,053; and from banks and bankers, $3,784,995. The taxation of business formerly went much further than at present. But even now it is not restricted to banks and bankers, as might appear from the above list. (The taxation of the capital and deposits of banks and bankers ceased March 3, 1883; they are, however, burdened with several other taxes.) Every manufacturer and dealer in tobacco or the liquors designated is still subject to taxation as such. The articles and occupations which had to be taxed during the war, but which have since been freed, yielded in 1866 an income of $236,236,037. The proceeds of the customs were, in 1884, $195,067,489. The total imports for the year 1883 represented a value of $723,180,914, of which $515,676,106 consisted of merchandise subject to duties. These goods paid an average duty of 41.63 per cent., equal to 29.68 per cent. on the total import. In 1884 the imports decreased to $667,697,993. On the questions here treated, see F. Hilliard, *Taxation*, Boston, 1885, and Cooley, *Law of Taxation*, Chicago, 1876.

those incurred under the articles of confederation as well as those contracted afterwards. The former are covered by the provisions of article VI., § 1, that the validity of existing obligations shall not be touched by the adoption of the constitution.[1] The latter are covered by the express grant of the right to contract new debts. Congress is empowered "to borrow money on the credit of the United States" (art. I., sec. 8, § 2). This power is granted without any limitation. Money may therefore be borrowed in every way known to modern mercantile life; nay, according to the decisions of the supreme court, in such a way that there is no borrowing whatever, even in the broadest sense of the term, but simply an advantage gained to the nation by the strengthening of its credit. The right to create the United States bank was deduced from this provision. Upon this clause, moreover, the constitutionality of the present system of national banks must be based.[2] Whether (and, if so, how far) congress has the power of making the federal currency a legal tender is a question which has formerly, and again quite recently, actively engaged the attention of the people, the politicians and the courts. But, in spite of the repeated decisions of the supreme court sustaining it, this power is

---

[1] In this connection the fourth section of the fourteenth amendment, which needs no commentary, may be cited. "The validity of the public debt of the United States, authorized by law, including debts incurred for payment of pensions and bounties for services in suppressing insurrection or rebellion, shall not be questioned. But neither the United States nor any state shall assume or pay any debt or obligation incurred in aid of insurrection or rebellion against the United States, or any claim for loss or emancipation of any slave; but all such debts, obligations and claims shall be held illegal and void."

[2] They are compelled to invest a large portion of their capital in government bonds, and thus the federal government can naturally borrow money much more easily.

not considered as definitely established, since public opinion looks upon these decisions and their motives, at least in part, as very doubtful. Efforts are therefore being made to settle this very important question beyond doubt by an amendment to the constitution. At this point I can supplement what has been stated in another connection concerning this great contest by pointing out another constitutional provision, which cannot be properly wholly disregarded in the argument, but, nevertheless, contains no certain indication of the intentions of the authors of the constitution on this question. The states are forbidden to "make anything but gold and silver coin a tender in payment of debts."[1] The question was therefore not overlooked by the Philadelphia convention. But what conclusion is to be drawn from the express prohibition on the one hand and silence on the other? Was there no need of prohibiting congress because it has only the powers granted it? Or may the disputed power be deduced from this silence, because without it the worth of the power to borrow money would have been substantially diminished and this power was granted without any limitation? No party and no political school has ever declared it to be a general principle of constitutional law that the federal government must be authorized to do whatever the states are expressly forbidden to do. And the very matters most closely related to the question in hand are not so treated by the constitution as to necessitate such a conclusion. In the very same paragraph the states are forbidden to coin money, but although this right must rest somewhere and could appertain only to the federal government if denied the states, yet the constitution does not let the matter rest with that

[1] Not "their" debts, as Schlief (p. 469) very arbitrarily translates this.

express prohibition, but expressly grants congress the power (art. I., sec. 8, § 5) "to coin money, to regulate the value thereof and of foreign coin."[1] But on the

[1] The coinage act of April 2, 1792, provided that the dollar should have 371¼ grains of pure silver (416 standard) and the ten-dollar gold piece, the eagle, 247¼ grains of pure gold (270 standard). The relation of gold to silver was fixed at 1:15. The disadvantages which soon arose in commerce were not traced back to the principle of the "double standard," but were attributed simply to the circumstance that gold had been valued too low. This difficulty was relieved by a law of June 28, 1834, which fixed the legal proportion of the two metals at 1:16. Thereafter the eagle was to contain only 232 grains, pure gold (258 standard). But if the former rule prevented the coinage of gold, the silver dollars, now above par, vanished out of circulation still more rapidly. A new coinage act of February 12, 1873, made the gold dollar the unit of coinage, but did not change the weight or fineness of gold coin ($1 equals 25.8 grains troy). The same law demonetized the silver dollar, i. e., thereafter only silver coins of fifty cents or less and also a new coin, 420 grains troy, called the trade dollar, because it was struck off solely in the interests of trade with Asia, were issued. The reason of the demonetization of the silver dollar was because, on account of its being above par, it had long since disappeared from circulation. In the preparation of the Revised Statutes, which became law June 20, 1874, the demonetization of the silver dollar — probably simply by an oversight — was made complete. The act of February 12, 1873, had provided that the silver thereafter coined should be legal tender only for $5 or less. The Revised Statutes extended this provision to all silver. Scarcely had the act of February 12, 1873, been passed than the value of silver began to sink rapidly in consequence of the extraordinary yield from the mines of Nevada, the adoption of the gold standard in Germany, etc. The result of this was an energetic agitation for the remonetization of silver, which speedily won over public opinion. A bill which President Hayes had refused to approve became a law February 28, 1878. The secretary of the treasury was directed to buy every month not less than two and not more than four million dollars' worth of silver at its market value and to coin it into silver dollars. The efforts to put the silver into circulation have, nevertheless, had only scant success. Of the $175,355,829 coined up to June 30, 1884, only $39,794,913 could be issued. In addition to this, there are $96,427,011 of "silver certifi-

other hand the states are forbidden to issue "bills of credit," and the right of the federal government to do so is unquestioned, although this right was not expressly granted to it, but is merely deduced from the authority to borrow money.[1] Yet the debates of the Philadelphia convention leave it very doubtful whether the intention was to give the federal government the right to issue paper money. An express grant of this power was in the draft of the constitution[2] and was stricken out by a vote of nine states to two. The views of the delegates differed, however, as to what rights congress would have in this respect, if nothing were said about it. The prevailing, if not quite unanimous, view was that congress would not be able to make the federal notes a legal tender.[3] On the other hand it may be alleged that the original idea was simply to forbid the states to issue bills of

cates" which are received in payment of taxes and customs by the government. There is a growing fear that the government will soon be no longer able to make its payments in gold, and that then there will be a great crisis. President Cleveland, shortly before his inauguration, declared himself in favor of the discontinuance of the coinage of silver, but in February, 1885, both houses of congress defeated proposals to that effect.

[1] "Bills of credit" are simply direct obligations of the state intended to circulate as money. Bank-notes do not fall under this description, even if the state is the sole holder of the bank stock. *Craig vs. Missouri*, Peters, IV., 410; *Briscoe vs. Bank of the Commonwealth of Kentucky*, Ibid., XI., 257; *Darrington vs. Bank of Alabama*, Howard, XIII., 12.

[2] "And emit bills on the credit of the United States."

[3] Madison had proposed to declare this expressly instead of striking out the clause, but thereafter he voted to strike it out because he, as he says, had convinced himself that it "would not disable the government from the use of public notes, as far as they could be safe and proper; and would only cut off the pretext for a paper currency, and particularly for making the bills a tender, either for public or private debts." Elliot's *Debates*, V., 434, 435.

credit and make something else than gold and silver a legal tender when, and only when, congress did not consent.¹ There is much to be said in favor of the view that this is one of the cases where, by force of circumstances, an actually valid constitutional right has been created which runs counter to the true intent of the constitution. This cannot, however, be asserted with certainty. The provisions of the constitution and the debates of the Philadelphia convention show beyond doubt that the intention was to place the entire monetary system in the hands of the federal government, not only for the sake of uniformity but because the states were distrusted.²

---

¹ Elliot's *Debates*, V., 484.

² Here it must be noted that congress is expressly authorized to enact penal laws against counterfeiting both coin and paper currency. Art. I., sec. 8, § 6.

The national debt of the United States reached its highest point in 1865. It was then $2,844,649,626. At the close of the fiscal year 1883-84, it had been reduced to $1,830,528,923. The annual payment of interest has been diminished from $150,977,697 in 1865 to $47,926,432 in 1884. The *per capita* debt of $78.25 in 1865 has been reduced to $25.89 in 1884, and the *per capita* interest from $4.29 to 86 cents.

The history of paper money in the United States economically, politically and legally has formed one of the most significant chapters in the story of national development. Upon the recommendation of the first secretary of the treasury, Alexander Hamilton, the act of February 25, 1791, created a "Bank of the United States." Its capital was not to exceed $10,000,000 in shares of $400, of which the government might take one-fifth, in consideration of which it was bound to receive the notes of the bank in payment. Its franchise was good for twenty years. When the bank sought a renewal it was refused. In the meantime the states had evaded the provisions of the constitution which forbade them to issue bills of credit by authorizing the creation of banks with the right of issuing notes. These small banks, the jealous complaints of which had much to do with preventing a renewal of the franchise of the United States Bank, now had a free field. Like mushrooms after a warm summer shower, they

§ 37. THE BUDGET AND ADMINISTRATION OF FINANCE. The axiom, that "the purse strings must be in the hands of the representatives of the people," *i. e.*, of the legislature, the Americans obtained from England. In its application, however, it has undergone an important change and won a much wider range. In this connection it becomes particularly clear and evident that there is a

sprung into existence, and very often did business in a most extraordinary manner.

The "wildcat currency" period still survives in the memory of the people. Scarcely was the United States Bank dissolved than the United States had to create a substitute for its notes. Trouble with England, finally leading to war, produced financial embarrassments which induced congress in 1812 to authorize the issue of interest-bearing treasury notes. They were the first federal notes under the constitution of 1789, which, although not legal tender, were nevertheless issued in order to circulate as money. In 1815 the issuance of non-interest-bearing notes was begun. The cessation of cash payments in almost the entire country and the innumerable different bank-notes produced boundless confusion. The report of the secretary of the treasury in 1815 says: "Hence it has happened (and the duration of the evil is without any limitation) that, however adequate the public revenue may be in its general product to discharge the public engagements, it becomes totally inadequate in the process of its application, since the possession of public funds in one part no longer affords the evidence of a fiscal capacity to discharge a public debt in any other part of the Union." The treasury notes varied in market value in different portions of the country as much as fifteen per cent. Congress sought to stem the evil by creating a new United States bank, again for a period of twenty years. The chief provisions of the law of April 10, 1816, were as follows: There was a capital of $55,000,000, of which the United States took a fifth; all the government offices had to take bank-notes at par; the bank was bound, under heavy penalties, to redeem its notes in coin; the government funds were to be deposited at the bank, and it was to pay the government $1,500,000 annually for its privileges.

From the outset the bank had to contend with difficulties of the most diverse kinds. Vigorous and, in part, not unfounded complaints were made of its business management, and President Jackson made its annihilation a chief end of his administration. When the bank

substantial difference (in the proper sense of this word "substantial") between what is called in Europe the "government" and in the United States the "administration." It is the duty of the president and certain organs of the executive authority to administer the affairs of state in the manner prescribed by law. But so far as their determination is concerned, his constitutional,

in 1832 asked for the renewal of its franchise, the bill was passed by congress, but vetoed by the president July 10. The bank held, it is true, a charter from the state of Pennsylvania, but was nevertheless unable to maintain itself. It is now generally accepted as a good thing that the connection of the government with the bank was dissolved, but the new order of things was ushered in at the time of a general bank and monetary crisis. When the conflict between the north and south had ripened into a catastrophe, the government in its embarrassment laid hold of the means used before and issued treasury notes. Besides this it negotiated a number of loans in coin in exchange for interest-bearing bonds from the state banks whose notes were at par. While its necessities grew apace from day to day to gigantic proportions, it nevertheless continued to issue treasury notes and refused to receive the bank-notes. These were presented to the banks in large amounts for redemption. The banks thereupon, on December 27, 1861, suspended cash payments. On January 1, 1862, the government did likewise. Secretary Chase now wished to issue irredeemable paper money. The law of February 25, 1862, passed after a long debate, authorized the government to issue $150,000,000 in notes, the lowest denomination to be $5, which should be "legal tender" for all public and private debts then existing or thereafter contracted, and exchangeable for six per cent. bonds. The import duties were to be paid in gold. Even though the law did not explicitly declare it, it was nevertheless understood that the sum of $150,000,000 should not be exceeded. But necessity soon compelled the issuance of new notes, likewise made a legal tender; at the same time, the provision forbidding the issue of notes in sums less than $5 was repealed. Moreover, the law of March 3, 1863, authorized interest-bearing notes: provided that the right to exchange the paper currency for six per cent. bonds at par should lapse July 1, 1863; and burdened the notes of the state banks with a tax of two per cent. But this taxation was not, however, the only means with which the secretary of the treasury and congress attacked the sixteen hundred

legal, and practical influence is restricted to the fact that he can recommend to congress such measures as seem good to him, and that by refusing to approve an act he can put before congress the alternative either of stopping the wheels of government in whole or part or else changing its conclusions, unless both houses by a two-thirds majority persist therein. In European countries one of

state banks, the notes of which at the beginning of the war comprised the largest part of the circulating medium. The attack was justified, for the genuine notes were about seven thousand in number, and the counterfeits—Upton distinguishes between "altered, spurious, imitated, and other kinds more or less fraudulent"—also ran up among the thousands. The system of national banks, towards which Chase gave the first impetus in December, 1861, put the axe to the root of this wretched confusion. The first law about the national banks (approved February 25, 1863) has in the course of time received manifold, more or less substantial, amendments. The most important of the provisions in force at present are the following: A minimum capital is fixed, which increases with the size of the place; a minimum number of stockholders is likewise fixed; at least one-half of the capital must be paid in immediately, and the rest in monthly instalments of at least ten per cent.; at least one-third of the paid-up capital is to be deposited with the treasurer of the United States in the form of interest-bearing, registered United States bonds; for ninety per centum of the market value of the bonds deposited — provided that does not exceed the par value — the bank receives notes of different denominations engraved in blank; if the bank desires to diminish the note circulation, it pays the United States treasurer "legal tender notes," receiving a corresponding amount of its bonds on deposit, and the treasurer redeems the notes of the bank to an equal amount when they are presented to him; each bank must deposit an amount equal to five per cent. of its notes in the United States treasury, and the treasurer uses this deposit to redeem the notes presented to him; every national bank must receive the notes of every other national bank at par; the government pays out the notes at par, except for interest on the public debt; the notes redeemed by the treasurer are destroyed, and in lieu thereof new notes are given the bank upon its making its deposit for redemption good; no limit of time is fixed for the redemption of the notes of banks which have ceased to exist for one or the other reason, and the part

the chief tasks of the government is to prepare and present the budget. The legislature must accept it, after making such corrections as it may see fit. The ministers are free to escape any responsibility for these corrections by resigning. In the United States, on the other hand, so far as the constitution is concerned, the labor and the entire responsibility of the budget rest upon congress. It is permitted to summon the organs of the executive to its aid as much and in whatever way it may see fit. If

of the five per cent. deposit not used for redemption must finally fall to the United States, as no other use for it is provided. At the conclusion of the civil war there were still $143,000,000 of the state bank notes in circulation, against $146,000,000 of national bank notes. But as from July 1, 1865, the state banks had to pay a tax of ten per cent. on their notes, the state bank currency disappeared entirely. All the notes of the United States of every kind whatever added together reached at the time $695,000,000. With the spring of 1866, measures were taken to reduce this monstrous mass of depreciated money. The speculations of the exchanges ran the price of gold in a wild whirl up and down and at times staggered even the policy of congress and of the administration. Under the operation of the general business crisis of 1873, congress resolved, in April, 1874, to increase the amount of notes outstanding, but President Grant refused to sign the bill. An act of January 14, 1875, fixed the resumption of specie payments for January 1, 1879, and despite all opposing prophecies this was carried out without any difficulties, fourteen and a half years after the legal tender notes had sunk to about one-third of their face value. (On the 11th day of July, 1864, gold was quoted at its highest point, 285.) But the national banking system, which has finally given the country a uniform and safe circulating medium, and even in the judgment of its original opponents has proved itself of substantial excellence, is approaching a crisis. The basis of the system is the deposit of United States bonds, and this basis is being destroyed by the rapid extinction of the public debt and the vigorous reduction of the rate of interest. See E. G. Spaulding, *History of Legal Tender Paper Money*, 2d ed., Buffalo, 1875; F. Q. Ball, *National Banks*, Chicago, 1881; W. G. Sumner, *A History of American Currency*, N. Y., 1874; J. J. Knox, *United States Notes*, 1884; J. R. Upton, *Money in Politics*, Boston, 1884.

it does so, in so far as it makes their co-operation a legal duty, it imposes a legal and political responsibility; but the constitutional responsibility belongs to congress alone, *i. e.*, it cannot hide itself behind the cabinet. As the administration can present no bills, and consequently cannot be made responsible either for the public revenue or for the manner and means of its collection, so also, in regard to the public expenditures, it can make no demands, but can simply work out estimates of expenses and make suggestions. So far as the initiative is concerned, the administration has no will of its own, but only an opinion. The only right or duty the secretaries can have in the matter is to report as experts upon the business affairs of the state.

After making such a report — when congress permits or desires it — the whole matter is constitutionally and legally at an end from the standpoint of the administration. The president and the heads of the departments cannot even take a stand against a proposition which is opposed to their well considered recommendations, while it is under discussion in congress. And when the final conclusions of congress reach the president, he can send back the bill concerned only as a whole. Only the particular bill, and not the whole budget, for the entire budget is not framed at once. The appropriations are made in groups, each of which is covered by a separate so-called appropriation bill.[1] These bills always originate in the house of representatives and they are in fact prepared by

[1] The legislative, executive and judicial expenses appropriation; civil expenses appropriation; consular and diplomatic appropriations; army appropriation; Indian appropriation; pension appropriation; military academy appropriation. To these are added special appropriations and a greater or less number of deficiency appropriations.

its "committee on appropriations."[1] They must emanate from this house, because the constitution provides: "All bills for raising revenue shall originate in the house of representatives."

It has always been undisputed in the United States that "bills for raising revenue" include all the so-called "money bills," but there have often been different views as to the legitimate application of this doctrine.[2] The house of representatives has always asserted that its functions embraced the framing of the appropriation bills, and the senate has never succeeded in its occasional efforts to maintain the contrary. A literal interpretation of the constitutional provisions must evidently decide the matter against the claims of the house of representatives, and, too, the discussions of the Philadelphia convention tell more against than in favor of these claims. But Seward was right in saying, February 7, 1856, in the senate, that the fact that from the beginning the house claimed the framing of the appropriation bills as its privilege and that the senate did not contest it, was weightier than these arguments.[3] The question whether the doctrine should be narrowed or widened is, however, as experience has taught, one without practical significance, as

[1] The committee on appropriations bears the same relation to the expenditures that the committee on ways and means does to the public revenue. There are thus two budget commissions and no budget. Congress does not place the revenue and expenditures in juxtaposition and thus make a simple whole of the public finances. How far congress has made it the duty of the secretary of the treasury to elaborate a sketch of the budget for it, was explained in discussing the organization of the treasury department.

[2] See especially the debate in April, 1872, *Congressional Globe*, 2d session, 42d Congress, p. 2105 *et seq.*

[3] *Cong. Globe*, 1st sess., 34th Cong., 376. When the senate, despite this, sent some appropriation bills to the house, the latter simply laid them on the table.

the constitution itself reduced the idea, borrowed from the constitutional law of England, to a merely formal privilege of the house of representatives. The paragraph goes on to say that "the senate may propose, or concur with, amendments, as on other bills." In practice, however, the privilege of the house of representatives has become a public wrong of no slight consequence. The senate's amendments are not discussed in the house, but simply rejected. The senate persists, and the bill is referred to a conference committee in which both houses are equally represented. The proposals of this committee cannot be amended. They must be adopted or rejected as a whole. As action upon them is generally postponed until towards the end of the session, the house adopts the committee's report, because it shrinks from the responsibility of letting an entire appropriation bill go to wreck on account of a few questions of detail. While thus, in the senate, the appropriations suggested by the house are carefully investigated, amended at will and perfected, the house by its own beloved rules subjects itself to a certain moral compulsion by which it is forced to assent to the conclusions reached by only three of its members and a like number of senators. Occasionally indeed, one of the general appropriation bills has failed to pass.[1] But neither of the houses will lightly undertake this responsibility, because the constitution provides that no money shall be drawn from the treasury but in consequence of appropriations made by law (art. I., sec. 9, § 7). The administration therefore has no constitutional right to apply the moneys in the treasury to meet any public needs whatever, even if they be the most urgent, which congress has not provided for by making appropriations. In the event, therefore, of the failure of an appropriation

[1] See, for instance, my *Constitutional History*, V., 414.

bill, a most wretched and unendurable state of affairs must quickly come to pass.

Even under the most favorable circumstances the administration can get along for but a few months, because the appropriations are made only for one year. This is not due, however, to any constitutional necessity. On this point the constitution contains only the provision that congress may "raise and support armies, but no appropriation of money to that use shall be for a longer term than two years" (art. I., sec. 8, § 12). Congress, therefore, unquestionably has a right to substitute a biennial for the annual budget. It is, however, a different question, whether the provision just quoted implies the power of congress — except as to the army — to have a triennial or quadrennial budget. While it can certainly make appropriations for a longer time, it also certainly cannot frame an entire budget which shall be good for more than two years. And it can make one good for two years only when it does so at the beginning of its own existence.[1] No congress can bind subsequent congresses in such a way as to curtail their constitutional powers. And it is, moreover, evident not only that no congress would permit its predecessor to deprive it of its right of framing a budget, but that it could not constitutionally renounce its independent exercise of this right. Even a

---

[1] The constitution keeps a few appropriations beyond the control of congress. By several acts, however, the number of the so-called "permanent appropriations" has gradually grown to between twenty and thirty. Some years ago the senate passed a bill which repealed these altogether, save those for the president's salary, the salaries of the federal judges and the interest on the public debt. The assent of the house of representatives, however, could not be obtained, because the bill would have endangered the continuance of the act known as the "Bland bill," which requires the annual coinage of at least twenty-four million silver dollars.

single appropriation extending over a longer period must always presuppose the tacit sanction of the new congress. It is not likely that these questions will ever become practical. The United States is in too eminent a degree a popular state to let it seem possible that one congress would ever show a desire to usurp the prerogatives of future congresses in this respect. In fact the annual framing of the budget was probably not required by the constitution, only because it was regarded as a matter of course.

As the budget is fixed annually, the statement of the public revenue and expenditure, which must be published "from time to time" (art. I., sec. 9, § 6), is issued every year. The total revenue for the fiscal year 1883–84 was $348,519,869 (against $398,287,581 in the preceding year). The chief individual sources of revenue have already been mentioned. Here we may add that the sale of public lands yielded $9,810,705. The income from land sales exceeded these figures only in the three years 1835, 1836 and 1855, in the two former very considerably. But in the other years as a rule the receipts were much smaller. Congress appropriated for the fiscal year 1884–85 $137,451,398, distributed as follows: deficiencies, $4,385,836; legislative, executive and judicial expenses, $21,556,902; sundry civil expenses, $22,346,750; support of the army, $24,454,450; naval service (for only the first half of the year), $8,931,856; Indian service, $5,903,151; rivers and harbors, $14,948,300; military academy, $314,563; forts and fortifications, $700,000; pensions, $20,810,000; consular and diplomatic service, $1,225,140; agricultural department, $480,190; District of Columbia, $3,594,256; miscellaneous, $7,800,004.

COMMERCE, INTER-STATE AND NATIONAL.[1]

§ 38. TRADE AND COMMERCE scarcely came within the range of congress, under the articles of confederation.[2] The many and great evils resulting from this gave the most direct and vigorous impetus to the struggles for reform which led to the Philadelphia convention and to the adoption of its plan for a constitution. The convention therefore naturally considered it to be one of its greatest tasks to nationalize the Union in this respect. It has been rightly said that the consolidation of the industrial interests of the country has proved to be the strongest bond of the federal state.

Congress (says art. I., sec. 8, § 3 of the constitution) is authorized "to regulate commerce with foreign nations and among the several states and with the Indian tribes."[3]

---

[1] F. Chamberlin, *American Commercial Law*, Hartford, 1872; R. Desty, *Commerce, Navigation and Shipping of the United States*, San Francisco, 1880; L. Houck, *Law of Navigable Rivers*, Boston, 1868; J. G. Thompson, *Law of Highways*, 3d ed., Albany, 1881.

[2] So far as trade was concerned, only that with the Indians was subject to its control. As to its other powers in regard to commerce, see the fourth paragraph of article IX.

[3] The Indian appears in the constitution only here and in the provision concerning the apportionment of the number of members of the house of representatives and in the clause about direct taxes. The multifarious powers to regulate Indian affairs which the federal government has claimed and exercised must therefore be constitutionally based on all sorts of other constitutional provisions. Neither statesmen nor publicists have as yet, however, taken the pains to enter into the complicated questions involved therein and to analyze and explain them. In congress much has been frequently said concerning this or that question of law and the federal supreme court has rendered some important decisions. In general, however, the legal side of the problem has been pushed into the background by the practical. In respect to both of them, as Americans themselves admit without reserve, much has been overlooked and much seriously

From the extremely large number of judicial decisions rendered in interpretation of this provision, two most comprehensive principles are to be deduced: First, the word neglected. The first cause of the failures and mistakes has been in no small degree the lack of knowledge of and care for the fundamental question of law. Formal treaties have been concluded with the Indian tribes, as if they were independent nations with equal rights with whom and towards which the United States had an international relation. Yet, as a matter of fact, no such position has been granted them. It could not be granted. Urged on by the development of circumstances and by the fact that the domains of the tribes formed a constituent part of the territory of the Union, the government fell more and more into contradictions in its own actions towards the Indian and piled injustice upon injustice. By degrees men became aware of the blunders of the fathers of the republic. The law of March 3, 1871, put an end to further danger from this source. This law provided that in future no treaties should be concluded with the Indians, because they, as it expressly stated, are not independent nations. This put what are left of the unfortunate aborigines in a legal relation to the federal government corresponding with their actual one: They are wards who must be cared for so far as equity and humanity demand on the one hand, but on the other with due regard to the demands of civilization as it sweeps over the continent. They are still treated upon the theory that they are to be isolated as far as possible. Their domains are reservations. The largest is Indian Territory, which has a very peculiar *status*. It embraces over seventy thousand square miles, is bounded on the south by Texas and the Red river, on the east by Arkansas, on the north by Kansas, and on the west by Texas and New Mexico. A large number of tribes inhabit it and have legal relations with one another. The United States has only "executive jurisdiction," but certain law questions fall within its sphere to decide. A fuller discussion of the very peculiar structure of this semi-barbaric pseudo-state of the Union would be out of place here. Only the most important matters as to the regulation of Indian affairs can be brought forward. All tribes which have come to an agreement with the United States have their own districts, called reservations, which are sprinkled over the states and territories. The government is represented among the tribes by "agents" (and sub-agents), over whom are "superintendents" and "inspectors." At the head of the entire office of Indian affairs, forming a part of the department of the interior, is a commissioner. The

"commerce" has not the same signification as traffic, purchase and sale, *i. e.*, as "trade" in its more limited sense, but includes also the idea of "transportation." The author-

agents must give a bond, the amount of which is fixed by the president and the secretary of the interior. They must reside at a place fixed by the president within the limits of their reservation, or in its immediate vicinity, and must not leave their reservation without permission. Neither they nor the other officials of the Indian service are permitted to be interested in any business whatever with the Indians under a penalty of $5,000. Trade can be carried on with the Indians only by citizens of the United States, and these must give bond in the sum of $5,000 to $10,000 and procure a license, which can at any time be revoked by the superintendent, whenever he is convinced that the particular person is objectionable. The purchase of implements of the chase, and under some circumstances also the sale of weapons and ammunition, are subject to all sorts of restrictions. The sale, manufacture and introduction of intoxicating liquors on the reservations are most strictly forbidden. In order to prevent the violation of these rules, a comprehensive right of search is granted to the agents. Whoever carries on business without a license forfeits, in addition to all his merchandise, the sum of $500. Contracts can be made only with all sorts of formalities. As a general rule, the purchase of land is not permitted. A man who trys to buy land or surveys land in the reservation is liable to fine. Outsiders can enter a reservation, only if provided with a pass, and no one is permitted to settle there. Trespassers are expelled if necessary by the military. Any one who returns after being expelled must pay a fine of $1,000. The right of hunting and grazing in the reservations belongs solely to the Indians. Crimes are punished according to the laws of the places wherein the United States have exclusive jurisdiction. The Indian appropriation was $5,003,151 in 1884. The greater part of this is used in paying the tribes the moneys granted them and in supplying them with clothing, cattle, etc. In part it is a payment for lands ceded by the Indians according to treaties or other agreements and in part a gift without any legal obligation whatever. Without such assistance most of the tribes would soon succumb to hunger and misery. The federal government seeks by gifts to raise them gradually to such a degree of civilization that they will become able to support themselves. A business spirit has been stimulated by presenting individuals among them with cattle and rewarding them for the increase. In a similar manner, attempts are made to encourage agri-

ity of congress extends to all international and interstate commerce,[1] embracing all the means as well as the subjects thereof, including persons in either capacity.[2] Second, with commerce within the limits of one single individual state, congress has nothing to do. Thus if the authority of congress is far-reaching, it is nevertheless restricted, and the precise demarcation of its limits is for various reasons not an easy matter.

Among the infinite possibilities presented by the occurrences of real life, it is often very difficult to draw the line of distinction just indicated. The exclusive authority of the separate and individual state is not under all circumstances co-extensive with its geographical limits,

culture. In general the efforts of the government are directed towards dissolving the tribal relation and substituting the institution of individual property. New sources of industry were opened to these people and their self-respect heightened by placing in their own hands the distribution of the government goods and by organizing from their midst an Indian police force. And finally a number of schools have been successfully opened, in which the instruction given is especially adapted to their peculiar mental and bodily dispositions and desires. The good results of all these measures are already very noticeable. They have brought about a new era in the Indian policy. A great part of the credit belongs to Carl Schurz, who, as secretary of the interior under President Hayes, took especially to heart the care of the Indians. Still, only the beginning has been made of a more humane and just policy, corresponding better with the true interests of both parties; and the government has no little trouble in enforcing even the laws which now exist. It is not easy to impress the rough and reckless pioneer population with the idea that the Indians have any rights which must be respected. At the moment I write, it has become necessary to repel by force illegal invasion of the Indian Territory and of the other reservations.

[1] *Gibbons vs. Ogden*, Wheaton, IX., 189.

[2] *The Passenger Cases*, Howard, VII., 283. Five judges declare themselves against the view expressed by Judge Barbour in the earlier case of *New York vs. Miln* (Peters, XI., 102), that persons could not be "the subject of commerce."

even when these limits are in no wise overstepped in the case in question. Thus, for instance, in 1851, the supreme court decided that Virginia had no right to permit a company to put a suspension bridge over the Ohio river at Wheeling (when the stream was entirely within the territorial limits of the state) so as to interfere with navigation, because the Ohio was a navigable water way between different states, and congress must regulate interstate commerce, and that commerce included navigation.[1] In other cases, however, it has been decided that the states, if congress has not exerted its legislative authority, can permit the building of a bridge over a navigable stream flowing wholly within their jurisdictions, even if it interferes with navigation. These decisions were based upon the fact that bridges as well as navigable streams are means of commerce, and that the states must be able to determine whether and how far commerce across the water should be preferred to commerce on the water.[2] Finally, the right of the states to build bridges or let them be built over navigable streams within their limits, when there was no interference with navigation, has been repeatedly acknowledged. Whether there is or is not such interference is a question of fact that must, in every instance, be decided with regard to the circumstances of the particular case.[3]

[1] Howard, XIII., 518. But when congress legalized the bridge, as built, a suit brought by the state of Pennsylvania was dismissed by the supreme court because the assertion of an interference with navigation, accepted as valid by the court, had not been made good before congress.

[2] *Gilman vs. Philadelphia*, Wallace, III., 713; *The Passaic Bridges*, Ibid., 782.

[3] See *Wilson vs. Blackbird Creek Company*, Peters, II., 245, as well as the remarks of Justice McLean (Howard, VII., 397, 398), and Justice Clifford (Wallace, III., 743), upon this decision.

Further difficulties arise out of the question whether and how far the constitutional authority of congress is an exclusive one, *i. e.*, whether and how far the states possess concurrent power. When congress enacts a law, then, according to the judicial decisions, all state legislation is overruled, even if it does not immediately concern the same subject-matter.[1] Strictly taken, the authority of congress is an "exclusive" one, and a "concurrent" power of the states cannot be recognized.[2] But, in spite of this, legislative action on the part of the states, within the range of the constitutional authority of congress, is admissible. If congress has not made use of its powers, the inference may be drawn either that it does not wish any legislation on the matters in question, or else that it wishes to let the particular local circumstances control, and that it therefore commits the matter to the states or state concerned. Thus, for instance, if congress were entitled to enact a general pilot law on the ground that the pilot system belongs to navigation, and the regulation of navigation is included in the right to regulate commerce, and if it should nevertheless refuse to enact such a law, it would thereby say that it does not regard the pilot system as adapted to a general and entirely homogenous regulation. In such a case the state laws concerning pilotage could not be declared to be unconstitutional encroachments upon the domain of congress.[3] The states are by no means always entitled to legislate, if, and so

---

[1] *The Passenger Cases*, Howard, VII., 283. The reasons for the decision of the court as such were not given in this case; only the individual judges gave reasons; but five of them maintained the opinion stated in the text.

[2] See Judge McLean's remarks in the *Passenger Cases*, cited *supra*, upon Marshall's decision in *Gibbons vs. Ogden*, and Story's reference thereto in *New York vs. Miln*.

[3] *Cooley vs. The Port Wardens*, Howard, XII., 299.

long as, congress does not exercise its authority, but according to the above decision the exclusiveness of the authority of congress is not always absolute. In what case it is or is not to be regarded as such is manifestly not always quite certain from a legal standpoint. The courts must base their decision more or less upon considerations of a practical political nature, and therefore it may often be highly doubtful to which category the case in hand should be referred.

Difficulties grow apace because, as the federal supreme court has decided, " it is not everything that affects commerce that amounts to a regulation of it, within the meaning of the constitution;"[1] and the states, moreover, have certain powers by the exercise of which they may very easily come into conflict with the congressional legislation which regulates commerce. First and foremost of these are the police powers of the states. Drawing the line up to which a direct or indirect invasion of the province of congressional legislation on trade and commerce will be acknowledged as authorized, must necessarily be a somewhat arbitrary process. Thus, for instance, health and quarantine laws fall within the domain of the state.[2] It is very evident, however, that such laws could readily be made to interfere with many of the provisions of congressional legislation about trade and commerce. Moreover the supreme court in the *License Cases* (Howard, V., 504) decided that the states might, under certain restrictions, require the trade in liquors imported or brought from another state to be licensed, while in an older case (*Brown vs. Maryland*, Wheaton, XII., 419) it was decided that in general the importer's right of sale must not be interfered with by the state's requiring him

[1] *State Tax on Railway Gross Receipts*, Wallace, XV., 293.
[2] *Gibbons vs. Ogden*, Howard, IX., 203.

to buy a license. The judges, however, assigned the most diverse reasons for their decision in the *License Cases*. And it can by no means be discovered from these reasons how far the states may go in the exercise of their police power in restricting commerce in articles which they regard, for any reason whatever, as injurious or dangerous to the community. Similar conflicts may arise from the right of taxation possessed by the states. In inter-state or international commerce, neither the goods nor the transportation of property or persons can be taxed by the states.[1] But the business as such and the capital used in it are subject to the state's right of taxation. The correctness of this principle certainly cannot be attacked, but just as little can it be disputed that it gives the states the power of encroaching very seriously upon the congressional domain, if they are only careful about the way in which they do so.[2] The courts indeed are in no wise bound to permit the simple question of the sufficiency of the form in which a state carries out its right of taxation to determine their decisions, and they do not do so. As soon as they enter upon the question, whether the tax-laws of a state materially encroach upon the right of regulating international and inter-state commerce, subjective views are again given more or less sway.

These observations will be sufficient to show why an accurate judgment of the extent of this constitutional provision in all its ramifications is possible only in connection with all the judicial decisions to which it has

[1] *State Freight Tax*, Wallace, XV., 232; *The Passenger Cases*, Howard, VII., 283.

[2] How easily and in what various ways this may occur will be sufficiently indicated by pointing to the decision in *Liverpool Insurance Company vs. Massachusetts*, Wallace, X., 566, according to which a state can tax a foreign corporation higher than similar corporations created by its own laws.

given rise. And they also show why no general and fixed commercial law, in the European sense of the word, has been developed in the United States. The narrow frame of this work makes it necessary to let this suffice and only to mention briefly the matters subject to the authority of congress, under this general provision, either by force of custom or of judicial decisions.

This authority extends to the places, the means and the subjects of trade and commerce.

As to the places, congress must not only provide where, under what conditions, and how certain events in international and inter-state commerce — such as the departure and arrival of vessels, the discharge of their freight, the payment of duties, etc. — shall take place, but it must also take care that the places meet the demands of commerce and trade. That is, it must put and keep the harbors in good condition, must improve the navigability of the rivers, must build light-houses, piers, etc.

As to the means, the principle prevails that the authority of congress is not restricted to those means which were known and in use at the time of the adoption of the constitution. Steamboat and railroad traffic and the telegraph system are as much subject to congressional regulation as were the media of commercial intercourse of earlier times. Its powers " keep pace with the progress of the country and adapt themselves to the new developments of time and circumstances. . . . As they were entrusted to the general government for the good of the nation, it is not only the right but the duty of congress to see to it that intercourse among the states and the transmission of intelligence are not obstructed or unnecessarily encumbered by state legislation."[1] Whether and how far congress is entitled to itself provide media of

[1] *Pensacola Tel. Co. vs. Western Union Tel. Co.*, Otto, VI., 124; Cooley, *Principles*, 65, 66.

commerce, *i. e.*, to establish highways, to build or materially aid in building railroads, etc., is one of the oldest and most important questions, and one which has not yet received a final and comprehensive legal decision. But the tendency of actual development has always been towards the subordination of legal arguments to considerations of expediency. On the other hand the power of congress to use its authority to regulate trade in such a way as to indirectly accomplish other objects is generally recognized.[1] Congress has done this in the numerous laws usually referred to under the name of registration and navigation laws. These are in great part designed to give American ship-builders and ship-owners an advantage over their foreign competitors. To the power to regulate the means of commerce we must also refer the laws as to building and outfitting of vessels, the number and safety of the crews, as well as of the passengers, the discipline, the legal rights and duties of the sailors, etc.[2]

[1] How far congress may do this has, however, been a hotly contested question in the battles between protection and free trade.

[2] The influence of the federal government upon the means of commercial intercourse — apart from those used in navigation — has been up to the present time comparatively very limited. As to the railroads, it has reserved a somewhat more comprehensive power only as to the roads in the construction of which, to be discussed further on, it assisted in part. In the discharge of its constitutional duties, in which it could not do without the railroads, as in the carrying of the mails, congress promptly used its legislative powers as far as the public interests seemed to demand. But as to the rest, the federal laws contain little more in reference to the railroads than the provisions that relate to all "common carriers." But that this is not due to any doubts as to its own authority is plain from the act of March 3, 1873, which was dictated solely by a humanitarian regard for the rest, feeding and watering of cattle transported by rail or water. (*Stat. at Large*, XVII., 584, 585.) For years, however, congress has debated a considerable number of proposed laws of every kind which cut deeply into the autonomy of railroad companies and in part also

Under the authority of congress as to the subjects of commercial intercourse, the laws which regulate the import and export of certain commodities and the movements of certain persons have been passed. Many of the powers of congress under this division of its authority enure also to the states from their police power. Restrictions on the importation of poisons and explosives, prohibitions of the introduction of indecent publications and pictures, etc., could be imposed also by the states. The application of the principles of constitutional law in this respect may easily lead in disputed questions to no slight difficulties. As far as persons are concerned, the author-

sharply invade the realm of legislation which the states have thus far been permitted to monopolize. The opposition of material interests, however, and especially the general political considerations against such action, have thus far defeated every effort for a more uniform regulation of the railroad system by federal legislation. As late as the spring of 1884, congress considered, but again without result, a number of proposals as to railroad freights, a matter which Leyen justly designates as the "true germinal point of the so-called railroad question" in the United States. It will probably depend to a large extent upon the conduct of the railroad companies themselves as to whether, or how soon, the tendency manifested by such attempts at legislation will finally, however, begin to triumph over difficulties to be overcome. What decisive action congress might think itself authorized to take, under certain circumstances, appears from the act of January 31, 1862, which authorized the president to take possession of all railroads and telegraph lines, as far as he thought public safety required, and invested the secretary of war with sole control of the transportation of troops and of all military stores. (*Stat. at Large*, XII., 334.) See J. F. Lacey, *Digest of American Railway Decisions*, Chicago, 1875; E. L. Pierce, *Law of Railroads*, Boston, 1881; D. Rorer, *A Treatise on the Law of Railways*, 2 vols., Chicago, 1884; A. v. d. Leyen, *Die Nordamerikanischen Eisenbahnen in ihren wirthschaftlichen und politischen Beziehungen*. Leipzig, 1885.

As to the telegraph companies, the federal government has somewhat more extensive rights. An act of July 24, 1866, grants the tele-

ity of the states goes to the full extent required by the "law of preservation." As they may protect themselves by their health and quarantine laws against the introduction of contagious disease, so they may guard themselves likewise against the "moral pest" of vagabonds, paupers and criminals. But apart from this the regulation of immigration is the exclusive domain of congress. Thus, for example, a state cannot prohibit the immigration of persons (Chinese, for instance) because it fears that they will not obey the laws, or because it regards them, for economic or other political reasons, as a pernicious element of the

graph companies organized under state laws the right of way along post-roads or military lines, along navigable streams and over public lands, and permits them to take from the public domain wood, stone and other material for the building of their lines and station-houses, provided they bind themselves to send government telegrams ahead of all other dispatches at rates fixed by the postmaster-general, and to sell their lines upon demand by the government to the United States, at a price to be determined by five impartial men, two of them named by the postmaster-general, two by the company, and the fifth by the four. I am not, however, aware that any telegraph line has actually been bought under this law. Telegraphs and railroads are both still private enterprises and private property, but the continuous consolidation of these important instruments of commerce in the hands of mammoth corporations disturbs public opinion more and more. Discontent is widespread and has at times attained such proportions that the "monopolies" would probably have been already broken, if it were clear what should take the place of the existing circumstances, and if an agreement could be reached on this point. As long as the appointment of nearly fifty thousand postmasters is not wholly withdrawn from party politics, the thoughtful part of the people will scarcely be persuaded to add to the post-office department the telegraph employees, who are counted by tens of thousands (the Western Union Telegraph Company alone had, in 1883, twelve thousand nine hundred and seventeen). President Grant recommended this in his annual message of December, 1871.

population.¹ Whenever congress exercises its legislative authority in this respect, it must always be in a general way, treating all the states alike.² This is, indeed, nowhere expressly declared; but it would be opposed to the general spirit of the constitution to give certain parts of the Union a separate and distinct position, because this would too readily excite at least the suspicion that the conclusions of congress were influenced by partiality for one section or dislike of another.

So far as the regulation of trade is concerned, this fundamental doctrine of complete equality is expressly ordained in regard to certain matters. Art. I., sec. 9, § 5, provides that "no preference shall be given by any regulation of commerce or revenue to the ports of one state over those of another." And it declares further: "Nor shall vessels bound to or from one state be obliged to enter, clear or pay duties in another." The freedom from taxes of the entire coast trade and of the commerce on inland waters is thus firmly established by the constitution, and it has been rightly said that this provision alone is sufficient to show the immense worth of the Union.³

§ 39. NATURALIZATION. Immediately after the provision as to the regulation of trade and commerce, the right is granted to congress "to establish a uniform rule of naturalization." To this is added the power already men-

---

¹ The states are not only not authorized directly to prohibit immigration, but they cannot even indirectly hinder it by laws about the landing of passengers from foreign ports. *Chy Lung vs. Freeman,* 92 U. S. (Otto, II.), 272.

² A law of May 2, 1882, "suspended" the immigration of Chinese for ten years.

³ In this connection it should also be said that in the clause already discussed as to exports, the states are also forbidden to tax imports.

tioned, to enact a uniform bankruptcy law, and further provisions relating to trade and commerce follow. It seems from this juxtaposition that the authors of the constitution regarded naturalization especially from the standpoint of the industrial interests, and that therefore, in the adoption of this provision, they had in mind mainly the encouragement of immigration. In this sense, too, congress has made use of this power. The debt of the United States to this for their unexampled development is well known. If the efforts of the different nativist parties and especially of the "Know Nothings" in the fifties to substantially increase the time of probation, fixed at five years (they wished to make it twenty-one), had been successful, the stream of immigration would unquestionably have been very considerably reduced.[1] From a legal point of view, it need be observed only that the power of congress is exclusive,[2] but is of course restricted to the grant of the right of citizenship of the United States.[3]

Among the other powers of congress over commercial

---

[1] A person must have resided five years in the United States and at least one year in the state or territory where he wishes to be naturalized. Two years prior to naturalization, the immigrant must declare under oath in court his wish to become a citizen. This is not necessary if he came to the United States at least three years before attaining his majority. The widow and the minor children of an immigrant who had declared his intention to be naturalized in the manner required, need only take the prescribed oath to obtain the right of citizenship. Children of immigrants obtain citizenship without naturalization, if they reside in the United States and at the time of their parents' naturalization are still in their minority. Titles of nobility must be expressly renounced at the time of naturalization.

[2] *Chirac vs. Chirac*, Wheaton, II., 259, 269.

[3] The peculiar consequences of the right of the states to grant state citizenship have already been discussed.

intercourse are those in regard to money, already stated in another connection.

§ 40. MEASURES AND WEIGHTS. So far as the right "to fix the standard of weights and measures" is concerned, it need but be noted that it is not an exclusive one. Congress may make a uniform system of weights and measures obligatory, but it has contented itself with legalizing the metric system, by an act of July 28, 1866, and with fixing the relations of the customary weights and measures (mile, foot, inch; acre, yard, inch; gallon, quart, gill; pound, ounce, grain).

§ 41. THE MAILS. Of the power given congress "to establish postoffices and post-roads," Pomeroy (p. 264) rightly says that the words express the intention in the most insufficient manner. "To create and regulate the entire postal system of the country is the evident intent." Accordingly congress has always done so without any opposition. But this clause has given rise to a more significant controversy, namely, whether congress can simply convert existing roads into "post-roads" or whether it itself may build post-roads. It has done the latter, but very seldom.[1]

[1] The act of April 30, 1802, for the admission of the state of Ohio, involves a claim of the right to build such roads, but with an important limitation. Whether congress thought this limitation was required by expediency in the particular case, or generally as a matter of constitutional law, does not appear. The act provides that the twentieth portion of the net proceeds from the sale of public lands within the state should be applied to the building of roads "leading from the navigable waters emptying into the Atlantic, to the Ohio, to the said state, and through the same, such roads to be laid out under the authority of congress, *with the consent of the several states through which the road shall pass.*" *Stat. at Large*, II., 175. The building of the Cumberland road, which was authorized by act of March 29, 1806 (*Ibid.*, 357), and its maintenance gave occasion to repeated and very incisive discussions of the question as to how far the power of the

§ 42. PROTECTION OF INTELLECTUAL PROPERTY. The power to do this quite naturally follows the powers as to commerce, because this has to do to a certain extent with commercial intercourse. Congress may " promote the progress of science and useful arts by securing for

United States to build roads extended. President Monroe, in a message of May 4, 1822 (*Statesman's Manual*, I., 402–537), defended the view " not only that the power necessary for internal improvements has not been granted, but that it has been clearly prohibited; " but he adds: " To the appropriation of the public money to improvements having these objects [to facilitate the operations of war and the transportation of the mail] in view, and carried to a certain extent, I do not see any well-founded constitutional objection." Jackson adopted Monroe's views in substance; but, in the application of the principles laid down by Monroe, Jackson took his position more decisively with the state's-rights party, and emphasized more sharply " the general principle that the works which might be thus aided should be of a general, not local, national, not state, character." See his Maysville Road Veto of May 27, 1830; *Statesman's Man.*, I., 719–728. Subsequently, the interest in the question, as one of constitutional law, became much less. The power of the United States to construct roads is deduced, however, not only from this clause about post-roads, but also from the duty of taking care of the country's defenses, and from the right to regulate commerce. The railroads, the building of which was aided in any way whatever by the United States, are under an unconditional legal obligation to carry the mails at prices fixed by congress. All railroads which carry the mail must do so, if required, on every train, and can make no extra charge for the transportation on such train of mail matter, or of the persons in charge of it. If the postmaster-general can make no bargain, such as the law allows, with a railroad to carry the mails, he is authorized to send the letters by messengers on horseback, and the rest of the mail by wagon. Contracts for mail carrying are let, after public advertisement, to the lowest bidder, if he gives a sufficient bond. Yet a letting of this sort is obligatory only where the mail is not carried by rail or steamer. It is only letters which must be sent by mail. Packages are usually forwarded by express companies, and latterly the larger newspapers have availed themselves in great measure of these means, because this costs less than sending the papers by mail. The act of June 8, 1872, introduced the money-order system for sending money by mail.

limited times to authors and inventors the exclusive right to their respective writings and discoveries." The authority of congress to promote art and science is thus a very limited one, but as far as the power extends it is exclusive and plenary, *i. e.*, it extends also to the enactment of special laws. The exclusive right acquired under national law does not, however, in itself, embrace an unlimited right to use and sell an invention.[1] For, in this respect, the possessor of a patent is subject to state laws, which may impose conditions upon the use of the article and may, under some circumstances, even forbid its use as dangerous to the community. Copyrights and patents under the existing law are granted citizens and inhabitants of the United States for seventeen years. They may be extended on a proper petition for fourteen years more. The widow and children of a deceased author or inventor can also obtain this extension. The words "authors and inventors" and "writings and discoveries" have received an extraordinarily broad interpretation in legislation. All kinds of printed matter, mechanical reproductions of works of art of every sort, photographs, etc., may be legally protected. According to recent decisions of the supreme court (*United States vs. Steffens* and *United States vs. Wittemann*, 1879) congress cannot, under this clause, enact laws as to trade-marks. The right to do so may, however, be deduced from the provision as to the regulation of commerce, but the trade-marks would then be protected only in inter-state commerce. In the separate states, however, trade-marks are protected by the common law. Foreign countries are not considered at all in the legislation on copyrights and

---

[1] The common law grants an author protection only against the unauthorized publication of his manuscript, but not an exclusive right of property in his published work.

patents.[1] The agitation for international agreement on these subjects has been vigorously carried on of late, but as yet without result.

JUSTICE.

§ 43. GENERAL POWERS. After the observations already made as to the organization of the judicial system, the right of constituting inferior tribunals (art. I., sec. 8, § 9) needs no further commentary.

The next paragraph in this section grants congress a legislative authority as to piracies and felonies committed on the high seas and offenses against the law of nations. To give a more distinct idea, we must treat these provisions in connection with those found in other parts of the constitution which also relate to the administration of justice.

It belongs to congress to fix the penalties for piracies and for felonies committed on the high seas and to define what shall be considered as crimes falling under either of these two heads. As piracy is covered by international law, congress is not bound to define it; but whatever is made piracy by international law is subject to the penalty for piracy fixed by congress.[2] It is, of course, also authorized to declare certain crimes to be piracies, and to punish them as such, which by international law are not piracies.[3] Various views have been held as to the correct interpretation of the expression "high seas" in this clause. It is, however, established that the authority of congress to enact penal laws is not restricted to crimes committed on the high seas, but that it is co-extensive with the criminal-law jurisdiction of the admiralty and maritime courts,

[1] *Brown vs. Duchesne*, Howard, XIX., 188.
[2] *U. S. vs. Smith*, Wheaton, V., 153.
[3] *The Antelope*, Wheaton, X., 66.

a jurisdiction which, according to art. III., sec. 2. § 1, is within the scope of the federal sovereignty. The federal supreme court has, moreover, decided that the large inland lakes and the navigable rivers also fall within the jurisdiction of the admiralty and maritime courts.[1]

The act of June 30, 1864 (*Rev. Stat.*, § 5413), defines what is meant by the "securities and current coin of the United States," the counterfeiting of which congress may punish by law.

§ 44. TREASON. Finally, the crime of treason against the United States falls within the criminal jurisdiction of congress. Art. III., sec. 3, sets forth: "Treason against the United States shall consist only in levying war against them, or in adhering to their enemies, giving them aid and comfort. No person shall be convicted of treason unless on the testimony of two witnesses to the same overt act, or on confession in open court. The congress shall have power to declare the punishment of treason; but no attainder of treason shall work corruption of blood or forfeiture, except during the life of the person attainted." Determining what shall be treason lies entirely without the sphere of congress, for this the constitution has itself done with painful care. Congress has solely the power of fixing the penalty for the crime. The interpretation of this highly significant provision of the constitution is to be sought, not among the laws of congress, but amid the decisions of the courts.[2] These decisions lay down two important principles: first, the crime of "con-

---

[1] *The Hine*, Wallace, IV., 555. See S. R. Betts, *Admiralty Practice*, N. Y., 1838; E. C. Benedict, *Am. Admiralty*, 2d ed., N. Y., 1870; R. Desty, *Admiralty and Shipping*, San Francisco, 1879; T. M. Etting, *Admiralty Jurisdiction of the United States*, Phila., 1879.

[2] An act of April 30, 1790, contains, indeed, a definition of treason, but the substance of it is a verbal transcript of the constitutional provision. Compare *Revised Statutes*, sec. 5331.

structive treason," which in England has caused more than one noble head to fall below the axe, does not exist in the United States;[1] second, only a citizen of the United States can commit treason, for the crime presupposes allegiance.[2] Apart from these principles, the decisions, gauged by both moral and political standards, present many striking features. War is "levied" as well by inciting war as by carrying on war. But a conspiracy to overthrow or coerce the government, as well as the enlistment of men for such a purpose, is not, however, treason. Treason is committed only when persons assemble for the purpose of carrying out a treasonable plan. In such a case, all are guilty of treason who have taken part in the meeting, even in the slightest degree, and if ever so far removed from the place of action, provided they are connected with the general conspiracy.[3] The act alone does not of itself constitute treason; there must also be a treasonable intent. The intent need not, however, be the overthrow of the government. Even the attempt to prevent the execution of a single law, or to compel its repeal, is treason, if force is used and the resistance is of a public and general character. The amount of force used is a matter of indifference. These observations explain the provision — at first sight a curious one — of the act of July 17, 1862, that treason is punishable either by death or by imprisonment in the penitentiary for not less than five years and a fine

[1] See my *Constitutional History*, V., 292, 293.
[2] *U. S. vs. Wiltberger*, Wheaton, V., 79. The act of April 30, 1790, already quoted, is in unison with this. On the other hand, quite a modified doctrine is stated in *U. S. vs. Greathouse*, 2 Abbott's U. S. Rep., 380. See Hurd, *Theory of Our National Existence*, 61.
[3] *Ex parte Bollman*, Cranch, IV., 75.

of at least $10,000.[1] From the power of congress to fix the punishment for treason, its power also to fix punishments for crimes of lesser degree but of like character, such as insurrection, conspiracy, etc., is inferred.[2] The expression "attainder of treason" must be understood as referring only to a judicial sentence. "Bills of attainder," that is, legislative sentences, which at one time played such an important part in English history, are unconstitutional.

The authority of congress is limited to cases of treason against the United States. The clause providing for the extradition of fugitive criminals (art. IV., sec. 2, § 2) shows that the constitution recognizes the possibility of treason against a single state. This is an important matter, for the usual assumption is that treason can be committed only against a sovereign power. If the separate states are, however, really "sovereign," and if treason can be committed against them, there may then be a dangerous and unfair conflict of duties for the individual

---

[1] The act of April 30, 1790, provided that every traitor should "suffer death." *Stat. at Large*, I., 112. The same act further declared that whoever had knowledge of a treasonable crime, and did not as soon as possible give information of it, should "be adjudged guilty of misprision of treason and be punished by imprisonment of not more than seven years and by a fine of not more than $1,000."

[2] The civil war gave extensive occasion for the use of this implied power. On July 31, 1861, an "act to define and punish certain conspiracies," and on August 6, 1861, an act in regard to the enlistment of soldiers and sailors "to engage in armed hostility against the United States," became laws. The penalties provided by these laws are extraordinarily mild. Then followed the law already mentioned, the act of July 17, 1862, "to suppress insurrection, to punish treason and rebellion, to seize and confiscate the property of rebels, and for other purposes," and finally, on February 25, 1863, an "act to prevent correspondence with rebels." *Stat. at Large*, XII., 284, 317, 589, 696.

citizen. This was pointed out when the constitution was being drafted and when its adoption was being discussed.[1] This appeared on a broad stage during the civil war. Many southerners, like General Robert E. Lee and Alexander H. Stephens, the vice-president of the Confederate States, were opposed to secession, but, after secession was once ordained by their respective states, they declared themselves not only willing to go with their states, but bound to go with them unless they were to be guilty of treason, for they owed allegiance to their respective states and indeed only to them. The federal government naturally refused to admit this, and Chief-justice Chase decided, in *Shortridge vs. Macon*, that no "rebel" could defend himself from the charge of treason by pleading the ordinances and commands of his state. Logically, however, this question, on account of its connection with other problems of constitutional law brought to the surface by the civil war, leads to a whirlpool of conflicting conclusions. But a further discussion of the question (upon which Hurd throws a penetrating light in the book already cited) must not be attempted here. This remarkable fact, however, should be stated, that the doctrines of constitutional law in relation to treason were not clearly stated and sharply defined by reason of the civil war, but were rather obscured thereby.

§ 45. OTHER CRIMINAL LAW POWERS. Further express authorizations to enact criminal laws are not to be found in the constitution. It is, however, self-evident, and it has never been seriously denied, that congress may not only punish all violations of the federal laws, but may also impose penalties upon acts which, if committed with impunity, would render impossible the effective exercise

---

[1] See Elliot, I., 382, 383; V., 488.

of its constitutional powers.[1] This right is based upon the provision authorizing congress "to make all laws which shall be necessary and proper" to carry out the powers belonging to it or to any other factor of the government (art. I., sec. 8, § 18). That the constitution did not intend to charge the respective states with the duty of enforcing the observance of the federal laws by means of their own penal laws is so certain that, according to the decision of the federal supreme court in *Martin vs. Hunter* (Wheaton, I., 304), not even a part of the criminal-law powers of the United States can be conferred upon the state courts.[2]

§ 46. IMPEACHMENT. Impeachment is a judicial proceeding, and its discussion therefore belongs to this chapter on the powers of congress in regard to the administration of justice. It has undoubtedly nothing in common with the powers hitherto discussed, and is absolutely *sui generis*. Congress, as such, is not in question. It is not a legislative but a judicial power which comes into play. In this proceeding the two houses have entirely different functions: the house of representatives acts as accuser, and the senate as judge.[3] It is evident, therefore, that the constitutional provisions concerned cannot be interpreted by judicial decisions, because any controverted questions under them do not come before ordinary courts.

---

[1] The latter principle was established by the decision of the supreme court in *U. S. vs. Marigold*, Howard, IX., 560.

[2] See T. F. Waterman, *U. S. Digest of Criminal Cases*, N. Y., 1877; J. P. Bishop, *Criminal Law*, 6th ed., 2 vols., Boston, 1877; Ibid., *Criminal Procedure*, 3d ed., 2 vols., Boston, 1880; F. Wharton, *Criminal Pleading and Practice*, 8th ed., Phila., 1880; Ibid., *American Criminal Law*, 8th ed., 4 vols., Phila., 1881; R. Desty, *American Criminal Law*, San Francisco, 1882.

[3] Art. I., sec. 2, § 5, and art. I., sec. 3, § 6. Both clauses use the phrase, "the sole power."

Impeachment is a political process. The decision as to what the law is is made by the powers which act in this process as accuser and judge, inasmuch as they carry out the constitutional provisions in accordance with the interpretation which seems to them just. There is no appeal from their decision.

The constitution presupposes that it is well known what an impeachment is. And as it is a technical expression, this implies that the proceeding known in English law by this name is meant. But it is by no means to be said that the English idea must be accepted without any modification. Whether it has been changed, and if so how, must be deduced from the further provisions of the constitution on this point, as interpreted by both houses of congress, when engaged in their respective functions in conducting impeachments.

Art. II., sec. 4, reads: "The president, vice-president, and all civil officers of the United States shall be removed from office on impeachment for and conviction of treason, bribery, or other high crimes or misdemeanors." The wording of this paragraph raises a most significant question. Farrar (p. 436) thinks that emphasis must be laid upon the effect which conviction is to have upon the designated persons impeached for the causes assigned, and thus he comes to the conclusion that any other person may also be impeached. But since there is nowhere else in the constitution anything said as to who shall be subject to impeachment or in what cases it shall come to pass, while another paragraph contains more definite provisions as to the consequences of conviction,— in view of this it has always been the opinion of the most prominent jurists and statesmen as well as of the entire public, that the clause cited must be held to settle these two questions, and, of course, that only the persons named are subject to impeachment and they only for the causes mentioned. This must be held to be the valid constitutional law, as long as the house of representatives does not impeach, and the senate does not hold itself competent to try, under impeachment, a person who is not a "civil officer" of the United States. The two houses did not at first agree as to the limit of the power. Senator Blount was impeached by the house in 1798, but the senate, by a majority vote, declared itself incompetent to hear the case. It is self-evident that neither the house of representatives nor the senate is bound by this decision. But it will scarcely be questioned that members of congress are not "civil officers" of the United States, within the meaning of this constitutional provision. It has never been disputed that judges come under this designation. It has been asserted, however, that impeachment is admissible only as long as the person concerned remains in office. One effect of this would be that every official threatened with impeachment could escape it by resignation. The house of representatives decided against this doctrine, in 1876, by the impeachment of Secretary of War Belknap.

There have been more vigorous discussions over the proper interpretation of the constitutional provisions in regard to the grounds of impeachment. It is agreed that the incriminating acts must have some relation to the official action of the person concerned, since impeachment aims at the preservation of public interests. But the two houses have by no means assented to the view, so energetically defended, that only official acts present a constitutional ground for an impeachment. Just as little have they ever held that the words "high crimes and misdemeanors" are to be understood in their technical sense, and that an impeachment can be based only upon acts which the federal laws have expressly declared to be "felonies" or "misdemeanors;" that is, "indictable offenses." Some authorities — and they agree in this with congress — are, nevertheless, of the opinion, that the words are not to be understood in the misty and vague sense they have in ordinary speech, but are to be interpreted by the rules of the common law. This opinion will never go unquestioned, because the very existence of a general "common law" of the United States is strenuously denied.[1] Practically the matter takes this form, that the individual views of the then members of congress must always determine what they will regard as high crimes and misdemeanors within the meaning of the constitution. Neither the arguments of authorities on jurisprudence nor precedents can bind them any further than they wish to be bound.

As to the effect of impeachment, art. I., sec. 3, § 7, says: "Judgment in cases of impeachment shall not extend further than to removal from office and disqualification to hold and enjoy any office of honor, trust or profit under the United States; but the party convicted shall, nevertheless, be liable and subject to indictment, trial, judgment and punishment according to law." It is evident from the second clause that the purpose of impeachment is not the punishment of the guilty person,

[1] Apart from this, the common law, as is well known, plays nearly as large a part in American as in English legal life. An American common law may therefore be spoken of even by one who, like myself, holds the opinion stated in the text, provided that the expression is understood to mean the common law *in* the United States and not the common law *of* the United States. On the common law in the United States, see J. D. Wheeler, *American Common Law*, 8 vols., N. Y., 1833-1836; W. A. Cocke, *Common and Civil Law in the U. S. Courts*, N. Y., 1871; O. W. Holmes, Jr., *The Common Law*, Boston, 1881.

but the protection of public interests from danger or injury by abuse of official power, neglect of duty or conduct incompatible with the dignity of the office. The punishment of all crimes and punishable misdemeanors according to law remains entirely with the ordinary courts, in the regular course of judicial proceedings. As to the consequences of a conviction in an impeachment trial, the wording of the constitution admits of a twofold interpretation. In theoretical circles it is usual to assume that, according to the constitution, conviction incapacitates the culprit for filling any federal office. This view is, however, not only not shared by the most profound jurists, but the senate has already in one case (that of John Pickering, 1804) passed sentence of only a removal from the office then held. The theory which has also been advanced, that a less penalty than removal from office may be imposed (Farrar, pp. 434, 435), will probably never be approved by the senate. It is founded, indeed, only upon far too subtle verbal criticism, and it conflicts with the very substance and purpose of impeachment. In cases of impeachment the president has no right of pardon (art. II., sec. 2, § 1).

As to the method of procedure, the constitution contains three provisions. The senators shall be on oath or affirmation when the senate meets as a court of impeachment; if the president is impeached, the chief justice of the supreme court shall preside; and for conviction a two-thirds majority of all the members present shall be necessary (art. I., sec. 3, § 6). Everything else as to procedure is left to congress.[1] But it is self-evident that congress is bound by all the provisions of the constitution in point. Tiffany's view (p. 354) is therefore to be rejected

---

[1] See the detailed description in Story, § 807 *et seq.*

without question. He holds that congress may arrest an impeached president and suspend him from office during the proceedings. But this would place the president, who is a co-ordinate, and within his constitutional sphere an independent, factor of the federal government, completely in the hands of a hostile majority of both houses of congress.[1] Pomeroy (p. 494) may be cited against Tiffany. He holds that, in the case of an official whose term of office is not fixed by the constitution,[2] the question is to be decided upon grounds of equity and expediency, because there are no insuperable constitutional objections to suspension in such a case.

INTERNATIONAL RELATIONS AND MILITARY SOVEREIGNTY.

§ 47. INTERNATIONAL RELATIONS. The powers of congress in regard to international relations are few in number. The first provision on this point which authorizes congress "to define and punish . . . offenses against the law of nations" (art. I., sec. 8, § 10), considered from a certain point of view, should be discussed in the paragraphs concerning justice. The right in this case is clearly also a duty, and the duty has been met and discharged by the passage of so-called neutrality laws, which have often played an important part in the inner history of the United States.[3]

The other powers of congress in this respect all relate to the condition of war, and must be discussed in con-

---

[1] The disposition prevailing against Andrew Johnson in 1868 leaves little room for doubt that congress would have proceeded against him in this way if it had considered itself able to do so.

[2] Judges are thus excluded.

[3] The other laws enacted by virtue of this provision need no special mention.

nection with the question of military sovereignty. Moreover, foreign relations are placed in charge of the president, with the co-operation of the senate. They will therefore be treated in the chapter on the powers of the executive. Here it is necessary simply to lay stress on the fact that foreign relations are the exclusive domain of the federal government. The constitution does not content itself with sharing among the different factors of the national government all the powers concerned. It expressly withholds them from the states. The latter are absolutely forbidden to enter into any treaty, alliance or confederation (art. I., sec. 10, § 1). They can make agreements or compacts of any kind whatever with a foreign power only with the consent of congress.[1]

§ 48. MILITARY SOVEREIGNTY. In a military aspect the consolidation or nationalization of the Union has not been carried as far as in reference to the regulation of peaceful relations with foreign powers. Experience has shown, however, that the constitutional provisions on this point render the highest development of national strength possible.

The right "to declare war" belongs to congress alone (art. I., sec. 8, § 11). Of course, the United States may get into a war without congress's having declared war. War is, in the first place, a state of fact, the appearance of which cannot be made wholly dependent, by any constitutional provisions whatever, upon the pleasure of one of the nations concerned. As far as that is possible, however, congress has the exclusive right of the initiative.

[1] The other constitutional provisions on this point will be mentioned later in another connection. The "agreements and compacts" are distinguished from "treaties and alliances" in this: that the latter have a more permanent character, while the former have only a momentary purpose and are ended when it is accomplished. *Holmes vs. Jennison*, Peters, XIV., 540, 572.

If a foreign power begins war against the United States, then it is not only the right, but the duty, of the president to oppose the enemy with all the means placed at his disposal by the constitution and the laws. But he is not to regard every act of hostility as the opening of an aggressive war and thereupon begin on his own part actual war. It is for congress to decide whether he has exceeded his constitutional authority in this respect, or has actually found himself face to face with an accomplished fact by the initiative of a foreign state.[1] That the latter may be the state of the case is expressly acknowledged by the constitution's providing that without the consent of congress "no state shall . . . engage in war, unless actually invaded, or in such imminent danger as will not admit of delay" (art I., sec. 10, § 3). The states can no more begin war than can the president; they can take into account the presence of actual facts only as far as the inalienable right and imperious necessity of self-defense demand it. If a state gets into serious trouble of this sort when congress is not in session, the president is in duty bound to call forth the entire federal power, if necessary, for its protection; for the United States must "protect" every state "from invasion" (art. IV., sec. 4).[2]

It appears, therefore, that the right to declare war may become a duty, and further, that this right implies the powers needed for the effective conduct of a war.[3] If the

[1] The importance of this question appears from the ante-bellum history of the Mexican war, which was quite certainly brought about by the president in an unconstitutional way. See my *Constitutional History*, III., chs. 6–9.

[2] The two clauses last mentioned apply in case of threats or acts of violence, not only by foreign enemies, but also by sister states.

[3] The question as to whether a "war" against rebellious states was admissible or even possible, constitutionally, has been discussed with much acuteness and much learning. Many stout volumes have been

most essential of these powers were expressly granted to congress, this was done, not only to save all doubt, but because they must be vested in congress in time of peace as well, partly for the sake of preparing for war and partly for other reasons.

The right to grant letters of marque and reprisal, conferred upon congress in the same paragraph which treats of the right to declare war, is expressly withheld from the states (art. I., sec. 10, § 1). This is not the case as to the authority to enact laws concerning captures on sea or land, as this right in its very nature is an exclusive one. The property of an enemy can be legally confiscated only in accordance with laws passed by congress,[1] but the power

---

filled with demonstrations *pro* and *con*. Even if space allowed, however, further discussion of this controverted question must be waived. It certainly is not without interest and it has a practical, important side. Thus the blockade imposed by Lincoln gave foreign powers a formal legal basis for the recognition of the Confederate States as a war-making power. But from the stand-point of constitutional law, the question at bottom involves only an idle exercise of the wits. If abstract logic be followed, it becomes very easy to construct an interminable labyrinth of contradictions. Examine it more closely and the labyrinth is only a house of cards. The American statesmen upon whom devolved the duty of overthrowing the rebellion did not from the outset keep clearly enough in view the fact that it was not a law-suit, which should or could be carried on in accordance with constitutional provisions, but a state of fact, which had as its legal basis, in principle, so far as the rebels were concerned, the annulment of the entire constitution. Legally they were and they remain rebels. Whether and how far it was expedient and necessary, to give the form of a war, conducted according to the laws of nations, to the attempt to subdue the rebels,—an attempt which was a constitutional right and duty,—depended solely on matters of fact and has nothing to do with constitutional law. As far as the rebels were concerned, the whole constitution was reduced for the federal government to the single right and duty of forcing them back to obedience; all else was a question of policy.

[1] *Brown vs. United States*, Cranch, VIII., 110.

of confiscation possessed by congress is subject to no legal restriction of any kind whatever. This clause has become of great practical significance, because the right of emancipating the slaves in the rebellious states was deduced from it.

The right to raise and support armies and to provide and maintain a navy (art. I., sec. 8, §§ 12, 13) is not entirely exclusive in congress. The states are forbidden only to "keep troops or ships of war in time of peace . . . without the consent of congress" (art. I., sec. 10, § 3). But if, in times of war, the states are free to act independently in this respect, yet this in no way limits the power of congress to call forth the force of the people under the immediate and sole control of the federal government in whatever measure it sees fit. It alone is to decide upon how strong the army and navy should be and how the men are to be got. On account of the smallness of the regular forces needed in ordinary times — at present not quite thirty thousand soldiers, seven thousand five hundred sailors (officers excepted), and one thousand five hundred marines — free enlistment supplies all the men needed. During the civil war, however, congress made use of conscription.[1] The constitutionality of the law was, it is true, vigorously contested. The sound sense of the people was, however, so decisively opposed to the legal subtleties, intended to prove the law's unconstitutionality, that the strange doctrine gained no foothold, despite some decisions in its favor. This assertion, that congress was not authorized to act solely upon grounds of necessity and expediency, was the more sur-

[1] Able-bodied immigrants from twenty to forty-five years of age, who had declared under oath their intention to become citizens, were made liable to conscription just as citizens were. For certain exceptions and more detailed information, see *Stat. at L.*, XII., 731 *et seq.*

prising, because the constitutional provisions concerned have always been interpreted to mean that congress can do everything demanded by the defense of the country. Upon these provisions have been based the right to build forts and all other fortifications, the right to found and maintain the military school at West Point and the naval school at Annapolis, the right to grant rewards and even pensions to soldiers, etc.[1]

Better founded occasions for constitutional criticism might be found, indeed, in the methods adopted by the federal government to create, before the conscription act of March, 1863, the army needed to make war upon the rebels. The first seventy-five thousand men were called to arms by Lincoln, under an act of 1795 relating to the mustering of the militia. Then, however, "volun-

---

[1] The military school at West Point was founded May 16, 1802. Applicants for admission must be from seventeen to twenty-two years of age. The president appoints the pupils, one from each congressional district, each territory and the District of Columbia, and ten at large. The appointees are subject, however, to an examination for admission and are dismissed from the academy if they do not pass the examinations held during the course of studies. These examinations are controlled by a board of visitors consisting of thirteen members. The president appoints seven, the vice-president appoints three senators, and the speaker of the house of representatives appoints three members of the house. The cadets, who must bind themselves to serve for eight years, are supported wholly at the expense of the United States. They receive rations and pay. At the head of the military academy there is a "superintendent." The immediate control of the "battalion of cadets" is vested in a "commandant of cadets." These two military principals as well as the professors are appointed by the president. The corps of teachers is completed by army officers detailed by the secretary of war. The organization of the naval school is substantially the same as that of the military academy. The pupils are appointed, one from each congressional district, upon the recommendation of the representative from that district. The age for admission is from fourteen to eighteen years.

teers" were asked for; that is, required. This was done, manifestly, upon the ground of the power "to raise armies," and the "volunteers" were designated and treated as a constituent part of the United States army. On some essential points, however, they were treated as militia. Regiments were organized according to states; the entire number of men called for was divided into quotas for the several states; and the inferior officers were appointed by the respective governors. It would, indeed, be difficult to prove that this was actually unconstitutional, but, at all events, the federal army and the militia were not kept so distinctly separate as they should have been, or at least might have been, according to the true intent of the constitution.

§ 49. MILITIA. There is no militia of the United States. The constitution recognizes only a militia of the several states, and the authority of the federal government as to them is precisely defined. It is nowhere made the express duty of the states to have a militia. But not only does the constitution take the existence of a state militia for granted, but the states can be compelled to maintain one by federal legislation, for congress is authorized "to provide for organizing, arming and disciplining the militia." [1]

[1] "Every able-bodied male citizen of the respective states, resident therein, who is of the age of eighteen years, and under the age of forty-five years, shall be enrolled in the militia." *Rev. Stat.*, sec. 1625. But, as it further says that "all persons who now are or may hereafter be exempted by the laws of the respective states shall be exempted from militia duty," the states are absolutely bound only to have some sort of a militia. Even if this is not the spirit of the law, its letter permits them to make the exceptions so extensive as to become the rule. Their freedom of action is expressly restricted only in so far that they must regard the exceptions made by the federal law, especially the exemption of federal officials. If a state abuses the freedom left it by the letter of the law, it might not be able to

The training of the militia, according to the rules laid down by congress, and the appointment of officers, are strictly reserved to the states (art. I., sec. 8, § 16). The militia can be called into the service of the Union only for three distinct purposes: "to execute the laws of the Union, suppress insurrections and repel invasions" (*Ibid.*, § 15). The militia cannot be taken out of the country. Moreover it can be directly called into service to suppress an insurrection only when the insurrection is against the United States. In case of domestic violence, directed solely against a state government, the federal government can interpose only on application of the state legislature, or of the governor if the legislature is not in

raise an armed force for its own protection. For, when the militia of several states is called into the service of the United States, the total number of men required must be distributed among these states in proportion to the number of their representatives in congress.

By an act of July 17, 1862, the call must not be for more than nine months. If the militia is taken into the service of the United States, it is subject to the same rules and articles of war as the regular army, but also receives "the same pay, rations, clothing and camp equipage." Its court-martials, however, are made up only of militia officers. A law of July 14, 1862, put militia in the national service upon the same footing as regular soldiers, so far as pension-rights were concerned. The first militia act (May 8, 1792) prescribed exactly the arms and equipments with which every officer and soldier should be provided. As early as 1808, congress appropriated $200,000 per annum for the militia, for the supply of arms, etc.,—an amount which was to be annually divided among the states in proportion to the number of their representatives in congress. As a result of this arrangement the seceded states were able to begin war against the Union with arms furnished them by the government of the Union. The federal laws contain no absolutely binding directions as to how the militia should be subdivided into divisions, brigades, regiments, etc., but the composition of the corps of officers is carefully prescribed. Each state must have an adjutant-general, and he must send a report to the president at the beginning of each year. Army regulations as to discipline and drill are to be taken as a model.

session. In this instance, however, it is bound to lend its aid (art. IV., sec. 4).¹ The constitution does not say in so many words whose duty it is to call out the militia for any of the purposes mentioned. The wording of the particular clause —"to provide for calling forth"— shows, however, that congress need not act directly in every case, but may pass general laws providing under what circumstances and in what way a call shall be made. This it has done, and has transferred the power, with all the implied powers and duties, to the president. When the militia is called into the service of the United States, the provision applies to it, which authorizes congress "to make rules for the government and regulation of the land and naval forces" (art. I., sec. 8, § 14). The wording of this paragraph, which forms the basis of the whole "military law," is not sufficiently clear to permit the line between the authority of congress and that of the president as commander-in-chief to be always drawn with certainty.²

§ 50. QUARTERING SOLDIERS. Traditions of English history caused the passage of the third amendment. This provides that "no soldier shall in time of peace be quartered in any house without the consent of the owner, nor in time of war, but in a manner to be prescribed by law."

---

¹ This provision has this weighty result, that, when two legislatures or two governors are opposed to one another in the same state, the president must decide which government is the legal one. Whether there really is domestic violence is a question of fact, as to which, according to law, the president has the exclusive right of decision. If his decision is held to be erroneous by congress, the latter can administer whatever remedy seems fit, but there can be no appeal to the courts from the judgment of the president. *Luther vs. Borden*, Howard, VII., 43–45; *Martin vs. Mott*, Wheaton, XII., 29–31.

² See Pomeroy, p. 297, for a case of conflict resulting from this.

THE SEAT OF GOVERNMENT AND THE SEPARATE PROPERTY OF THE NATION.

§ 51. DISTRICT OF COLUMBIA. When, after the termination of the war of independence, the wretched effects of a weak government became daily more and more manifest, the evils due to the fact that congress had to meet within the limits of a state's jurisdiction were especially felt. This made congress dependent to a certain degree upon the state government, a dependence which was always improper, and under critical conditions might have become fatal. These evils led the authors of the constitution to think of a means of preventing them for the future. And they concluded that they had discovered it in the provision authorizing congress to acquire by cession from any of the states a district of not more than ten miles square as the seat of government over which it could "exercise exclusive legislation in all cases whatsoever" (art. I., sec. 8, § 17). The territory called the District of Columbia was acquired from Virginia and Maryland. The part ceded by Virginia was afterwards ceded back to her. The history of the slavery question teaches on every page the eminent significance of the fact that the capital was built within the domain of slavery. Against the clear wording of the constitution, the south asserted that congress could not, without the consent of Maryland (and Virginia), abolish slavery in the District. Until civil war had come, the representatives of the north acknowledged the "moral" obligation of letting it continue. The seat of government was withdrawn from the influence of a state government, but instead it was brought under the infinitely more potent influence of the slavocracy. Apart from the slavery question, this paragraph has given rise to no far-reaching controversies. The principles laid down by the supreme court, that the exclusive legislative power involves exclusive jurisdiction, and that congress is not the local legislature of the District, but possesses, as the national legislature, exclusive legislative power over it, have never been seriously assailed.[1] The power of giving the city of Washington its own municipal government has therefore always been regarded as self-evident. On the contrary, the constitutionality of organizing the District into a territory like the ordinary territories has been disputed, because a partial delegation of the legislative power is inadmissible, on account of the expressly stated exclusiveness of this power. It is, however, generally admitted that "exclusive" does not mean the same as "unlimited." Congress cannot grant the inhabitants of the District any rights which, according to the general political nature of the Union, belong only to the population of the states — such, for instance, as representation in congress, participation in the presidential election, etc. And just as little can congress rule the District without regard to the provisions of the so-called "bill of rights." But what congress cannot do in regard to the District in matters not involving the rights of the states as such, that it also cannot do in reference to anybody or anything.[2]

[1] *Cohens vs. Virginia*, Wheaton, VI., 424.

[2] Congress has tried all sorts of experiments as to the local government of the District, some of them with very unfortunate results. At present there are three commissioners at the head of the administration of the District. The inhabitants cannot well grieve over the loss of their short-lived enjoyment of a limited autonomy, for while their rights have again become more limited (necessarily so under the present system) their interests are better cared for. They must bear the same burdens as the rest of the people, have the same taxes to pay and are bound to serve in the militia. But in spite of their full

§ 52. NATIONAL PROPERTY. In the same paragraph equally exclusive authority is given congress " over all places purchased, by the consent of the legislature of the state in which the same shall be, for the erection of forts, magazines, arsenals, dock-yards, and other needful buildings." Real estate within a state may also be acquired by the nation without the consent of the state legislature, but it is only when that consent is given that this provision applies. The inhabitants of such places are legally no longer inhabitants of the state, that is, they do not possess the civil and political rights which would belong to them as citizens of the state. In spite of this provision, the seceded states demanded the evacuation and surrender of the forts and arsenals as their right, on the plea that the "places" had not ceased to be a portion of the territory of the state on account of congress's acquiring exclusive legislative power and jurisdiction over them, and that consequently they must *ipso facto* revert to the states if the latter by virtue of their sovereignty cut loose from the Union. If the premises, that is, state sovereignty and the resulting right of secession, are admitted, then the correctness of the conclusion must be granted, and the Union would have had only a right of reasonable indemnification. But what legal claims could the seceded

---

citizenship political rights are withheld from them solely because they have their domicile at the seat of government. This is an anomaly that has never been justified theoretically, and its necessity — not to say its expediency — has become at least doubtful since the power of the federal government has become so firmly established and so far beyond the power of each separate state. This anomaly, moreover, will always remain a thorn in the flesh of the American disciples of the doctrine of natural political rights. The creation of the District of Columbia is one of those steps which it is scarcely possible to retrace, even if the circumstances, which at one time made them seem wise, have given room to a completely changed state of things.

states, upon these premises, make in regard to that federal property,— the territories,— which had most directly led to the development of the clash of interests between the north and south into an "irrepressible conflict" which had to lead to a rupture? The abstract logic of this method of interpreting constitutional law would have obliged the south to demand the partition of the territorial domain among the several states. This would have been the final practical result of the doctrine, and it puts its absurdity in the most glaring light.

§ 53. THE TERRITORIES. The slavery question, which every year became more and more the central point of the whole inner history of the United States, culminated in the struggle over the territories; that is, in the question what rights the slave-holder had, or ought to have, in them. While the southern states had originally preferred to rely upon a claim of equity, and had triumphantly celebrated the fact that their "peculiar institution" could be unconditionally and forever excluded only from the territorial domain north of 36° 30', the rapid development of the north forced them to constantly increase their claims, until they finally laid down the principle that slavery could not be prohibited in a territory either by congress or by the people of the territory through its legislature, but that, independent of the constitution, the slave-holder could go with his slaves into any territory, and must be protected in his ownership until the territory became a sovereign state and thus acquired the right to determine for itself whether or no slavery should exist within it. The so-called Douglas democrats also denied the power of congress to legislate as to slavery in the territories, but declared that the population of each territory was authorized to permit or prohibit slavery. The republicans, on the contrary, advocated fully and completely the doctrine, at first generally acknowledged, of the exclusive and unlimited legislative authority of congress over the territories. The assertions of the radical southerners and of the Douglas democrats found not the slightest positive support in the constitution. Neither of these two parties asked what the law was according to the constitution, but constructed by general reasoning from pretended "principles" outside of the constitution the "right" which they claimed existed. This was made possible because the only express constitutional provision that could be invoked as bearing on this question certainly gave no sufficiently solid and broad foundation for the correct doctrine. The latter, therefore, had to be to a great extent based upon deductions from other clauses of the constitution, or wholly upon general principles. The constitution says nothing whatever about "territories." And, moreover, the word "territory" is used but once, and that in the following provision: "The congress shall have power to dispose of, and make all needful rules and regulations respecting, the territory or other property belonging to the United States" (art. IV., sec. 3, § 2). "Territory" is thus named in connection with "other property." It was argued from this that the word was used only in reference to land as a salable object, and that the "rules and regulations" related only to the methods of turning it into cash.

Even statesmen and jurists who were by no means "strict constructionists" have recognized that it is at least very doubtful whether there could be deduced from *this* paragraph a general legislative power of congress over the territories, limited only by the constitution. They based the right upon the power of acquiring territory. This power itself was originally doubted; but the opinion of the supreme court that it is implied in the grant of power to declare war and make treaties received general assent. If, however, the right of legislation can be inferred only from the right of acquisition, does it not exist, then, only as to the domain acquired by war or treaty under the constitution? But one of the first laws of congress related to the territorial domain acquired before the existence of the constitution. This law provided that the "ordinance of 1787" as to the territory northwest of the Ohio river, which became inoperative upon the adoption of the constitution, should remain in force.[1] The constitutionality of this law was questioned by no one, although it was admitted that the congress of the confederation had no authority to enact the ordinance, and that its usurpation could be pardoned only on the ground of an imperious political necessity. Moreover, as it had cost a long and difficult struggle to persuade the states to transfer to the Union the unsettled "backwoods" districts they claimed under their colonial patents, the great importance of the question must have been very plain to the authors of the constitution. These facts lead to one of two conclusions, either that the right of legislation seemed to the authors of the constitution a self-evident consequence of ownership, or else that the provision cited does not refer simply to the value of "territory" as part of the national wealth.[2] The preference must be given to the latter assumption. For, in the first place, the right of sale is a direct legal

[1] It has, however, been disputed whether or no the adoption of the constitution affected the validity of the ordinance. Cooley, *Principles*, 169.

[2] Georgia and North Carolina ceded their "backwoods" country only after the adoption of the constitution. It is to them that the final clause of the paragraph quoted refers: "And nothing in this constitution shall be so construed as to prejudice any claims of the United States or of any particular state."

12

consequence of the fact of ownership, and if an express declaration of the smaller power were deemed necessary, the express declaration of the greater could not be regarded as superfluous. It would have been quite possible, however inexpedient, to transfer to the president the administration of the territorial domain regarded simply as property, if the regulation of territorial relations by law was to be renounced. But the general right of legislation for this most important part of the national domain *could* belong only to the national legislature, if it existed at all. That it must exist was never disputed by the most extreme advocates of states'-rights. It was constantly exercised, with their co-operation, in the most comprehensive manner, although they utterly denied its existence in regard to slavery as a question *sui generis*.

In spite of the greatest differences of opinion upon the constitutional basis of the powers in question, legislation as to the territories has thus always had, by common consent, two entirely different sides. On the one side the laws refer to the territorial domain as *ager publicus*, and on the other to the territories as such, *i. e.*, as political structures entirely peculiar to the United States, pointedly called embryo states,—states in chrysalis form. As to the former, we need only emphasize here that thoughts of immediate monetary returns were thrust more and more into the background as the country developed and greater stress was laid upon the encouragement of settlement. Sales at low prices of course constantly continued, but the free grants increased extraordinarily. Among the more important of the latter were rewards to men who had shed their blood for the country, gifts for school purposes and for the promotion of railroad building, and above all things grants of homesteads, conditioned upon cultivation of the land a certain number of years.¹ If congress had limited itself to selling the land cheap and to giving it away, the process of settlement, however, would have gone on very slowly. In order to induce a

¹ The general land office was created April 25, 1812, to administer the national treasure of the public lands. Its head is a commissioner appointed by the president with the consent of the senate. It was originally part of the treasury department, but was afterwards attached to the department of the interior. How great the business extent of this bureau is may be inferred from the fact that it is the head centre of more than a hundred land offices. But it has already touched its high-water mark. In the near future there will be no *ager publicus* anywhere in the United States.

The survey of the public lands is made in accordance with a most comprehensive geometric plan. General meridian lines are first established. Then, between them, and at distances of six miles apart, parallel lines are drawn north and south, and east and west. The squares thus formed are called townships and are numbered continuously in both directions (from north to south Arabic and from east to west Roman numerals). Each township is divided in the same way into thirty-six sections, each one mile square, and every section into sixteen quarters of quarter-sections of forty acres each.

Acquisition by Purchase. The more the knowledge grew, how much the settlement of the "backwoods" was in the interest of the whole people, the more reasonable and moderate were made the prices of the public lands. The more also was attention directed to facilitating the settler's getting an indefeasible title to the land he had begun to cultivate. With this aim in view, very appropriate provisions were devised as to the right of pre-emption. An act of September 4, 1841, made subject to pre-emption all public lands with the exception of (1) the reservations made by treaty, law or proclamation of the president; (2) land within the limits of already incorporated or prospective cities and towns; (3) land already in use for purposes of trade or business; (4) lands on which salt-pits or mines were known to exist. Citizens of the United States of full age, and immigrants who have legally declared their intention of becoming citizens, can acquire the right of pre-emption at the lowest legal price, by beginning to cultivate the land they wish, provided that they do not already own in any state or territory three hundred and twenty acres,

larger number of people of culture to pull down their domestic altars and bear them into the wilderness, before all things they had to be assured that the principles of social and political order had already found a place there, and that the tribunal of law had been erected. In

and have not given up their property in that state or territory in order to take possession of public land. The president determines what public lands not claimed under pre-emption are to be offered at public sale. The necessary proclamations must be published from three to six months before the sale. As a rule the lands are offered for fourteen days, and the upset price is $1.25 per acre. Land offered at public sale and not sold may afterwards be sold privately. The alternate sections reserved in making land grants to railroads are doubled in price. There are special provisions as to mineral lands. Originally only the right of mining, and not the land itself, could be acquired. An act of May 10, 1872, permits the purchase, but restricts the right to citizens and to those immigrants who have made the often-mentioned declaration of intent to become citizens. This act authorizes the miners of each mining district to make rules "governing the location, manner of recording, amount of work necessary to hold possession of a mining claim," etc., under the self-evident restriction that these rules shall not conflict with the laws of the United States or of the state or territory in which the district is located. To receive a "patent" for a piece of mineral land, proof must be furnished that at least $500 has been expended in preparatory work upon the particular piece of ground. This provision assumes, what is true in fact, that the search for minerals in the public lands is entirely free. If within sixty days no counter-claim is made, the claim will be granted upon the payment of $5 per acre. A patent for a mining claim is issued only if the vein or lode has been found on the piece of ground to be patented. The claim cannot extend over one thousand five hundred feet along the vein or lode, and not more than three hundred nor less than twenty-five feet on either side of its centre line, to be measured on the surface. For placer-claims, that is, when the mineral to be excavated is not imbedded in rocks, a patent depends upon analogous provisions; but according to a law of July 9, 1870, no person or association can obtain a placer-claim of more than a hundred and sixty acres. An individual can buy one hundred and sixty acres of coal lands and an association three hundred and twenty acres, at a minimum price of $10 per acre if the land is more

the nature of things, this could happen in this instance only by virtue of federal law. And so the right or duty of congress to "make all needful rules and regulations" to make the territories worth as much as possible in money to the Union implied as its direct and necessary

than fifteen miles from a completed railroad, and at a minimum price of $20 per acre if it is within this limit. If an association of not less than four persons has already spent $5,000 in opening a colliery, it has a right to buy six hundred and forty acres (act of March 3, 1873).

Acquisition by Gift. "Mineral land" is excepted from all grants (resolution of January 30, 1865, and act of June 21, 1866). The land-grants made at various times to soldiers were assignable, and therefore, to a large extent, they were profitable only to speculators. The famous homestead law of May 20, 1862, absolutely forbids any assignment as long as the homestead has not become the sole property of the settler. Under this law citizens of the United States of full age (including women), and immigrants who have declared their intention to become citizens in the legal manner, can enter as homesteads either one hundred and sixty acres of public lands held at $1.25 an acre, or eighty acres of such land held at $2.50 per acre, upon paying a fee of $10 or $5 respectively. An affidavit must be made and filed setting forth that the entry is made for the purpose of actual settlement and cultivation, and neither directly nor indirectly for the benefit of any other person. When the settler has lived five years upon his land and cultivated it, it becomes his free property; but all right to it will be forfeited if he removes to another place or actually abandons the land entered for more than six months. For the benefit of minor children, both of whose parents die before perfecting the homestead title, the homestead may be sold within two years after the death of the surviving parent. Creditors cannot levy on a homestead if their claims are older than the patent. Pursuant to this law there were entered in the general land office from July 1, 1869, to June 30, 1884, about seventy-one million acres. Under the act hereafter mentioned, to encourage the planting of trees, twenty million acres more were entered.

Town and City Sites. By act of March 3, 1863, the president is authorized to reserve town sites at harbors, at the junction of rivers, important portages, or any natural or prospective centre of population. These reservations are divided into building lots and offered at public sale at prices fixed by disinterested persons. If not

result the general power of congress to legislate. Accordingly, congress has, as has been said, always and in fact, from the very beginning, made smooth the way for the pushing stream of settlers to the far west by organizing large sections of the territorial domain by law into territories bearing distinct names and possessing political sys-

sold at public auction they may be sold privately, but not for less than the estimated price. Private persons who have laid out a town upon the public lands or propose to lay one out must, pursuant to an act of July 1, 1864, record and submit an exact survey, covering at most six hundred and forty acres. The lots, which must not exceed four thousand two hundred square feet, are then offered at public auction at a minimum price of $10 each. At the subsequent private sales the secretary of the interior may raise or lower the price, as the development of the place seems to demand; but any change in the minimum price must be made known at least three months in advance. During these three months an actual settler on a lot can buy that and also any other one lot which he has substantially improved at the former minimum price. Pursuant to the act of March 2, 1867, the city authorities of an incorporated city (and in case of non-incorporation, then the judge of the county court) may enter in trust, for the benefit of the occupants of town lots, the whole area at the minimum price. The trust is then executed according to state or territorial legislation. The same law permits the area of the town to be enlarged as the population increases, and fixes two thousand five hundred and sixty acres as the maximum for five thousand inhabitants.

Certain parts of the public domain, distinguished for natural beauty or natural wonders, such as the Yellowstone Park, are reserved by law from sale, gift or other alienation.

W. W. Lester, *Land Laws, Regulations and Decisions of the U. S.*, 2 vols., Phila., 1860-70; H. N. Copp, *Public Land Laws*, Washington, 1875; J. B. Lewis, *Leading Cases on Public Land Laws*, Wash., 1879; D. H. Talbot, *Land Laws of the U. S.*, Sioux City, 1879; G. A. Blanchard and E. P. Weeks, *Leading Cases on Mines, Minerals and Mining Water Rights*, San Francisco, 1877; W. A. Skidmore, *Mining Statutes of the U. S. and Decisions*, San Francisco, 1878; M. B. Carpenter, *Mining Code of the U. S. and Colorado*, 3d ed., Denver, 1880; H. N. Copp, *U. S. Mineral Lands*, Washington, 1881; D. S. Sickles, *U. S. Mining Laws and Decisions*, San Francisco, 1881.

tems of their own under the control of the federal government. They are not limbs, but constituent parts of the Union. Therefore the doctrine that the constitution becomes valid as to the territories only by legislation — although Webster defended it — is utterly inadmissible. The constitution is not only the fundamental law of the united states, but it is the constitution of *the* United States; and this name comprehends within itself the whole domain of the Union. If the territories were not subject to the constitution, congress could pass no laws about them, for it possesses no power outside of the constitution. Webster's principle is true only in this: that a large part of the constitution does not apply to the territories. They have no rights of their own under the constitution, and cannot be granted any such by congress. The inhabitants of the territories, who are citizens of the United States by birth or naturalization, have all the rights guarantied or granted by the constitution or the laws to citizens of the United States as such. But they have not and cannot have the rights which belong to citizens of the states by virtue of the constitutional rights of the states. They can no more have representation in congress or a share in presidential elections than the District of Columbia can. In order to present their wishes, grievances and views directly to congress, the right has been given them by law to elect a "delegate" from each territory to the house of representatives. Delegates, like representatives, can discuss every question, but even if a territory were ten times as populous as one or another state, the right to vote in congress could be given its delegate only by a constitutional amendment. And such an amendment would overthrow a fundamental principle of the constitution.

On the other hand, congress can at any moment abolish the institution of territorial delegates and can subject the general organization of the territories to any change it sees fit. The form of organization has in fact varied. Different plans have been tried, not only as to minor details, but in matters of such an essential character that it is not incorrect to speak of territories of different grades. In the simplest form, the governor and the judges—both appointed by the president with the consent of the senate for territories of every grade—constitute the law-making body, while in territories of the highest grade the legislature is elected by the people and consists of two houses. Some of the territories have had both forms of government, besides undergoing a transition from one to the other. Now, there are only territories of the highest grade. Yet there is a substantial difference among them, because some of them have to submit their laws to the approval of congress, while in the case of others[1] this is not demanded. But even if congress has freely used its power of organizing the territories in each given case according to the peculiar controlling circumstances of the case, yet the same thought lies at the basis of every different form of organization. And this is made necessary by the tenor of the part of the constitution which precedes that which treats of the territories. It must be read and interpreted in connection with the latter. It relates to the admission of new states.[2]

[1] Dakota, Idaho, Montana and Wyoming.

[2] The territorial organizations have become, as stated in the text, more and more alike. The following provisions hold good for all of the territories: The executive power is in the hands of a governor, who is appointed by the president with the consent of the senate for a term of four years. In the same way and for the same time are appointed the secretary, the judges of the supreme court, the district attorney and the marshal. The term of office may also be ended by removal, before the expiration of the four years. The governor is

§ 54. THE ADMISSION OF NEW STATES. "New states may be admitted by the congress into this Union." It is evident that the authors of the constitution, in adopting this provision, had in mind, in the first place, states which were to develop in and out of the then territorial domain of the Union, because the constitution goes on to say: "But no new state shall be formed or erected within the jurisdiction of any other state, nor any state be formed

commander-in-chief of the militia. He possesses the right of pardon in cases of violation of territorial laws, and in cases of violation of federal laws he has the right of postponing the execution of the judgment until the president's decision can be got. He appoints certain officials. He has the same qualified "veto"-power over territorial enactments as the president has over congressional legislation. Other important powers of the governor need not be cited here, because they simply call into life the organs of self-government and themselves expire with the meeting of the first legislature. The secretary discharges the functions of the governor, in case of the latter's absence, resignation or removal, until the governor can again attend to his office or another governor is appointed. The secretary keeps the legislative as well as the executive records. He sends the laws to congress and to the president, and to the latter, besides, the journals of the legislature, the pardons and the official correspondence of the governor. The legislative power — in striking contrast with the corresponding provisions of the federal constitution, although the governor has in this respect only the same powers as the president — is vested in the governor and a legislative assembly. The latter consists of a council and a house of representatives. Members of both houses are elected for two years. The legislature meets each second year. The sessions cannot last more than forty days, and the printing expenses of a session cannot exceed $4,000. A candidate for the legislature must reside in the particular district and must have the franchise. The conditions of the right of suffrage are fixed by the legislature; but it can be granted only to citizens of full age and to such immigrants as have legally declared their intention to become citizens. As the constitution and all federal laws, so far they are not "locally inapplicable," are valid in the territories, the political equality of the colored people is protected in the territories as far as it is in the states under the constitution and federal laws. The authority

by the junction of two or more states, or parts of states, without the consent of the legislatures of the states concerned, as well as of the congress" (art. IV., sec. 3, § 1).[1] It is certain that this is what the fathers had in mind, because in the ordinance of 1787, already mentioned, the formation of "not more than" five new states out of part of this territorial domain and their admission into the Union had been taken into view.

Accordingly, congress, in organizing territories, has always aimed, not to act from the stand-point of colonial administration, but, on the contrary, to ascertain the life-forms adapted to an embryonic state. This explains, too, the different "grades." The more nearly a territory approaches the end of its territorial existence,— its transformation into a state,— that is, the more the number of its

of the legislature extends "to all legitimate objects of legislation," but congress reserves "the primal disposal of the soil." Federal property cannot be taxed at all, and the property of non-residents cannot be taxed higher than that of residents. The legislature cannot grant private franchises and special privileges; that is, corporate rights can be granted only by general laws. Justices of the peace and general officers of the militia are chosen in the manner prescribed by the legislature. Whether and how the township, district and county officers are to be appointed or elected is left to the legislature. Members of the legislature are paid $6 a day, besides mileage. All payments for the support of the territorial government from the national treasury are made only upon vouchers signed by the secretary of the treasury. The supreme court consists of a chief justice and two associate justices. Two judges must be present to decide a case. The territory is divided into three judicial districts. Each of the judges of the supreme court is judge of one of the districts. He must live in his district. Cases are heard in the supreme court only upon appeal. Probate courts pass upon matters of inheritance. Justices of the peace have no jurisdiction in litigation over real estate. All other regulations as to the different courts are left to the legislature.

[1] Congress nevertheless held itself authorized, after the secession of Virginia, to empower the loyal part of the state to organize itself as an independent state, under the name of West Virginia.

people, the density of its population,[1] and its wealth,[2] correspond to the claims which a state must meet, the greater is the freedom of action granted it. The times and methods of admitting new states have varied greatly. Congress is under no constitutional obligation either in the one or the other respect, since it *may*, but never *must*, admit new states. As to the time of admission, the general rule has been that a territory must have as many inhabitants as are necessary to elect a member of the house of representatives, but this rule has not been always strictly followed.[3] As to the manner of admission, the general rule has been that congress, by an "enabling act," has permitted the people of a territory to frame and adopt a state constitution in a constitutional convention. It is true that several territories went to work without this authorization of congress, and were nevertheless admitted by it. Other irregularities, too, at least extra-legal if not illegal, have occurred, and, although objected to, have not been regarded as sufficient reason for refusing admission.[4] A

[1] The very large territories have been repeatedly divided by congress, partly in order not to let the new states be too unequal in size, and partly in order not to hamper the more densely settled portions with those slower of development. The boundaries of a state thus by no means always coincide with the original limits of the territory out of which it is formed. Indeed, parts of different territories may, under certain circumstances, be made into one state.

[2] The expenses of territorial government are borne by the Union, while the state governments are, of course, supported by their respective peoples.

[3] Not only have states been admitted before the population had reached the required number, but territories with a population far in excess of this number have been refused admission. The latter was the case with Utah and New Mexico. Mormonism with its polygamy kept out Utah, and the predominance of Spaniards and Indians in the population kept out New Mexico.

[4] All the instances in point will be found in Jameson, *The Constitutional Convention.*

popular vote on the work of the convention has not been deemed absolutely necessary. The new constitution, however, is always subject to the approval of congress, which has virtually already, by the enabling act, ordered the admission of the state in case the conditions set forth in that act are fulfilled. The question of the limits of the right to impose conditions has repeatedly given rise to violent parliamentary contests. The equality of the states is a fundamental principle of the constitution. Hence it has been argued that conditions which limited the right of self-government, in comparison with the position in constitutional law of the other states, were inadmissible, and that they could not be enforced; because, as soon as the admission has taken place, the state has become complete master of its freedom of action. Congress, however, in a considerable number of instances, has imposed such conditions, and has also demanded the assurance that the state constitution should never be changed in this or that respect.[1] But, as congress never *must* admit a state, the imposition of conditions of any sort cannot be hindered, if they be not directly unconstitutional. And if a state promises not to make use of a certain right guarantied it by the constitution, this is not unconstitutional; it is simply not obligatory, from the stand-point of constitutional law. The imposition and adoption of such conditions are to be regarded as a political pact, to the maintenance of which the state is bound by truth and faith, but not by constitutional law. It must be admitted that such compacts do not respond

[1] This latter occurred particularly in regard to the seceded states before they were again allowed representation in congress. The argument against the constitutional authority of congress applies to these cases in the same degree as to new states about to be admitted. For a collection of the facts in question, see Cooley, *Principles*, 174–177.

to the spirit of the constitution. Congress would hardly have required them, and, if it had done so, would hardly have commanded public approval, if the slavery question, and later on the civil war and the abolition of slavery, had not brought about a condition of affairs in which legal opinions were, and had to be, pressed into the background by political and moral considerations. Conditions of another kind, as to boundaries, etc., of course cannot be objected to as in any way opposed to the constitutional law. If congress has not provided that the state shall be admitted upon the fulfillment of the conditions imposed by it, this happens as a matter of law by a proclamation of the president. According to the theory of American politicians and publicists, the transformation of the territory into a state has already taken place before its admission; for, they allege, a state must exist in order to have a state admitted. They have never, however, answered, to my knowledge, the question as to what relation prevails if congress, after the passage of an enabling act, and the consequent formation and adoption of a constitution by a constitutional convention, should nevertheless, for some reason, exercise its undoubted right to refuse admission to the state. In my opinion, the failure to regard the admission of a state as the completion of its transformation from a territory involves some serious results. The territorial domain of the United States can be transformed, as a matter of constitutional law, only into states of the Union, and a state can therefore come into existence only when it is one of the states of the United States; that is, a co-ordinate and recognized constituent member of the Union. The change of a territory into a state has no legal effect upon the *status* of the public lands. Except so far as they are granted expressly to the state by congress for definite purposes (schools), they do not pass into its possession, but remain property of the Union, and are subject to the same legal provisions as before.

The admitted states have all been formed out of parts of the states of the original Union or from the territorial domains of the Union. Texas is the only exception. It was an independent republic. Its incorporation into the Union met with vigorous opposition, on not only political but constitutional grounds. The way in which this was done — by a "joint resolution" of both houses of congress after a treaty of annexation had failed to receive the necessary majority in the senate — was a good cause for serious objection. Nevertheless the assertion that an independent nation cannot be directly transformed into a state of the Union seems unfounded, for the power to admit new states is granted wholly without conditions.

THE POWERS OF THE PRESIDENT.

§ 55. POWERS AND DUTIES OF THE PRESIDENT. It has been said that the president of the United States is mightier than the rulers of modern England. This is undoubtedly true.[1] To correctly estimate the powers of the president, one fact must be taken into consideration, which is often wholly overlooked or insufficiently appreciated. He has of course certain very important powers which he exercises in full independence of the other factors of government. But this full independence in the most essential matters is restricted to taking the initiative. His acts require the sanction of the senate in order

---

[1] Of those powers of the president already discussed in another connection — the right to require written opinions from the heads of departments, the so-called veto, his powers as to convening and adjourning congress and his right and duty to report to congress upon the state of the Union and to make recommendations — no further mention will be made here.

to be perfected. In another set of his powers he is likewise independent of congress to this extent, that it cannot of itself either diminish or increase them. But the opportunity for the exercise of these powers is given the president only by law and the way in which he shall exercise them is defined by law. To a great extent congress can determine how widely or how narrowly it will draw the limits of his independence. It can grant him a fullness of power that under certain circumstances is little inferior to that of a Roman dictator. It can also bring him so sharply under its own control and bind his hands so closely, that his constitutional position as a co-ordinate factor of the government is seriously endangered and the interests of the country are gravely injured by the weakness of the executive power. If congress wishes to abuse its powers, it can easily bring down the president — so far as a number of his most important powers of an eminently political character are concerned — to the level of the third duty imposed upon him by the constitution,— that of acting merely as the executive organ of the legislative will of congress.[1]

[1] It has been boldly asserted that parliamentary government as it is known in Europe was entirely excluded in the United States by the constitutional organization of the federal government. On the contrary the government vests directly in congress to such an extent that in a book just published, which deals incisively with this question, the author says: "I know not how better to describe our government in a single phrase than by calling it a government by the chairmen of the standing committees of congress." (W. Wilson, *Congressional Government: a Study in American Politics*, Boston, 1885.) This exaggerates, as all statements must exaggerate which seek in one pointed phrase to define great and complicated relations. Not only, however, is there much truth in the assertion, but this truth is so clear, and its pre-eminent significance is so plain, that for some years public attention has been more and more strongly drawn to it. The framers of the constitution did not expect this develop-

§ 56. MILITARY POWER. The president is commander-in-chief of the army and navy, and also of the militia, when the latter is called into the actual service of the United States (art. II., sec. 2, § 1). This is all the constitution has to say as to the military power of the president. This clause in its blunt simplicity is the best illustration of the maxim of American constitutional law already mentioned, that the constitution enumerates but does not define the powers of the federal government. Congress can appoint no other commander-in-chief, and can withdraw from the president not the slightest part of the powers appertaining to the commander-in-chief. This is without doubt, as the constitution confers that office upon him with a categorical "shall be." But what are the powers appertaining to the office *proprio jure?* The constitution cannot possibly mean that the expression "commander-in-chief" should first be given a concrete meaning by legislation, for the thought underlying

ment. It undoubtedly runs directly counter to their intentions. They created a separate executive because their experience led them to reject congressional government on principle. They had recognized the fact that the many-headed legislative power not only could not govern well, but in the long run could not govern at all; and so far as the facts correspond with Wilson's assertion, they have demonstrated this truth anew. He calls his study "*Congressional Government;*" yet he does not say that congress governs, but that its standing committees or rather their chairmen do; and that, too, not in the sense that they are together actually the government, but that each of them is a particular and isolated part of the government. So far as his assertion is well founded, this "congressional government" is therefore in a great measure a systematic laxity of government, because the organic coherence, the uniform guiding thought and will, and the legal binding of the parts into a comprehensive whole are wanting. Yet, however, matters of constitutional law and of fact may be considered from a political stand-point, this is certain, that in law and in fact America is partly in advance of Europe and partly behind her in parliamentary government.

this provision is manifestly that of ensuring the greatest energy in the application of the military strength of the country by entrusting its direction to one hand. But, as we have seen, all military legislation is entrusted to congress, and the president is simply the commander-in-chief and not at all the lord of peace and war. It is thus very difficult, if not impossible, to draw the line of demarcation with absolute certainty between the authority of congress and that of the president. The general principles of demarcation, however, can be established without difficulty, and their practical application has hitherto led to relatively very few important conflicts. Congress must regulate by law whatever is of general importance and bears a permanent character, but considerations of expediency may demand that even within this, its own domain, it should leave the president free to act at his own discretion, especially in the more technical matters. Of course it is not forbidden to do this. On the other hand, the president alone must determine how the military force shall be employed, and he must make all provisions, temporary and not general in their nature, because, from the nature of things, these must be adapted to special circumstances. Congress — to make this relation clear by some illustrations — provides where forts shall be built and what kind of forts they shall be, how many and what kind of arms are to be provided, and how the men are to be distributed among the different branches of the service; but as to what the strength and composition of the garrisons are to be, how the arms and ammunition are to be distributed, how and where the army and navy are to be stationed and moved,— as to all this, congress can give the president no directions whatever. In war the entire technical direction of affairs is thus incumbent upon the president. Congress has only to decide whether there shall be war and what means it will grant the president with which to conduct the war; but how the war declared by congress shall be conducted by the means granted by it is the exclusive affair of the president. Congress may criticise, may express wishes, may pass resolutions, but it can prescribe absolutely nothing to the president, even though his acts and omissions be fraught with political consequences of the most pre-eminent importance, as, for example, the declaration of a blockade may be under certain circumstances. This principle was extended so far during the civil war that it was acknowledged to be his right to determine whether and how far the rebels were to be regarded as a war-making power; that is, how far the war should be conducted pursuant to the provisions of the law of nations.[1] Accordingly, this war-power of the president is not limited to matters involved directly in the conduct of war, but extends beyond purely military actions into the domain of the exceptional relations which may result from war. If, for instance, in a war with a foreign power a territory has been conquered, the president can put a military governor over it, and this military government will end only upon the conclusion of peace, and in case of a cession of the territory only upon legislation in the matter by congress. This is also true of rebellious states vanquished in civil war. In both cases the president may establish a provisional civil government, with power to organize courts, so that a well-ordered administration of justice is rendered possible. In the case of a conquered rebel state, the quickest practicable supplanting of military government by a provisional civil government is to be regarded as a duty, in so far as the principle applies that the president is not authorized to use military power

[1] *The Prize Cases*, Black, II., 635.

where the laws can be enforced without such aid. The president has the greatest liberty in the choice of means not only to attain the most immediate purpose of war,— the subjugation of the enemy,— but also to meet the further task implied in this, to deprive the enemy of the power of levying war again.[1] But in all this he must steadily keep in mind that the ultimate purpose is the restoration of the normal, the constitutional condition of peace. This maxim leads to the further principle of constitutional law, that the immense power which the president has as commander-in-chief in time of war must be exerted to its full extent only where the authority of the federal government cannot be exerted by peaceful methods; that is, where the actual condition of war exists. It is only when this is the case, and the ordinary courts in consequence of the war cannot exercise their functions, that military courts can sit. Where these premises do not exist, no one, unless he belongs to the army, can be punished by the military authorities.[2] Spies are an exception. As this exception must be acknowledged to be a necessity, and as it is not always certain whether the premises already mentioned exist or not, prominent American publicists take the view that it is not possible to bring all cases under a fixed rule, but that the special circumstances of each must be taken into account, even in a decision upon grounds of constitutional law.[3] It is unquestionable that the constitution recognizes the possibility of its being necessary in time of war,

[1] Lincoln justified his emancipation proclamation, as is well known, upon the ground that the freeing of the slaves was a means of subjugating the rebels.

[2] *Ex parte Milligan,* Wallace, IV., 127.

[3] The difficult chapter of the so-called " war-powers " of the different factors of government has been treated by W. Whiting in a strong volume entitled *War Powers under the Constitution of the*

even where the efficiency of legal authority is entirely unimpeded, to suspend the operation of law. It expressly grants a "war-power" by which every inhabitant of the Union — whether or no the district in which he resides is within the limits of the theatre of war or not — may be deprived for the whole duration of the war of one of the most substantial safeguards of the law. It is, however, another question whether the president as commander-in-chief can bring about this condition of affairs. This question may now be regarded as decided against him.

The constitution provides that "the privilege of the writ of *habeas corpus* shall not be suspended unless when, in cases of rebellion or invasion, the public safety may require it" (art. I., sec. 9, § 2). This states only in what cases the writ may be suspended, but not who is to order the suspension. At the beginning of the civil war, Attorney-general Bates claimed for the president the right to refuse obedience to a writ of *habeas corpus*.[1] The final result of the conflicts between the president and the courts, and the earnest discussions caused by them, was, however, a decided victory for the doctrine that the suspension is a legislative act, and can therefore be ordered only by congress or by the president when and only when he has been authorized to do so by congress.[2] An

United States. The conclusions which the author reaches have, however, been much questioned.

Indisputably the doctrine last mentioned in the text must not only be assented to, but must be given great scope, in order to hold constitutional the sentence by a military commission of Mrs. Surratt, an accessory of Booth in the assassination of Lincoln. The District of Columbia was at the time, however, under military law.

[1] *Op. of the Attorneys-General*, X., 74.
[2] See Horace Binney, *The Privilege of the Writ of Habeas Corpus*, and, also, *Martin vs. Mott*, Wheaton, XII., 19. A vote of the house

act of March 3, 1863, authorized the president during the continuance of the rebellion to suspend the privilege in the entire domain of the Union or any part thereof, if he deemed it necessary. In a proclamation of September 15, 1863, Lincoln made use of this permission. This law, declared to be constitutional by the federal supreme court, shows that this war-power may be given the widest scope, but the same decision holds that the provision must be strictly construed, in accordance with its verbal tenor.[1] Not only in case of a war with a foreign power must the writ be suspended only in the event of an invasion, but the suspension simply denies to a prisoner the right to sue out the writ; it does not authorize arrest without legal cause.[2]

It is beyond doubt that the president has the power of putting himself personally at the head of the army in war and of taking its immediate direction into his own hands, but the view has always prevailed that this would not correspond with the intent of the constitution.[3]

of representatives, February 19, 1807, can, however, be interpreted as a direct recognition of the principle that there may be circumstances under which the privilege of *habeas corpus*, even without a legislative act, must give way to the public safety.

[1] *Ex parte Milligan*, Wallace, IV., 133.
[2] *Ex parte Milligan*, Wallace, IV., 133.
[3] Jefferson Davis, the president of the Confederate States, also tried the *rôle* of a general.

Some of the powers granted by law to the president as commander-in-chief deserve special mention. His right of promotion is very limited. In general the principle prevails that promotion from rank to rank shall depend upon the time of service. In war, however, the president may, with the consent of the senate, as a reward for distinguished services against the enemy, grant a higher rank " by brevet." The legal position of an officer in the service will not be changed of itself by brevet-promotion, but the president may assign the brevet-officer to duty according to the rank of which he has only the title. In time of peace, there can be no dismissal from the

FOREIGN RELATIONS.

§ 57. INTERCOURSE WITH FOREIGN POWERS. In American works on constitutional law the statement is frequently found that the foreign relations of the Union are

service, except upon the judgment of a court-martial or in mitigation of a judgment. If an officer is absent without furlough for more than three months, the president can cashier him for desertion. If he has served forty years, he is entitled to be retired from active service. After thirty years' service, an officer may petition to be retired; it is then optional with the president whether or no to grant the petition. If an officer is sixty years of age, or has served for forty-five years, the president may retire him. The secretary of war, when directed by the president, convokes from time to time an army retiring board, formed of officers and military surgeons, in order to examine and determine whether and how officers have become disqualified for service. The decision of the retiring board must be approved by the president. Courts-martial are of two classes: the "general" and the regimental or garrison courts-martial. The former, in times of peace, can be organized only by direction of the general-in-chief commanding the entire army or by a general in command of a separate army or "of a particular department;" in time of war, they may be convened also by division and brigade commanders. They should when possible consist of thirteen officers and must consist of at least five. Their judgments are subject to the confirmation of the president in the following cases: When the commanders named are accusers and the accused is an officer under their command (in this case the president appoints the members of the court-martial); when in time of peace the sentence is dismissal from the service; when the sentenced person is a general; when the sentence is death, except in war in cases of a spy, of mutiny, of desertion, of murder, of "guerilla-marauders," and also of other high crimes. A death sentence, moreover, requires a two-thirds majority of the court-martial. Officers cannot be tried before the lower military tribunals; the decisions of these latter can extend only to the deprival of a month's wages, and imprisonment for a month, with or without "hard labor." There is a bureau of military justice, composed of a judge-advocate-general, an assistant judge-advocate-general, and eight judge-advocates. Justice is administered in the navy in substantially the same way. R. A. Ives, *Military Law of the United States*, N. Y., 1879.

the exclusive domain of the president, or in a manner, of the president and the senate. This is manifestly incorrect. Congress has, as we have already seen, a number of the most important powers in relation to international affairs.[1] Unlimited, that statement is true only in regard to the *intercourse* of the Union with foreign powers. This is accomplished only through the president, but he must have the consent of the senate as to the persons by whom he is to be served in this respect. He " shall receive embassadors and other public ministers " (art II., sec. 3), and he is to appoint, with the consent of the senate, " embassadors, other public ministers and consuls " (art. II., sec. 2, § 2).[2] He is not the sole bearer of the

[1] On April 4, 1864, the house unanimously adopted a resolution, which declared that the United States were not indifferent spectators of the occurrences in Mexico and could not recognize a monarchical government erected in America under the auspices of a European power upon the ruins of a republic. (*Congressional Globe*, 1st Session, 38th Congress, p. 1408.) The secretary of state, W. H. Seward, at once instructed Dayton, the ambassador at Paris, to inform the French government that foreign affairs did not fall within the jurisdiction of congress. The house of representatives in turn, on December 19, 1864, declared its position in the following resolution: " Resolved, That congress has a constitutional right to an authoritative voice in declaring and prescribing the foreign policy of the United States, as well in the recognition of new powers as in other matters; and it is the constitutional duty of the executive department to respect that policy not less in diplomatic negotiations than in the use of the national force when authorized by law; and the propriety of any declaration of foreign policy by congress is sufficiently proved by the vote which pronounces it; and such proposition while pending and undetermined " (the resolution of April 4 was a " joint " one and the senate had not yet passed upon it) " is not a fit topic of diplomatic explanation with any foreign power." The first part of this resolution was adopted by a vote of one hundred and eighteen to eight, and the second — beginning " and the propriety "— by sixty-eight to fifty-eight. (*Congressional Globe*, 2d Session, 38th Congress, 65-67.)

[2] There has been much controversy over the question as to whether

power of the state in relation to foreign countries, but
he alone represents it, and that, too, not only where
one nation confronts another, but also where the rights
and interests of individuals are involved,— so far as they
do not come within the jurisdiction of the courts. This
exclusive right of the president to represent the state-
power in all international relations must not, however,
be considered as only a formal right. He is also a co-
bearer of the state-power, and the exclusive representative
right involves his having the exclusive right of initiative
with the exception of the powers granted congress in art.
I., sec. 8, §§ 10, 11.[1] Congress is, indeed, free to express
its views on everything affecting relations with foreign
powers, not only by criticism of the president's policy on
the part of individual members, but also by formal resolutions and positive propositions. But although such
action always has considerable actual weight and will
often be the decisive factor in the conclusions of the
president, it nevertheless cannot legally bind him in any
way whatever. At most, there may be a doubt as to
whether the constitutional provision which requires the
concurrence of the senate to conclude a treaty is to be so
understood that the senate has a certain, so to speak, direct participation in the right of initiative so far as treaties
are concerned.

§ 58. THE TREATY POWER. The constitution says that
the president "shall have power, by and with the ad-

and how far the president is to determine at what foreign courts the
United States shall have representatives, and of what kind these
representatives shall be. The actual state of things is, that the president without any special legal authorization nominates ministers
whom the senate either confirms or does not confirm. Fnally, however, the decision rests with congress, for congress cannot be compelled to appropriate the money needed for the ministers appointed.

[1] The powers "to declare war, grant letters of marque and reprisal,
and make rules concerning captures on land and water," etc.

vice and consent of the senate, to make treaties, provided two-thirds of the senators present concur" (art. II., sec. 2, § 2). The words "by and with the advice and consent of the senate" appear also in the provision as to the senate's confirmation of nominees to office. And although debates often take place over the nominations sent in by the president, yet the action of the senate is limited to the exercise of the right of saying yea or nay. The provision was never interpreted to mean that the senate was empowered as such, and officially, to advise the president to nominate a certain other person for the particular office. The question is, therefore, whether in the clause concerning the making of treaties the same words are to be interpreted in the same manner, that is, that the senate is also authorized only to say yea or nay when a treaty is placed before it for ratification by the president. The actual practice has always been for the presidents to call for the "advice" of the senate only when they sought its "consent," that is, when they presented to it the treaties perfected up to the point of its assent. And this was never held to be unconstitutional. But it has also happened that a president before negotiating a treaty has asked the senate for advice; and his right to do so has never been disputed.[1] And it has likewise happened that the senate has said neither simply yea nor simply nay, but has amended the treaty laid before it; and this has not been regarded as unconstitutional.[2] I cannot therefore see why the senate should not be authorized to request the president to open negotiations for the purpose of concluding a treaty. But the president would unquestionably not be bound to obey the

[1] Washington did this repeatedly, and Polk did it in 1846 as to the treaty with England relative to Oregon.

[2] Thus, for example, the Gadsden treaty of December 30, 1853. See my *Constitutional History*, V., pp. 6–9.

request, and the expression of such a wish is undoubtedly also within the power of the house of representatives. A constitutional law claim of the senate to a share in the right of initiative, however indirect, cannot bear discussion, except in so far as the right of amendment is to be understood in that sense.

As to the extent of the treaty-power, the constitution says nothing, but it evidently cannot be unlimited. The power exists only *under* the constitution, and every treaty-stipulation inconsistent with a provision of the constitution is therefore inadmissible and according to constitutional law *ipso facto* null and void. Simple and self-evident as this principle is in theory, yet it may be very difficult under certain circumstances to decide whether or not it has been transgressed in fact. Indeed, the chief difficulty arises from the question of the relation the treaty-power of the president with the concurrence-power of the senate bears to the legislative power of congress. This question is answered by saying that these powers must be co-ordinate, for treaties like laws are " sovereign acts," which differ from laws only in form and in the organs by which the sovereign will expresses itself. It follows from this principle that a law can be repealed by a treaty [1] as well as a treaty by a law.[2] If a treaty and a law are in opposition, their respective dates must decide whether the one or the other is to be regarded as repealed.[3] Neither the principle nor the correctness of these conclusions from

[1] *Foster vs. Neilson*, Peters, II., 253.
[2] *The Cherokee Tobacco*, Wallace, XI., 616.
[3] *Foster vs. Neilson*, Peters, II., 253, 314; *Doe vs. Braden*, Howard, XVI., 635. " The courts of the United States cannot hold a law unconstitutional upon the ground that it violates treaty obligations. Such a question is an international one, to be settled by the foreign nations interested therein and the political department of the government." *Gray vs. Clinton Bridge*, 7 American Law Register (N. S.), 151; Hammond, I., 22, § 54.

it can well be disputed, and they are at any rate valid constitutional law. But in spite of this it must be admitted that the doctrine has its doubtful side, both in theory and practice. It must be called at least an anomaly, that by the *ex parte* action of the president and two-thirds of the senators present (who may be only a minority of the whole senate), a law can be repealed, the passage of which required the concurrence of the house of representatives with the senate and president or a two-thirds majority of each house of congress. The repeal of a treaty by the enactment of a law may, moreover, lead the more easily to serious consequences, because the incompatibility of the law and of the treaty may not be so clearly manifest that the foreign power concerned will immediately take notice of the law. It is in nowise inconceivable that congress itself might know nothing of what it had done, so that only after a long time would the fact be established by judicial decision, that in this indirect manner a treaty was overthrown, the repeal of which had not been contemplated by either of the two contracting parties.

On still another side this question of the direct relation between the treaty-power and the legislative-power makes it difficult to fix the limits of the treaty-power. It is certain that no authority granted by the constitution to any of the factors of government can be withdrawn from it by treaty. For that would be a change of the constitution and, as such, unconstitutional. But congress may be bound by a treaty not to exercise in a certain way a power belonging to it, although it might exercise it in that way if not bound by the treaty. The freedom of action of the house of representatives can thus easily be restricted by a treaty to such a degree that the restriction must be admitted to be a violation of the constitution, even if not strictly of its letter, yet still of its spirit. Thus, for instance, the framers of the constitution certainly did not wish that duties should be fixed in a way repugnant to the views of the house of representatives, and yet this might be brought about at any moment by a commercial treaty. Of course it must not be inferred that in general there should be no commercial treaties. But Daniel Webster was certainly right in advising his countrymen to consider carefully before beginning to handle questions of duties in connection with treaties.[1] The considerations which led him to give this advice are of even more importance now. The president and senate in concluding commercial treaties, and indeed treaties of all kinds, must keep steadily in mind the house of representatives, not only in order not to excite its sensitiveness and jealousy and to avoid any con-

---

[1] See his letter of November 25, 1842, to Everett, in Curtis, *Life of D. Webster*, II., 174. The *Nation* of January 29, 1885, says: "There have been treaties negotiated by President Arthur and now before the senate, that make, or will make if ratified, a new departure in our diplomacy. A series of commercial treaties, that tie the hands of the government in the future levy of duties on merchandise from all or a large part of the states and colonies on the south of us, must be of tremendous significance. The consequences of such treaties for good or for evil the country is just beginning to appreciate, and does not yet fully comprehend. Fortunately, President Arthur has inserted in the Spanish treaty, and presumably in all the commercial treaties that are on the way, a stipulation that they shall not be exchanged and proclaimed as binding till not only the senate, but the law-making power, has ratified them." As to the important results of this proviso it says farther on, in the same article: "If ratified by the senate, those treaties must then by the president be submitted to congress as a legislative body, and President Cleveland [a president, thus, who had nothing to do with the negotiation and conclusion of the treaties] may be called on to approve or veto the doings of congress thereon. Therefore, the responsibility of ratifying, exchanging and proclaiming the Spanish treaty may, and probably will, rest in the end on President Cleveland. He will probably be called on to deal with the whole subject *de novo*."

flict with it, but also in order not to act in opposition to the spirit of the constitution. It need but be suggested that the treaty-power embraces also treaties of peace to make it clear at the first glance that president and senate may remain fully within the letter of their constitutional authority and yet be in conflict with the fundamental ideas of the constitution. Nobody will assert that no treaty of peace should be concluded which did not in all its parts receive the approval of the house of representatives. But since the constitution gives congress the right to declare war, a treaty of peace, which a considerable majority of the house of representatives condemns *in toto* and with great emphasis, would seem to be a stretching of the authority of president and senate, according to the spirit of the constitution, although in a concrete case they may not only be politically fully justified but may also merit hearty thanks.

This leads to the last great question, to wit: Has the house of representatives the right to annul a treaty made in accordance with the constitution by the president by and with the advice and consent of the senate, by refusing its co-operation when this is necessary to carry out the stipulations of the treaty?

We already know the constitutional provision which declares that treaties, like the constitution itself and the federal laws, are "the supreme law of the land." As far as a treaty requires no legislation in order to become operative, federal and state judges are bound in making their decisions to regard it as valid from the very moment of its conclusion. If, however, the stipulations are of the nature of a contract, binding the powers concerned to perform certain acts, then the contract must be fulfilled by the action of the legislature (or executive) before the special provisions of the treaty become binding upon the courts.[1] But there can be no legislation without the co-operation of the house of representatives. The other factors of government cannot enforce this co-operation. The house, therefore, is always able in such a case to annul a treaty in fact, although it has no part in the power of making a treaty. Whether it has the right to do so has repeatedly given rise to very incisive and exciting debates. These debates have not led, however, to any certain decision of the question. The house has not withheld its co-operation; but it has also not dropped its claim of the right to act entirely in accordance with its own judgment, in cases when the fulfillment of the treaty requires it to make an appropriation or do anything else, as to which it may incontestably decide under all other circumstances with full freedom.

§ 59. THE APPOINTING POWER. Since the constitution, as has already been mentioned, imposes upon the president the duty of taking care that the laws be faithfully executed, it grants him, at the same time, the greatest influence in the selection of the persons by whom these laws are to be executed; that is, the federal officers. The right is unquestionably a necessary consequence of the duty, but only within certain limits. In no state, and least of all in a republic which is pre-eminently a state founded on law and governed "not by persons but by laws," can there be a reasonable ground for every inferior officer's being dependent for his office, that is, for his bread, immediately and absolutely upon the head of the state. On the other hand there are weighty reasons why in a republic the head of the state, even in the selection of those officers, who in a greater or less degree must be persons having his personal confidence, should not be free from all control. The provisions of the con-

---

[1] *Foster vs. Neilson*, Peters, II., 253.

stitution as to the appointment of officials are drawn from both points of view. Besides diplomatic representatives and consuls, only the members of the federal supreme court are explicitly designated as officials to be appointed by the president with the consent of the senate. For the rest, the general phrase is used of "all other officers of the United States whose appointments are not herein otherwise provided for and which shall be established by law." This provision is, however, limited by the clause already mentioned, that "congress may by law vest the appointment of such inferior officers as they think proper in the president alone, in the courts of law or in the heads of departments." It is difficult to understand how the question as to whether the heads of the departments themselves should be regarded as "inferior officers," within the meaning of this clause, could have been seriously mooted. For the rest, it is manifestly entirely within the discretion of congress as to how narrowly or how broadly it will fix the limits of this idea. If it regards it as necessary or expedient it can, consequently,— save as to the diplomatic corps and the consuls,— reduce the power of the president over appointments to a minimum, and could unquestionably do so in such a manner as not to increase the power of the heads of departments unduly. The legal regulation of the question is not confined to enumerating the offices and granting the power of appointment to the president, the courts of law or the heads of departments. This power, taken in connection with the duty of establishing the offices by law, is broad enough to embrace the right to establish all provisions deemed expedient as to the qualifications required in appointees, the time during which and the conditions under which their incumbency in office is to be ensured, the grounds of claims to promotions, etc. In a word, the so-called "civil-service reform," by which the federal offices are to be divested of the character of "spoils," with which party services are paid, is in no kind of opposition to any part of the constitutional law. The framers of the constitution cannot justly be held responsible for the grave abuses in the civil service since the presidency of Andrew Jackson. The constitution renders it possible to satisfy fully in every respect all the requirements of a modern civilized state as to the tenure of office.[1] Nor can they be reproached with having made

[1] A good beginning has been made herein by the law of January 16, 1883, the so-called Pendleton bill. The most important provisions of this very significant law are the following: The president is authorized to form a civil-service commission of five persons, of whom only three at most shall belong to the same political party; two must be federal officers of different departments, residing in Washington, and three occupy no other federal office. The task of the commission is to assist the president in formulating the regulations necessary for the execution of this law, on the basis of the following principles: The federal offices which have already been or will be classified for this purpose are to be filled by competitive examinations. Preference is to be given those applicants who have passed the best examinations. The offices in the departments at Washington are to be distributed as far as practicable in proportion to the population among the states and territories and the District of Columbia. A period of probation must precede permanent employment. The commission may order non-competitive examinations in such cases as it sees fit. It must regulate and control the examinations. It must annually report on everything covered by this law to the president for the use of congress and may use the report to make any further suggestions. The commission is authorized to appoint an examiner-in-chief, whose duty it is *inter alia* to see that the examining boards act alike. The commission appoints the examining boards, consisting of at least three federal officials in the particular state or territory; the heads of the departments to which these officials belong must be consulted in relation to their appointment; the examinations are to be held at least twice a year. The heads of departments must classify inferior officials in conformity with the intent of this law; officials whose appointment must be confirmed by

the president too dependent upon the senate as to the offices which he must fill with its consent. The nomination, that is, the selection of persons to be nominated, is left wholly to him. The co-operation of the senate comes into play only upon the nomination and is limited to that. If it refuse to confirm, the president again has full and free choice among all citizens, and it has happened that he has repeated his first nomination. And if the senate confirms he is still not yet irrevocably bound. The constitution provides in another paragraph that he shall commission all the federal officials (art. II., sec. 3). As long as he has not done this the appointment is not perfected, and he can send a new nomination to the senate. But the appointee has a legal claim to the office from the moment the commission is signed, even if it has not yet been delivered to him.[1] No difficulties arise from the fact that the senate does not remain in permanent session. Vacancies which happen during the senate's recess are filled by the president provisionally.[2] The commis-

---

the senate shall be classified and subjected to examination only upon the request of the senate. Four articles forbid members of congress and all federal officials from asking in any way whatever for money contributions for any political purposes whatever from federal officials and employees, and also from receiving such taxes, and especially from inducing by threats or promises such contributions for political purposes. The prohibition extends to all in all places where federal officials or employees have to perform their official duties. Violations of these provisions are to be punished by fines of as much as $5,000 or by imprisonment for three years or less, or by both fine and imprisonment. See J. M. Comstock, *Civil Service in the United States*, 1885.

[1] *Marbury vs. Madison*, Cranch, I., 156.

[2] The unanimous opinions of several attorney-generals claim for the president the right of filling provisionally any vacancies which may occur during the session. They construe the word "happen" as synonymous with "exist." Certain weighty reasons of expediency

sions he issues in such cases expire at the end of the next session of the senate (art. II., sec. 2, § 3).¹

§ 60. THE POWER OF PARDON. The president's power of pardon does not extend nearly as far as that of the rulers in monarchical states, but the interpretation of the constitutional provision concerned by various decisions of the United States supreme court has made this power so extensive that several of the principles set forth in these decisions have been most energetically attacked by leading American publicists. The president is authorized "to grant reprieves and pardons for offenses against the United States, except in cases of impeachment" (art. II., sec. 2, § 1). The president thus has not simply a right of pardon. He can pardon only for offenses against the United States, but as to these the power is entirely unlimited, for, according to the supreme court, the word "pardons" embraces everything which at the time of the adoption of the constitution was understood thereby in English law.² He can remit every punishment, from a money-penalty imposed for a violation of the internal-revenue or customs laws, up to and even including the death penalty. In cases of forfeiture, as far as others have acquired a legal right to the goods forfeited, the pardon naturally remains inoperative. And it does not effect a reinstatement in a forfeited office. For the rest, however, a full pardon annuls every legal consequence of a sentence. Indeed the pardon need not be a complete one. It may be coupled with a condition; and this, as a rule, tends to

---

certainly favor this interpretation, but the wording does not in my opinion justify it.

¹ The important question of removal from office has already been treated. It may be mentioned here that the president cannot refuse the resignation of an official.

² *Ex parte Wells*, Howard, XVIII., 309.

a mitigation of punishment.¹ Nevertheless, it is not necessary to put the mitigation in the form of a condition. It may be declared directly as a remission of part of the sentence. On the other hand, a penalty of an entirely different kind from the one imposed cannot be inflicted.² The most important of all the conclusions from the interpretation given the word "pardons" is unquestionably that a pardon may be granted before sentence has been passed, yea, even before any legal procedure whatever has been begun against the accused.³ From this comes the right to issue a general amnesty. The president is subject to no legal control in the exercise of these far-reaching powers. Any legislative encroachment by congress upon the pardoning power is excluded. The only remedy against a coarse abuse of it is the right of impeachment.⁴

THE JURISDICTION OF THE FEDERAL COURTS.

§ 61. GENERAL PRINCIPLES AND POINTS OF VIEW. The experience endured under the articles of confederation had impressed the more far-sighted patriots with the conviction that a real federal government could not be created as long as the sovereignty of justice was withheld from the Union. It followed directly from this principle that the jurisdiction of the federal courts must be co-extensive with the sphere of the federal legislature and the federal executive. Political considerations and grounds of expediency, however, determined the framers

[1] *Ex parte Wells*, Howard, XVIII., 307. This is the leading question decided in this case.
[2] *Ibid.*, 305.
[3] *Ex parte Garland*, Wallace, IV., 300. See Tiffany's (p. 336 *et seq.*) keen polemic against this doctrine.
[4] It may be noted that the president may withdraw and annul an undelivered pardon granted by his predecessor.

of the constitution to extend this jurisdiction even beyond these limits. But on the other hand, they did not deduce from that principle the conclusion that all litigation, in which the constitution, the federal laws or the acts and omissions of federal officials came into consideration, should be decided only in the federal courts. The constitution is a constituent part of the fundamental law of all the states and the federal laws are " the supreme law of the land " and consequently also of each several state. The federal constitution and laws must therefore come into question in innumerable litigated cases, which undoubtedly belong to the state tribunals as long as the Union bears the character of a composite state, so far as its legal existence is concerned. It was absolutely necessary to give jurisdiction to the federal courts in only two cases: first, where the preservation of the national authority — viewed from the stand-point of duties as well as of rights — demanded it; and, second, where uniformity of decisions was required. But in the second instance the existence of an invincible necessity can, however, be recognized only conditionally. The jurisdiction of the state courts need not be completely excluded on principle, in such cases. If the state courts are subordinated to the federal courts, in these cases, uniformity of decision is sufficiently assured. It is equally as true, however, that no principle requires that in all such cases the state courts **must be competent to decide in the first instance, while** there are **weighty** grounds of expediency to the contrary. As the constitution provides nothing on this point, the question must be regulated by federal legislation, and congress need guide itself in such legislation only by considerations of expediency. But as the constitution is silent not only in such cases, but in general, as to whether and when the federal courts shall have exclusive jurisdiction, congress must always determine this. This does not, however, override the fact that the fundamental ideas of the constitution imperiously demand in certain cases the establishment by law of exclusive jurisdiction, and in others, on the contrary, may as unconditionally require the concurrent jurisdiction of the state courts. Where this concurrent jurisdiction exists in accordance with the federal laws, it is not, however, *created* by them. Congress is not constitutionally capable of transferring even the slightest portion of the legal sovereignty of the United States to the several states or of delegating it to them; but the state courts have jurisdiction because the legal sovereignty indwelling in the states, before the adoption of the constitution, was not taken from them so far as these cases are concerned by the constitution or by the federal laws passed by virtue thereof.[1] Where the states have concurrent jurisdiction, their rules of procedure always prevail. Congress can vest the execution of the legal sovereignty of the United States only in federal courts and the authority of these courts rests exclusively upon the constitution and the federal laws enacted under it (*American Insurance Co. vs. Canter*, Peters, I., 511); they have no common law jurisdiction (*Wheaton vs. Peters*, Peters, VIII., 591, 658).[2] In the third place, where, from

[1] *Martin vs. Hunter's Lessee*, Wheaton, I., 304. On the other hand the supreme court in the noted case of *Prigg vs. Pennsylvania* (Peters, XVI., 539) laid down the principle that the states could not grant to their courts the right to carry out federal laws. Just as little can the authority of the federal courts be extended by state laws. But the federal courts may decide, when new rights are created by state laws, whether the law-suits arising thereunder fall according to federal law within the domain of the federal courts. *Ex parte McNiel*, Wallace, XIII., 243.

[2] In general — the exceptions to the rule will be hereafter noted — the legal sovereignty of the United States thus comes into play first only by virtue of federal legislation. The answer to the question, how far the sovereignty of law extends, can be found only in the

motives not of principle, but of expediency, the authority of the federal courts has been extended beyond the spheres of congress and of the president, the concurrent jurisdiction of the state courts is of course required and their subordination to the federal courts is not a matter of principle. In these cases the jurisdiction of the federal courts depends upon the person or the residence. Therefore the federal courts in their decisions in such cases regard as decisive the local law,— the common law, the law of custom, the statutory law and the constitution of the state, and that, too, as interpreted by the state courts,[1] provided, however, the judicial decision of the question at issue is dependent solely upon the legal *status* of the parties in the particular state.[2] If the decisions of the highest state court on the point at issue are in conflict with one another, the federal courts follow the last decision.[3]

In addition to the above three categories, which, if the cases be divided according to their objects, embrace all

constitution, but the laws must determine the authority of the federal courts. Congress can neither decrease nor increase the legal sovereignty fixed by the constitution, but the constitutional-law powers rest (they lie "dormant") till it has directed that — eventually also when and how — they are to be exercised by certain federal courts. In many cases, in which it could indisputably do so, it has not so ordered, or at least has not done so, to the fullest possible extent. But it is not congress, it is the constitution, which grants the federal courts their powers; congress provides only that, when and how the powers created by the constitutional law shall be exercised by the different courts.

[1] *Livingston's Lessee vs. Morse*, Peters, VII., 469; *Shelby vs. Guy*. Wheaton, XI., 361.

[2] The decisions of the state courts are therefore not followed as of course, when they involve passing judgment upon a national power, upon rights, privileges or exemptions claimed under the federal constitution, upon principles of law universally valid, upon state laws which have the nature of contracts, etc.

[3] *Green vs. Neal's Lessee*, Peters, VI., 291.

litigation of every kind in the federal courts, there is another triple division possible, based with equal clearness and just as naturally upon the particular constitutional provision concerned. It is not easy to find a perfectly appropriate name for the determining principle of this second tripartition, but the basis of division may be most correctly designated as the reason of the suit. And as "object" and "reason" are sometimes very difficult to separate or distinguish, while they are yet manifestly not synonymous, so the three classes of each partition are also co-extensive in great part, but by no means completely so. The sovereignty of law of the Union is based upon: first, the law to be applied; second, the parties to the suit; third, the thing involved.

§ 62. LAW-SUITS ARISING UNDER THE CONSTITUTION, THE FEDERAL LAWS AND TREATIES. The two first groups coincide most closely, for where the nature of the law to be applied is the condition of the legal sovereignty of the Union, this is always because the preservation of the national authority demands it. The constitution provides that "the judicial power shall extend to all cases in law and equity arising under this constitution, the laws of the United States and treaties" (art. III., sec. 2, § 1). It has already been said that the word "cases" is not synonymous here with "disputed law points." It must be understood as a technical term, and all "disputed law points" which are of a political nature are subject to decision by the political powers,— by the president or by congress, or by congress and the president. Moreover, all law cases in which, in a general way, the constitution, the federal laws or treaties come into question, do not "arise under" them within the meaning of this provision. The words "arising under" are to be understood as meaning that the correct decision of the legal dispute must depend upon the correct construction and interpretation of the constitution, of a federal law, or of a treaty.[1] If the constitution comes in this sense into question, the points involved may be whether or no a federal or state law, or the act of a federal or state officer, is constitutional. Congress has not thought it necessary to give exclusive jurisdiction to the federal courts in any one of these cases. In its opinion, it has sufficiently assured the preservation of the national authority and the uniformity of judicial decisions by giving the parties the power of transferring a case pending before a state court to a federal court. This can be done only on certain carefully defined conditions.[2] The federal supreme court is the court of last resort. Its decision may be, in fact, required when the constitutionality of a federal law or of a treaty is called into question, or where the action involves a power, a title, or a right of some kind claimed

---

[1] *Cohens vs. Virginia*, Wheaton, VI., 379.

[2] In all cases to which the legal sovereignty of the United States extends, congress may permit a removal of the case from the state to the federal courts (*Railway Company vs. Whitton*, Wallace, XIII., 270). This is not necessarily done by appeal. A case may be removed before it is decided. Even after a decision, the removal is not always by appeal in the technical sense of the word. It is usually by writ of error. On an appeal questions of both fact and law are re-examined. Under a writ of error only questions of law are re-examined. As to what is more properly called "removals of cases," that is, removals before judgments, see details in Cooley, *Principles*, 122-128. If the case involves only money, or money's worth, the sum claimed must be at least $500 to permit a removal. Federal officers or other persons sued under a tax or customs law of the Union have had, since 1833, special legal rights of removal. The central idea of the whole system of transferring cases is always more or less that of making surer of an impartial judgment. Every direct or indirect limitation, by state law, of the right of removal under federal laws is null and void. J. F. Dillon, *Law of Removal of Causes*, 3d ed., St. Louis, 1881.

to exist under the constitution, a federal law or a treaty, and the state supreme court has decided against the validity of the claim. If, however, the judgment depends upon whether or no a state law or a right claimed under the authority of a state is opposed to the federal constitution, federal law or a treaty, an appeal can be taken to the federal supreme court only in case the supreme court of the state has held the state law to be valid. Again, other cases "arise under" the federal laws or treaties, which question not their validity, but the correctness of their interpretation. Uniformity of judicial decision requires the federal courts to take jurisdiction of such cases, and congress has made this jurisdiction in part exclusive.

Next in order come four kinds of legal controversies to which, from the nature of the matter at issue, the legal supremacy of the United States must extend. In three of them the basis of jurisdiction is the personality of the parties. In the fourth — cases of admiralty and maritime law — the nature of the law to be applied is not to be understood as the basis of jurisdiction in the same sense as it has been in the preceding paragraph.

§ 63. EMBASSADORS, OTHER DIPLOMATIC AGENTS AND CONSULS. As to this provision of the constitution, I need observe only that these representatives and agents of foreign powers need not necessarily be "parties" to a suit. The jurisdiction extends "to all cases affecting" them,— an expression vague enough to leave its interpretation quite at the discretion of the judge.

§ 64. ADMIRALTY AND MARITIME JURISDICTION. The jurisdiction of the federal courts in admiralty and maritime cases is to a very large extent exclusive.[1] Congress and

[1] It is so in all cases " of prize, maritime torts and contracts, and liens for maritime services," as far as these are not processes *in per-*

the courts have given this grant of power a broad construction. In doing so they have relied especially on the phrase "maritime jurisdiction," in order to escape a too narrow technical explanation of the word "admiralty." The old opinion that the power extended only to tidewater has been wholly abandoned. Wherever navigation exists in the United States, there this constitutional provision extends (*Jackson vs. The Magnolia*, Howard, XX., 296, and *The Genesee Chief*, Ibid., XII., 443). The grant of jurisdiction implies the existence in congress of the right of legislation on these matters; but the jurisdiction extends only as far as congress has exercised its legislative power (*Ibid.*).

In all the subsequent provisions, the word "cases" is replaced by "controversies" and the word "all" is dropped. It is generally admitted that this change is not simply one of style but that it has a substantial meaning. So far, however, there has been no precise and authoritative establishment of this meaning. The doctrine that the legal supremacy of the United States does not extend to "all" legal controversies, especially those which barely come within the outer borders of these provisions of the constitution, is of no practical value, as long as nothing can be said as to which controversies are excluded. The explanation of the other point is less unsatisfactory. It is said that by "controversies" only civil proceedings are to be understood.[1]

§ 65. CONTROVERSIES TO WHICH THE UNITED STATES ARE A PARTY. The United States cannot be sued at all in a

sonam. Cooley, *Principles*, 114. See especially the decisions of the supreme court in *The Moses Taylor*, Wallace, IV., 411, and *Hine vs. Trevor*, Ibid., 555. Many American jurists declare that the jurisdiction of the federal courts in admiralty and maritime cases is entirely exclusive; but they have only "suits *in rem*" in view.

[1] *Cohens vs. Virginia*, Wheaton, VI., 264, 411, 412.

state court (*Ableman vs. Booth*, Howard, XXI., 506). They can be sued before their own courts only at their own pleasure, that is, only in those cases where the federal laws permit. Land bought by the United States within a state and used for no particular purpose is subject like private property to condemnation for public purposes under the authority of the state.

§ 66. CONTROVERSIES BETWEEN TWO OR MORE STATES. This provision is unquestionably of the utmost importance, for in case of a controversy between states, neither would be willing to commit the decision unconditionally to a court of the other. Just because a peaceful determination of such conflicts could only be assured by making them subject to the legal supremacy of the Union, the omission of the word "all" might become under certain circumstances of much significance. Since the abolition of slavery and the annihilation of the doctrine of state sovereignty — in its old form — by the result of the civil war, it is much less to be feared than formerly, that a controversy can ever arise between the states, in which the jurisdiction of the federal courts might be seriously and energetically disputed. Their jurisdiction over questions of boundary between the states has been established for many years by quite a number of decisions of the federal supreme court.

The legal controversies enumerated in the remaining provisions of the constitution all belong to those placed under the jurisdiction of the federal courts for reasons of expediency. Moreover, the decisions of the federal courts in these cases do not bind the state courts, which always have concurrent jurisdiction in them. The federal courts as a rule, as I have stated, follow the state courts in these cases, but there is no uniformity of legal decision in them.

§ 67. Controversies Between a State and Citizens of Another State. It is not sufficient that a state be interested in a legal controversy; it must be a party to it.[1] According to the original and undoubtedly the correct interpretation of this constitutional provision by the supreme court (*Chisholm vs. Georgia*, Dallas, II., 419), a state could be brought before the federal courts not only as plaintiff but as defendant. Public opinion was against this and the eleventh amendment was adopted. This withdrew from federal jurisdiction suits against a state by citizens of another state or by citizens or subjects of any foreign state. This amendment has led to serious complications, for different states have repeatedly failed to comply with their obligations as debtors. Attempts were recently made (1883) to bring them before the federal supreme court by having the owners of their defaulted securities assign the bonds to their own states which were then to appear as plaintiffs. The supreme court, however, has decided (*New Hampshire vs. Louisiana* and *New York vs. Louisiana*) that this was inadmissible, because it would be an evasion of the eleventh amendment. Whether the agitation begun to repeal the amendment will succeed, remains to be seen; but this can scarcely be hoped for, as quite a number of the states are at present directly interested in maintaining it. This amendment does not, however, prevent appeals to the federal supreme court if the decision of the state court has brought into question rights, titles, etc., under the constitution, the federal laws or treaties (*Cohens vs. Virginia*, Wheaton, VI., 264). A suit may be brought against a corporation chartered by a state, even if the state holds all the stock (*Bank of Kentucky vs. Wister*, Peters, II., 318).

---

[1] *Osborn vs. Bank of United States*, Wheaton, IX., 738.

§ 68. Controversies Between Citizens of Different States. The expression "citizen" is not to be understood here literally. It means "inhabitant." Even corporations are regarded as inhabitants. Inhabitants of the territories or of the District of Columbia, however, are not included. The jurisdiction granted by this provision to the federal courts has been by no means put in full force by congress in its legislation.

§ 69. Controversies Between Citizens of the Same State Claiming Lands Under Grants of Different States. This provision also applies when the states concerned originally constituted one state.

§ 70. Controversies Between a State or its Citizens and Foreign States, Citizens or Subjects. Foreign corporations, and also immigrants who have declared their intention of becoming citizens, are "foreign," within the meaning of this clause.

PRACTICE AND PLEADING.

§ 71. Rules of Practice were almost wholly left to congress to determine. But on one substantial point the constitution has given congress no discretion. "In all cases affecting embassadors, other public ministers and consuls, and those in which a state shall be a party, the supreme court shall have original jurisdiction" (art. III., sec. 2, § 2). These cases are the exceptions to the rule, according to which the judicial power of the United States can come into operation only after legislation by congress. Congress is authorized, here, as everywhere else, to enact the more definitive provisions of procedure, but if it does not do so, the supreme court may itself provide the *modus procedendi* (*Florida vs. Georgia*, Howard, XVII., 478). It is uncertain whether or no the constitution intended that this original jurisdiction should also have been exclusive. Jurists' opinions differ, and so do judicial decisions. The affirmative view has always had the more support, but legislation has not fully come up to it. For while a suit against embassadors, consuls, etc., can be maintained only in the supreme court, they may bring suits in other courts as well. On the other hand, it is generally admitted that congress cannot extend the original jurisdiction of the supreme court. The extent of its jurisdiction in appeals is practically left wholly to the discretion of congress. The constitution says: "In all the other cases before mentioned, the supreme court shall have appellate jurisdiction, both as to law and fact, with such exceptions, and under such regulations, as the congress shall make." Congress must therefore give original jurisdiction to other federal courts, as far as this is not granted in the first sentence to the supreme court. Congress may also give them an appellate jurisdiction. The supreme court has this appellate jurisdiction only so far as it is expressly granted by the laws. The circuit courts, consequently, sit in some cases as courts of first as well as last resort.[1] A case in which a jury has rendered a verdict does not come within the category of those in which the supreme court may re-examine a question of fact on appeal. The seventh amendment, to be hereafter discussed, establishes this.

[1] Details as to practice and pleading in the different federal courts are beyond the scope of this work. The most necessary are grouped in Cooley, *Principles*, 120 *et seq.* Among the comprehensive books on the subject are: St. D. Law, *The Jurisdiction and Powers of the U. S. Courts*, Albany, 1852; G. T. Curtis, *Commentaries on the United States Courts*, Phila., 1854; A. Conkling, *Treatise on the Organization, Jurisdiction and Practice of the Courts of the U. S.*, 5th ed., Albany, 1870; B. R. Curtis, *Jurisdiction, Practice and Peculiar Jurisprudence of the Courts of the U. S.*, Boston, 1880; R. Desty, *Federal Procedure*, 5th ed., San Francisco, 1881.

The United States therefore cannot appeal in a criminal case, for in "crimes"—impeachments, of course, excepted—the decision must be by jurors (art. III., sec. 2, § 3). Everything which is a crime by the common law or state laws does not come within the limits of this paragraph of the constitution. It refers only to those crimes which are within the jurisdiction of the federal courts. The conditions precedent of the exercise of this jurisdiction are that the act in question has been declared to be a crime by federal law, and that congress has conferred the requisite jurisdiction upon a certain court.[1] In the latter respect, congress has not complete freedom of action. If the crime was committed in a state, the trial must take place within that state and in the particular federal district.[2] If the crime was not committed in a place geographically or legally within a state, but in a territory, in the District of Columbia, in Indian Territory, in a fort, arsenal or other place subject to the exclusive jurisdiction of the United States, then the place of trial must have been fixed by law.

EXPRESS LIMITATIONS OF AUTHORITY AND PROHIBITIONS.

Many of the provisions belonging under this head have already been treated elsewhere, and may therefore remain unnoted here. So, too, those provisions which concern the rights and legal safeguards of individuals will be passed over here, because they are to be treated in a special section.

§ 72. BILLS OF ATTAINDER AND EX POST FACTO LAWS. "No bill of attainder or *ex post facto* law shall be passed" (art. I., sec. 9, § 3). It is not stated who is forbidden to

[1] *U. S. vs. Coolidge,* Wheaton, I., 815; *U. S. vs. Hudson and Goodwin,* Cranch, VII., 32.
[2] Sixth amendment.

pass such measures. The next section of the same article, however, says: "No state shall pass any bill of attainder [or] *ex post facto* law." Hence follows directly the important principle that (as the courts have always held) all prohibitory clauses of the constitution containing no words extending their import bind only the federal powers.[1] According to a decision of the supreme court (*Cummings vs. State of Missouri*, Wallace, IV., 323, 324) the expression "bill of attainder" is to be understood here in the broadest sense, so that it includes also the so-called bills of pains and penalties. In other words, not only can no death sentence be imposed by an act of the legislative power, but the latter cannot take the general exercise of justice in criminal cases into its own hands. In the United States a punishable crime is only one which is declared to be such by existing laws, and a man accused of such a crime can be made answerable only under existing laws and before a competent court.[2] A correct definition of the expression "*ex post facto* laws" is not to be got by translating and taking the Latin in its literal sense. The framers of the constitution used the Latin words because they desired to speak only of what this technical term means in English law, and not of all retroactive laws. Indeed, all *ex post facto* laws are retroactive, but all retroactive laws are not *ex post*

[1] It suffices to mention *Barron vs. Mayor of Baltimore*, Peters, VII., 243.

[2] In the so-called Test-Oath Cases, viz.: *Cummings vs. State of Missouri*, *supra*, and *Ex parte Garland*, Wallace, IV., 333. the supreme court gave such a wide scope to this eminently technical expression, that most jurists will probably agree with the minority of the judges. The controversy in the Cummings case was over certain provisions of the Missouri constitution (and in the Garland case over certain federal laws) which made the capacity of occupying an office depend upon taking a test-oath as to non-participation in the rebellion. In both cases five judges were arrayed against four.

facto. The latter relate only to crimes and misdemeanors covered by the criminal law. Neither congress nor the states can give a law a retroactive force in such a way as to make an act, already done and not punishable when done, punishable now; or to increase the punishment or the legal grade of a punishable act; or to lessen the legal conditions of conviction;[1] or to withdraw a legally-vested right on account of an action now first made punishable;[2] or, finally, to deny to a person accused of crime the opportunity of pleading something — for instance, a declaration of amnesty, a former sentence or an acquittal — which would otherwise assure him immunity.[3]

§ 73. NOBILITY. Both the United States and the states are forbidden to grant any title of nobility (art. I., sec. 9, § 8,[4] and sec. 10, § 1).

§ 74. RELIGIOUS LIBERTY. The principle of the separation of church and state is as completely carried out in the United States as it can be in any nation based upon law; but religious liberty is not, as most Europeans believe, guaranteed by the constitution.. The latter contains only two clauses as to religion. It prohibits a "religious test . . . as a qualification to any office or public trust under the United States" (art. VI., § 3).[5] The word "test" is unquestionably to be understood in the

[1] In 1798, in *Calder vs. Bull*, Dallas, III., 390, Justice Chase defined these four classes.

[2] See the convincing criticism of this part of the Test-Oath Cases by Pomeroy, pp. 340–347.

[3] Cooley, *Principles*, 286.

[4] Here, too, belongs the provision that no officer of the United States "shall, without the consent of the congress, accept of any present, emolument, office or title of any kind whatever, from any king, prince or foreign state."

[5] The federal and state officers who must pledge themselves to support the constitution are free to take a mere affirmation in lieu of an oath.

15

technical sense which it possesses in the ecclesiastical-political history of England, but nevertheless it would be unconstitutional if — for example — faith in God should be declared necessary in order to become a federal officer. The United States are not legally a Christian state; they are not even a theistic state; but just as little are they a pagan state. They are simply a state. The religious convictions of the people and the churches as communities of believers do not exist, so far as the United States are concerned, *i. e.*, all these things lie without their sphere of action.[1] The federal government has only the powers granted by the constitution, and the latter mentioned religion only because it appeared safer to express explicitly what complete silence would have implied. The second provision also contains but a single prohibition. The first amendment forbids congress to enact any law "respecting an establishment of religion or prohibiting the free exercise thereof."[2] "An establishment

---

[1] The attempt has been repeatedly made to bring into the constitution in some form or other a recognition of God, but the people have never taken kindly to the thought, perhaps less because they are quite conscious of the objections to it on principle, and regard them as decisive, than because they consider the matter simply unnecessary.

A treaty concluded with the Bey of Tripoli November 4, 1796, says: "The government of the United States is not in any sense founded on the Christian religion." *U. S. Statutes at Large*, VIII., 155.

[2] The Mormons, on account of this amendment, declare that the laws against their polygamy are unconstitutional. And it has seemed doubtful to many non-Mormons whether congress was authorized to assail this "remnant of barbarism" with penal laws. The question is certainly not wholly without difficulty, for it is well to note that the free "exercise" of a religion cannot be prohibited. But the demands of sound common sense have won the victory over scruples of constitutional law. A state cannot be in duty bound to look with folded arms on the subversion of its fundamental principles of morality because the attack is cloaked under the form of practicing

of religion" is also a technical expression borrowed from England, but it must not be understood in its narrowest technical sense. Congress is not only prohibited from making any religion whatever a state religion or any church whatever a state church, but it cannot make any laws favoring one religion or church more than any other. As far as the federal constitution is concerned, not only are all religions and churches tolerated, but they have all perfectly equal rights, inasmuch as congress has no powers whatever in relation to any of them or all of them. On the other hand, neither of the two constitutional provisions as to religion imposes any obligation or limitation upon the states. But the constitutions of the states themselves, without exception, contain provisions substantially the same as those of the federal constitution. This is not, however, because the latter binds them to this. Actually and legally the complete religious liberty

a religious dogma. But although, undoubtedly, no such insane and suicidal obligation can be deduced from this constitutional provision, it must, nevertheless, be admitted that the limits to which congress may proceed, in its application, cannot be defined with absolute certainty. If its application has once become a necessity, only the sound sense of the people can prevent the transgression of the correct line of demarcation on any other occasion. In the United States public opinion offers sufficient security, however, against any such transgression. From a political stand-point it is a more important fact that so far no effective means have been found for suppressing polygamy by legislation. The final reason why all penal laws have remained substantially ineffective is perhaps the unanimity of passive resistance which the Mormons oppose to them. Neither accusers nor witnesses can be found, and there is therefore no opportunity to apply the law. The latest penal act (that of March 22, 1882; the so-called Edmunds bill) punishes polygamy in the territories and in other places under the exclusive jurisdiction of congress with a fine not exceeding $500 and imprisonment for not more than five years, and also deprives a polygamist of the franchise and of the right of occupying any public office.

and separation of church and state exist throughout the Union, but not as an effect of the constitution. The latter guaranties this only so far as the federal government is concerned. The separation of church and state is manifestly not to be understood as implying that the churches can do and not do what they please. As corporations, they are subject like other corporations to the legislative power of the states, especially as to their property. They are also subject to the police power, and they cannot any more than individuals escape from the laws of the state prohibiting and punishing violations of public morals by appealing to their religious convictions.[1]

§ 75. FREEDOM OF SPEECH AND OF THE PRESS. The general observations in the last paragraph apply here also. Freedom of speech and of the press are guarantied by the constitution, only so far as the federal government is concerned; but they are also guarantied by all the state constitutions.[2] It is to be observed that congress is

---

[1] On the ground that the Christian religion was always acknowledged by the common law, and further, that it is the prevailing religion of the United States, the power to punish "blasphemies" has been claimed. The relations of church and state will be more fully discussed in the chapter on the public law of the several states.

[2] The provisions in point are collected by Cooley, *Constitutional Limitations*, 414–417. Hammond, I., 23, § 67, says, nevertheless, in reference to *United States vs. Hall*, 13 *Int. Rev. Record*, 182: "The right of freedom of speech, and the right peaceably to assemble and other rights enumerated in the first eight amendments to the constitution, are thereby protected only against the legislation of congress and not against the legislation of the states. These rights, therefore, were not secured to the people of the United States until the fourteenth amendment to the constitution, because till then they might be impaired by state legislation; but now they are not only secured from congressional interference, but by the amendment, from state interference also." He can refer here only to the clause in the first section of the fourteenth amendment, which prohibits the states from making or enforcing "any law which shall abridge the privileges or

forbidden to "abridge" the freedom of speech or of the press. They were therefore recognized as existing rights. Hence it has been argued that the correct interpretation of the words must be found in the common law. In the opinion of the most prominent English jurists, however, the common-law freedom of the press is in substance merely freedom from a censorship, while in the United States the idea has always been given in fact and in law a far wider range. Cooley defines it as meaning that everything can be published which does not injure public morals or private reputation in a way punishable according to the principles of the common law. There is no responsibility for publication only in those cases which for various reasons are recognized as "privileged."[1] Even proof of the truth of the alleged libel does not always assure immunity from punishment. In civil cases it is always sufficient; but if the complaint is a criminal one, the motive of publication must have been justifiable. In cases of the latter kind, the jury in many states decides not only questions of fact but also questions of law. In some states this principle extends to all actions for libel and slander. Juries always decide the questions of fact. That attacks against the government ought not to be punished as libels has been generally recognized, since the "sedition law," passed during the presidency of John Adams, was condemned by public opinion with great decision and bitterness as unconstitutional. Even attacks upon the form of the state cannot be punishable as long

---

immunities of citizens of the United States." In my opinion this clause cannot be given so comprehensive an interpretation. Compare § 82. See, also, *U. S. vs. Cruikshank*, 92 U. S., 542.

[1] See Cooley, *Constitutional Limitations*, 425, 426; and *Principles*, 275 *et seq.* A distinction must be drawn between cases of conditional and unconditional privilege.

as the change is sought in a constitutional way. In case of plans for the violent subversion of the government or the state, seditious publications can, however, be produced before the criminal judge as part of the *res gestæ*.

§ 76. THE RIGHT TO ASSEMBLE AND TO PETITION. These rights are likewise guarantied in all the state constitutions. In them, as well as in the federal constitution, the former right is subject only to the condition that the people assemble "peaceably." Public authority can, therefore, interfere with a public meeting under no circumstances, unless a violation of law has become an accomplished fact. This right has never been in danger in the United States. The right of petition, on the contrary, during many years, occasioned the most heated contests in congress. This aroused much of the opposition of the free states to the steady, reckless and domineering advance of the slave-holding interests.

§ 77. "THE RIGHT OF THE PEOPLE TO KEEP AND BEAR ARMS shall not be infringed" (second amendment); because a well-regulated militia is necessary to the security of a free state. It has therefore been argued that the constitutional provision refers only to arms necessary or suitable for the equipment of militia; although it must not be inferred from this that the right is restricted to those citizens who belong to the militia. As to whether or no the bearing of other arms can be forbidden, judicial decisions are far apart. It is, however, generally admitted that the secret carrying of arms can be prohibited.

§ 78. SLAVERY is prohibited throughout the entire domain of the Union by the thirteenth amendment. So, too, is "involuntary servitude," except as a punishment for crime, after due conviction.[1]

[1] I pass over all other provisions relating to slavery, as they have now only an historic interest.

§ 79. CONTRACTS.[1] No state shall pass any "law impairing the obligation of contracts" (art. I., sec. 10, § 1). This provision, unlike those in the first two amendments, relates wholly to the states. It does not follow, however, that congress may pass such laws. Here, as in all cases, the principle obtains that it has only the powers which are granted it by the constitution. The claim of an express grant of power to pass such laws can scarcely be made. Unquestionably, congress can as little impair the obligation of contracts as a state. If the federal government wishes, however, to violate any of its contracts, there will often be practically no legal remedy for this; for the right of suit against the United States exists only so far as they establish it by law. But as to claims for money under such contracts, the right to sue is granted. The court of claims has jurisdiction of all claims founded on a federal law, upon an order of an executive department or upon a contract, express or implied, with the government of the United States, and also of all claims referred to it for decision by either house of congress. But the obligations incurred under contracts are not always of such a kind that in case of non-performance the injured party can give his suit the form of a claim for money, or that damages in money can atone for his real damages. The proceedings under this constitutional provision in the federal and state courts furnish a mass of proofs of this. If these are studied more closely the student is inclined to regard it as, on the whole, a matter of good fortune that the prohibition is not expressly extended to the United States. If it had been, the labyrinth of judicial decisions, through which it is scarcely possible to thread one's way now, would probably be still more extensive and confusing. This apparently

[1] J. P. Bishop, *Contracts*, St. Louis, 1878.

simple clause, which was hardly mentioned in the debates over the adoption of the constitution, has proved to be one of the most important, has given occasion to as many legal controversies, perhaps, as all the rest of the constitution put together, and has laid the heaviest tasks upon judicial brains. Becoming complete master of the whole matter involved would be the task of a life-time, and the trouble taken would be ill repaid; for the decisions vary in manifold ways, and cut across each other at every imaginable angle. Indeed, a number of recent decisions let it seem quite possible that the very ground lines of constitutional law on this question, once supposed to be irrevocably and firmly drawn, will by and by be twisted into a radically different outline. I must therefore renounce the attempt to state, even in the most general way, what the actual constitutional law on this point is. I do so with the less hesitation because most of the questions involved scarcely come within my idea of the public law, although they form an important part of constitutional law, and are therefore, as a rule, treated in great detail in American books. I shall simply note as briefly as may be those points which are really of especial importance from the stand-point of public law.

As the constitution speaks simply of contracts, all kinds of contracts come under the provision — executed and executory, express and implied. The word covers, in fact, not only contracts between private persons, but also those between a state and private persons. On both these fundamental principles there is no difference of opinion. This is a scanty gain, however, for the importance in public law of these principles depends wholly upon the definition of the word "contract." Giving the word the narrowest possible meaning would have resulted in no difficulty worth notice. But the supreme court has given the word a scope far beyond what is understood by it in ordinary speech. It is generally admitted that laws are not contracts; but contracts may be entered into by the state under the form of laws, and legislative donations to private persons, which come under the head of "grants," are contracts within the meaning of the constitution.[1] Upon these two statements rests the whole significance in public law of this clause of the constitution. Their consequences reach to the very root of the whole body of constitutional law and involve the question of the political character of the constituent members of the Union. The legislative power of the states within their constitutional sphere is limited by this interpretation of the contract-clause in a way which, in the opinion of many, is absolutely incompatible with the existence of the autonomy of the states. All acts incorporating private corporations by general or special laws and all charters are contracts. In every such contract the state surrenders *pro tanto* its legislative will.[2] A legislature binds all future legislatures as to the entire extent of the "contract." The provisions which are not in the proper sense of the word essential to the accomplishment of the object, but serve only to advance it, cannot be changed by the state alone any more than the essential provisions can be; for the constitution forbids not only the annulment, but every impairment of contracts.[3] The state retains only the

[1] *Fletcher vs. Peck*, Cranch, VI., 87, 137; *Providence Bank vs. Billings*, Peters, IV., 560.

[2] Charters of municipal corporations are not "contracts" (*Dartmouth College vs. Woodward*, Wheaton, IV., 659, 694). Privileges granted them in the charter, such, for instance, as a ferry franchise, can be again withdrawn by the legislature. These privileges would be inviolable if granted to a private corporation. *East Hartford vs. Bridge Co.*, Howard, X., 510.

[3] *Planters' Bank vs. Sharp*, Howard, VI., 327. If, for instance, a state in incorporating a bank has agreed not to tax it beyond a cer-

powers which come from the right of eminent domain.¹ The "contract" must always be strictly construed in favor of the state. No public obligations are to be inferred; the courts recognize only those which are clearly expressed. Some of the state courts — especially in Ohio during the fifties — made repeated and energetic efforts to overthrow the principles which led to consequences of such enormous practical significance. The result, however, was the very opposite of that striven for. The federal supreme court kept steadily on for a long time building upon the foundations already laid, especially on those outlined in the Dartmouth College decision, the leading case for the interpretation of the contract-clause.² Nevertheless, the states have found a way to break the chains which this put upon their legislative freedom of action. By general legal provisions, or in the very contracts concluded by law, they reserve the right to modify or repeal the obligations entered into. Against this the federal supreme court has had nothing to say, for the reservation is a part of the contract, and therefore a modification or repeal does not impair the obligation of

tain amount, the state is bound forever. One legislature can thus limit the right of taxation for all future legislatures. It binds, in fact, the people themselves, for even a change in the constitution of the state cannot repeal the contract-obligations entered into by an earlier legislature. See *Dodge vs. Woolsey*, Howard, XVIII., 331; *Mechanics & Traders' Bank vs. De Bolt*, Ibid., 380; *Same vs. Thomas*, Ibid., 384; *Skelly vs. The Jefferson Bank*, Black, I., 436; *The Binghamton Bridge*, Wallace, III., 51. In this last case Justice Grier, who with Chief-justice Chase and Justice Field dissented from the decision, said: "Although an act of incorporation may be called a contract, the rules of construction applied to it are admitted to be the reverse of those applied to other contracts." *Ibid.*, 82.

¹ *Bridge Co. vs. Dix*, Howard, VI., 507. See Cooley, *Const. Limitations*, 523–571.

² *Dartmouth College vs. Woodward*, Wheaton, IV., 519–715. Decided in 1819.

the contract. This has not, however, laid the storm against the principles of the Dartmouth College decision. It has raged more violently than before and with some results.[1] Those principles have unquestionably already lost the character of axiomatic truths which they had assumed in the minds of most jurists. The federal supreme court has itself begun to undermine them by its reasoning in the Granger cases,[2] although Chief-justice Waite does not directly attack either the decision in the Dartmouth College case or its foundation. The more recent decision in the Spring Valley Water Works case tends in the same way. These two decisions rest in substance upon the fundamental principle that in states which reserve the right of amending and modifying charters, stockholders in corporations must risk their investment upon the *hope* that future legislatures will not modify the legal conditions under which the former legislature invited the investment. But there is no legal remedy if this expectation is not fulfilled. If the rigid following-out of the principles of the Dartmouth College case to their ultimate consequences leads to results of the highest significance, politically and from the stand-point of public law, on the other hand this recent principle might produce economic and political results which make its unconditional acceptance impossible. Probably, therefore, a compromise between the two will be sought and finally found,— a compromise which will be in full accord with this clause of the constitution and will avoid the imminent perils of each of the present doctrines. However this may be, the constitutional law as to the obligation of contracts made

[1] See especially Shirley, *The Dartmouth College Causes and the Supreme Court of the United States*, 1879.
[2] 94 U. S., 113–187.

by legislation is still in embryo, despite the numberless judicial decisions upon it.[1]

EXPRESS OBLIGATIONS.

§ 80. GUARANTY OF A REPUBLICAN FORM OF GOVERNMENT. "The United States shall guaranty to every state in the Union a republican form of government" (art. IV., sec. 4). This is the only constitutional provision which lays an obligation upon the "United States" without saying anything as to who shall determine whether action of any kind is needed for the fulfillment of the duty and what means shall or must be used. Though the framers of the constitution certainly attached great importance to this clause, they do not seem to have put these questions to themselves or at least to have been thoroughly clear in their own minds as to the possible significance of the provision. Manifestly they set out with the thought that the Union would stand on feet of clay if its constituent members had not homogeneous political institutions, and that therefore, so far as might be, every possibility of the growth of monarchical tendencies by reason of internal conflicts or external influences should be cut off. The history of the Union since the rebellion of the colonies against the mother country presented many reasons for the fear lest under certain circumstances tendencies of that kind might be aroused here and there, if a curb were not provided in the constitution, that is, if the entire Union were not explicitly and unconditionally pledged to use all its powers to suppress these

[1] The most concise compilation of all the important decisions of both federal and state courts under this clause is to be found in the second edition (1884) of Desty's *Constitution of the United States*, pp. 124-186 and 304-311.

tendencies wherever and however they might appear. For this is and should be implied in this clause. It not only promises the states that the Union will interpose with all its might on their behalf, if internal or external enemies threaten or overthrow their republican form of government, but it absolutely forbids them to adopt any other form of government under any conditions, or for any reasons whatever. The United States give a pledge to themselves and to their constituent members that they will always remain a republic and, indeed, a federative republic. Within the limits of the republican idea, the federal and state constitutions can be subjected in constitutional methods to every imaginable modification, but the least transgression of these limits on the part of the Union is, *ipso facto*, a legal dissolution of the Union, unless done with the consent of every single state. And even in the latter case legally a new Union will have taken the place of the old one. That is what the framers of the constitution had in view, and it is certainly of more than theoretical interest and importance. Up to the present time, however, its immediate practical significance has come wholly from another source, which certainly lies within it, but of which the framers of the constitution had either no idea at all or only an inkling of an idea.

While at the time of the adoption of the constitution it did not seem utterly impossible that under certain circumstances monarchical tendencies might appear in one or more states, still this was highly improbable. The Union in fact has never had occasion to interpose on this account. And yet the provision has been brought into play, through the prohibition implied in it against a state's assuming any other than a republican form of government.

As the United States must guarantee the states a republican form of government, they must also be allowed to judge whether the government of any state is republican, and as the United States can act only by means of the federal government, the latter must determine this. The only question is, to which of its departments the decisive judgment belongs. The supreme court has answered this question by saying that congress must decide, and that the courts and the president must recognize its decision as binding.[1] As the question is not legal, but purely political, this view certainly cannot be disputed. But is it not practically quite the same thing, no matter to whom the decision belongs, for could there ever be a difference of opinion as to whether or no a form of government is republican? At first glance it might appear that this was barely possible. More closely examined, it becomes evident that the matter is by no means always and necessarily quite so simple. For it is not the American idea that every form of non-monarchical government can be recognized as republican in the sense of this constitutional provision. There has never been an authoritative definition of the word "republican," but nevertheless attempts have been made to stake off, in a positive as well as a negative way, the approximate limits of the idea. Every form of government essentially the same as the governments of the states at the time of the adoption of the constitution must be recognized as republican, for it is self-evident that these were and remain republican in the sense of the constitution. Hence it has been argued that the system adopted must coincide with these original forms, at least to the extent of entrusting the legislative, executive and judicial powers to different organs.[2] Indeed a very competent authority has drawn

[1] *Luther vs. Borden*, Howard, VII., 42.
[2] Paschal, *The Constitution, etc.*, 243.

a distinction in principle between the democratic and republican form of government.[1] These assertions open a wide field for discussion, but it must be admitted that oligarchies and aristocracies do not come within the constitutional provision. No fixed line, however, can be drawn between an aristocracy and a representative republic in which but a small fraction of the people have full political rights. But no matter how much theories may differ, in practice public opinion is unanimous in deciding that even non-monarchical state-forms may also be non-republican. This may become of the greatest practical importance, for congress may get into such a position that it can, or even that it must, decide a concrete case. For instance, the question may be raised within a state which of two constitutions and which of two governments is the legal one. While the principle is generally understood that such a question should be decided by the state itself, nevertheless the federal government may be obliged to take sides with one or the other. And if it does so, its decision is absolutely final. In such cases, however, it is easily possible that considerations arising out of the question here discussed may be, or have to be, taken into account. The accepted interpretation of the word "republican" has given congress power to determine not only whether the form of government of the states is republican, but also whether the states are in substance republics. The exercise of this right, too, may, under certain circumstances, become an imperious duty. The judgment of history will certainly be that this was the case after the overthrow of the rebellion, even although in my opinion it will undoubtedly not exonerate congress from the charge of having greatly abused this power in its reconstruction policy. After

[1] Cooley, *Principles*, 194.

the seceded states had been forced back into the Union by the sword and the sword had destroyed the true root of the rebellion — slavery,— congress could not and should not have permitted the rebel states to become again full members of the Union until they had adopted constitutions which corresponded in all respects with the new condition of affairs; which were in harmony with the views of the victorious north; and which were republican in substance as well as form. But demands were made upon the southern states which went far beyond anything required by the most rigid interpretation of a republican form of government in the sense of the constitution.[1]

[1] When the question was discussed in the senate as to whether the state of Louisiana, on the basis of its constitution of 1864, should be recognized as again endowed with full constitutional and legal rights, Charles Sumner said, February 24, 1865, in reply to a question by Henderson: "I answer at once, as a constitutional lawyer, that at the present time, under the words of the constitution of the United States declaring that the United States shall guarantee to every state a republican form of government, it is the bounden duty of the United States, by act of congress, to guarantee complete freedom to every citizen, and immunity from all oppression and absolute equality before the law (!). No government that does not guarantee these things can be recognized as republican in form according to the theory of the constitution of the United States, if the United States are called upon to enforce the constitutional guarantee." (*Congress. Globe*, 2d Sess., 38th Congress, 1067.) Congress adopted this view, for in the reconstruction act of March 2, 1867, it made the re-admission of the rebel states to the right of representation in congress dependent upon, *inter alia*, the conditions that their new constitutions should be "framed by a convention of delegates elected by the male citizens of said state, twenty-one years old and upward, of whatever race, color, or previous condition," and that "such constitution shall provide that the elective franchise shall be enjoyed by all such persons as have the qualifications herein stated for electors of delegates." (*Stat. at Large*, XIV., 429.) Wherever congress could do so, it interpreted this constitutional provision in the sense given it by Sumner. The act of February 9, 1867, for the admission of Nebraska

It became evident during the reconstruction period that this clause of the constitution was a weapon of terrible weight and keenest edge. That the weapon was not always rightly used at a time when the country was confronted, constitutionally and practically, with an amazing labyrinth of extraordinary difficulties, is certainly no proof that the constitution was wrong in creating the weapon. Whether it will ever be used again to such an extent it is impossible to say definitely; but this is certainly improbable. An attempt against the republican form of a state has never yet been made, and it is almost inconceivable that such an attempt ever will be; for at the present time in each state the form and substance of the government are in harmony, and moreover all the state governments are becoming more and more alike in both form and substance. The civil war not only hastened the political consolidation of the Union in law and in fact, but also greatly promoted the nationalization of the people by making all the constituent parts of the Union, from ocean to ocean and from the great lakes to the Gulf of Mexico, actually and legally so homogeneous in their political and social structure that further

provided: "That this shall not take effect except upon the fundamental condition that within the state of Nebraska there shall be no denial of the elective franchise or of any other right to any person by reason of race or color, except Indians not taxed," and that the legislature should by a solemn public act adopt this condition. (*Ibid.*, XIV., 392.) The fifteenth amendment as originally proposed shows that congress sought to make this new and radical interpretation of the expression obligatory upon all the states, but it was not possible to force it upon the loyal states as a federal law. This, however, does not alter the fact, that for part of the states this clause was construed in a way which the rest of the states would not permit in respect to themselves,— in other words, the fundamental principle of constitutional law, the absolute equality of all the states, was overthrown in a matter of cardinal importance by federal laws.

development *must* go steadily on in the same direction until that degree of homogeneity is reached which, under the existing relations, is generally possible, justifiable and desirable. With the increasing density of the population and the growth of commerce the importance of this provision of the constitution diminishes from year to year in both ways, that is, so far as the duty it imposes upon the United States is concerned as well as in regard to the powers it grants congress. The guaranty offered by the actual condition of affairs is becoming so strong that each day there is less need of an express guaranty in the federal constitution.

§ 81. STATE COMITY. A study of details would show that the public laws of the individual states still present a variegated picture. Probably this will always be so. And though the differences are by no means all insignificant, none of them are of such a radical nature that an American, who moves from one state into another, cannot at once feel fully and entirely at home in this respect. On the other hand nothing makes him more conscious at every step that he lives, not in a national state, but in a federative republic, than the myriad legal relations of the individual in the different states. Even these, however, are unmistakably alike in type, and all the essential legal principles as well as legal institutions are common to all the states. But when the law relating to individuals is applied, the decision does not depend, in the great majority of cases, directly upon general legal principles, but rather on how these principles are stated in the specific provisions of the state laws. As a matter of course, although the relations between the citizens of the different states are so many-sided and so close, the state laws differ very much more than they would, if the Union were a single national state. So far as these relations are legal in their nature, however, they are regulated by the general principles and rules of international law as to individuals, unless, indeed, the federal constitution provides otherwise. It does so provide in some important respects, but by no means sufficiently so to make the legal relations correspond with the actual facts as far as might be desirable.[1] The nationalization of the Union in this respect is never to be expected. Even if it were possible, there are very many and very important objections to it. The immense extent of the territory, the great diversity of natural relations and the consequent diversity of customs and opinions, as well as of social and economic conditions, would count against it. But, nevertheless, many and great disadvantages result from the fact that every state has its own laws. And in certain directions these disadvantages will increase and become more serious, the more in all other respects actual nationalization progresses.[2] It is so much the more important and praiseworthy that the federal constitution has given parts of the legal system a national character or at least has deprived them of the purely international character which other parts bear.

The next clause to be considered provides that "full faith and credit shall be given in each state to the public acts, records and judicial proceedings of every other state," and authorizes congress "by general laws" to "prescribe the manner in which such acts, records and proceedings shall be proved, and the effect thereof" (art. IV., sec. 1). The manner of proof is purely formal and

[1] This comes most clearly to light in New York city, where the cities and towns on the right bank of the Hudson, in the state of New Jersey, are economically and socially simply parts or suburbs of New York.

[2] For example, much has recently been said as to what a great blessing a national divorce law would be.

of no interest here. The only question of importance is the meaning of "full faith and credit," that is, what actual effect the proceedings in one state shall have in another. This question has always been answered in one way. The constitution, it is said, never contemplated ordering or permitting the jurisdiction of one state to extend into the domain of other states; it intended only that every state should be in duty bound to recognize without reservation what other states have done in the exercise of their lawful jurisdiction. A judicial decision rendered in another state will not, for example, be enforced if the defendant can prove that the court had no jurisdiction,[1] but the correctness of the judgment *per se* cannot be called into question. If the defendant has no further defense under the laws of the state in which the judgment was rendered, it must be enforced in every other state. If, however, the laws of the former state vouchsafe him any kind of protection whatever against the judgment, he may avail himself of this protection in every other state, but of this protection alone. If, however, the judgment is barred by lapse of time under the laws of the state where it is sought to be enforced, the defendant may claim the benefit of these laws, but no state can pass a statute of limitation which makes it impossible to enforce judgments rendered in other states. The judicial proceedings of which the constitution speaks in this clause are only civil cases. In criminal cases another provision prevails.

[1] This is also true when the necessary formalities, such as due service of process, were not observed, provided the judgment is *in personam*. Service by publication is sufficient, however, to warrant a judgment *in rem* if the property concerned is within the jurisdiction of the court. On the other hand, no one is bound to pay any attention to a personal summons served in one state directing him to appear before a court in another state.

§ 82. EXTRADITION OF FUGITIVE CRIMINALS. "A person charged in any state with treason, felony or other crime, who shall flee from justice and be found in another state, shall, on demand of the executive authority of the state from which he fled, be delivered up, to be removed to the state having jurisdiction of the crime" (art. IV., sec. 2, § 2). The duty of extradition is absolute. If a requisition is made, it must be obeyed, provided the three following conditions are fulfilled: 1. The demand must be in the required form; 2, the charge must have been made in the manner prescribed by law before a court of competent jurisdiction; 3, the defendant must have saved himself from criminal prosecution by flight, that is, he must have departed from the state requiring his extradition. He must, therefore, have actually been in that state. If the crime were carried on from another state, as in the case of a conspiracy, the constitutional provision does not apply. The executive department of the state to which the requisition is directed cannot refuse extradition on the ground that the act with which the defendant is charged is not a crime, according to the laws of that state, but only a misdemeanor or even not an act punishable at all. A crime in the sense of this constitutional provision is whatever the laws of the state which makes a demand for extradition declare to be a crime.[1] This important doctrine of the supreme court of the United States has, however, been by no means unconditionally recognized in practice. Extradition has often been refused. This has led to wearisome and serious conflicts between states. The most violent and most threatening of these were caused by the slavery question. Certain acts, such, for example, as inducing slaves to run away, which were high crimes under the codes of slave

[1] *Kentucky vs. Dennison*, Howard, XXIV., 99.

states, seemed to the more earnest opponents of slavery in the free states to deserve reward rather than punishment. Different governors, such as W. H. Seward, of New York, afterwards senator and secretary of state, refused to obey a requisition in such a case, because they could not consider as crimes in the sense of the constitution what their laws and the moral judgment of almost the whole civilized world did not consider a crime. In these peculiar cases, it may be readily admitted that the refusal was morally and politically justified; but the rejection of the doctrine laid down by the federal supreme court might have been fraught with the most serious results. Now that all the states in all matters profess the same moral principles, no considerations of principle oppose the unconditional recognition of this doctrine, although in one or another case the question may be raised as to whether the law of the case is also the justice of it. But if a governor sees fit in his official conduct to determine this question subjectively against the demand, the state issuing the requisition has only the choice of submitting to the unconstitutional refusal under protest or of repaying like with like, and in its turn retaliating in kind and so committing the same unconstitutional act itself. For the supreme court has declared that it cannot compel the performance of the extradition duty.[1] This constitutional provision, certainly one of the most important,— an indispensable one, in fact,— cannot be quite sufficient, or else the act of February 12, 1793, which provides the means of executing it, must have omissions that should be supplied.[2]

---

[1] *Kentucky vs. Dennison*, Howard, XXIV., 107, 108.

[2] The next clause in the constitution treats of the duty of delivering up persons held to service or labor in any state. In order not to use the objectionable word slaves, in the constitution, its framers

§ 83. LEGAL EQUALITY. "The citizens of each state shall be entitled to all the privileges and immunities of citizens in the several states" (art. IV., sec. 2, § 1).[1] The great importance of this provision is evident at a glance. To it is chiefly due the fact that step by step with the progressive development of the United States the practical nationalization of the people proceeds. As far as the constitution does not expressly prescribe otherwise, the states have a perfect autonomy in all matters not made federal affairs by the federal constitution, but they cannot have two kinds of laws and two kinds of rights, one for their own citizens and one for the citizens of other states.[2] He who is a citizen anywhere in the Union can nowhere within its domain be an alien. If he crosses the boundary into another state he enters its legal jurisdiction as the possessor of equal rights with its own citizens. He is not simply tolerated; his rights are not given him as a favor; he has not to be contented with this or that being assured him; but wherever he sets foot he is *ipso facto* and *ipso jure* in the full enjoyment of all the privileges and immunities of citizenship. What are these privileges and immunities which belong to "citizens in the several states" as such? And does this mean all kinds of citizens or only a particular kind? Judicial de-

availed themselves of this circumlocution. In adopting this provision, indeed, they did not consider slaves exclusively, but apprentices as well. It obtained its historic significance, however, solely through slavery, and with the abolition of that it became purposeless.

[1] The corresponding provision of the articles of confederation expressly excepts "paupers, vagabonds and fugitives from justice."

[2] "Its sole purpose was to declare to the several states that whatever those rights, as you grant or establish them to your own citizens, or as you limit and qualify or impose restrictions on their exercise, the same, neither more nor less, shall be the measure of the rights of citizens of other states within your jurisdiction." *The Slaughter House Cases*, Wallace, XVI., 77.

cisions have asserted that the constitution means only citizens of the United States, and that the provision therefore has no application to non-naturalized immigrants to whom one state has granted its special state citizenship,[1] or to free colored people, because the latter could never be citizens of the United States.[2] The fourteenth amendment not only permanently set aside the latter doctrine, but also did away with the chief difficulties arising from the very obscure relation between the two kinds of citizenship, state and national. The only possible doubt now is in regard to non-naturalized citizens,[3] for "all persons born or naturalized in the United States and subject to the jurisdiction thereof[4] are citizens of the United States and of the state wherein they reside."

The special right of state citizenship is not *granted* citizens of the United States who immigrate. They *acquire* it *eo ipso* by their settlement in a state, and their settlement cannot be prevented. On the other hand, they lose their special state-citizenship by emigrating into another state or territory. The free right of emigration is not only as a matter of fact absolutely unlimited in the United States, but it is unquestionably one of the privi-

---

[1] *Davis vs. Pierse*, 7 Minn., 13, quoted by Bump, 290.

[2] *Dred Scott vs. Sanford*, Howard, XIV., 393.

[3] I cannot understand how Cooley (*Principles*, 244) can say: "It is impossible to conceive of such a *status* as citizenship of a state unconnected with citizenship of the United States." Even the fourteenth amendment has evidently in no way deprived the states of the right of granting their particular citizenship wholly in their own discretion. It simply restates what was already a recognized principle (*Pierre Gassies vs. Jean Gassies Ballou*, Peters, VI., 761; 1832), that no state can withhold its citizenship from citizens of the United States, and that the latter obtain this state-citizenship by the mere fact of domicile.

[4] This clause excludes Indians who live under the tribal system, for even if the tribe be within a state, the jurisdiction of the United States is only a limited and conditional one.

leges which the fourth article of the constitution guaranties all citizens. The state-citizenship of the citizen of the United States goes with him as long as he merely changes his residence, but retains his domicile. This makes it possible to determine what kinds of rights are not intended by the "privileges and immunities" spoken of in article four, and this again makes it easier to answer the question as to what kind of rights are meant thereby. Political rights, such as the franchise, the right to hold office, etc., are never an unconditional result of citizenship. This is evident from the fact that they are always withheld from minors, and almost without exception from women. The fourth article speaks only of privileges and immunities which are conditioned upon the right of citizenship. Political rights are consequently excluded. These are always and in all places inseparably bound up with the legal domicile. All rights appertaining to any citizens of the state are not guarantied to the citizens of all the states, but only those rights which the citizens of the particular state have under the same circumstances. The legislation of a state can make no distinction in favor of its citizens, but it goes without saying that the constitution did not intend to bind a state to give special privileges to the citizens of other states. And this would be the case if these latter could claim political rights. The law has never defined what kind of privileges and immunities belong to the citizens of the several states as such. Even the judicial decisions do not answer this question exhaustively. Justice Washington sought to enumerate them,[1] and lays special stress upon protection by the government; the enjoyment of life and

[1] *Corfield vs. Coryell*, 4 Wash. C. C., 380, 381. He takes as his predicate that only privileges and immunities are intended which must be regarded as "fundamental."

liberty, with the right to acquire and possess property of every kind, and to pursue and obtain happiness and safety, subject, nevertheless, to such restraints as the government may justly prescribe for the general good of the whole; the right of a citizen of one state to pass through or to reside in any other state for purposes of trade, agriculture, professional pursuits, or otherwise; to claim the benefit of the writ of *habeas corpus;* to institute and maintain actions of any kind in the courts of the state; to take, hold and dispose of property, either real or personal; an exemption from higher taxes or impositions than are paid by the other citizens of the state; the exercise of the elective franchise as regulated and established by the laws or constitution of the state in which it is to be exercised. It has never been disputed that all this falls within the limits of article four. In both legislatures and courts, however, the opinion of Judge Curtis has always prevailed.[1] He held that it was not possible to establish pertinently and exhaustively *a priori* what an immunity or a privilege in the sense of this clause really was, and that it was therefore safer to decide the question as presented in each case. This is of course true, too, of "the privileges or immunities of citizens of the United States," which, according to the fourteenth amendment, no state can abridge by law. Cooley (*Principles,* 247) expresses the indisputable view that the adoption of this provision is to be regarded as superfluous, inasmuch as the states manifestly had not the right to do this before. From the adoption of the provision it is evident, however, that the privileges and immunities of citizens of the United States and of the states do not correspond entirely, even if they coincide in part. The former must unquestionably be deduced from the federal constitution.

[1] *Conner vs. Elliot,* Howard, XVIII., 593.

The federal supreme court cite some examples of them in the Slaughter House cases.[1] It declares that as far as the jurisdiction of the federal government extends, such privileges and immunities also exist.[2] In the same case it decided, however, that so far as the privileges and immunities of the citizens of states were concerned, their "safety and protection" are incumbent on the states, and were not put, by the fourteenth amendment, under the "special care" of the federal government.

RIGHTS OF INDIVIDUALS AND THEIR SAFEGUARDS.

§ 84. DUE PROCESS OF LAW AND EQUAL LEGAL PROTECTION. "No person shall be deprived of life, liberty or property without due process of law" (fifth amendment). The fourth, fifth, sixth, seventh and eighth amendments are, in a certain sense, only a more detailed statement and explanation of this principle, which the fourteenth amendment has also made obligatory on the states, and has enlarged for them, so that they cannot refuse to any person under their jurisdiction the equal protection of their laws. It must not be concluded from the fact that the latter provision was not also made expressly obligatory on the federal government that it can at pleasure and constitutionally violate this principle. So, too, the adoption of the first clause of the fourteenth amendment must not be interpreted as meaning that the principle contained in it first became binding upon the states, or upon a part of the states, when this amendment went into force. Except in the case of the slaves, and in part

[1] Wallace, XVI., 79, 80. For further examples see Cooley, *Principles*, 245-247.
[2] "We venture to suggest some which owe their existence to the federal government, its national character, its constitution or its laws."

also of the free colored people, it was always a fundamental principle of the constitution of every single state. But as it was deemed necessary to take care lest, in the former slave states, the colored people should be exposed to all kinds of oppression and wrong, it was also thought necessary to guarantee them safety under the law, and also equality under the law, through the constitution of the United States. But although this is the real cause of the origin of this part of the fourteenth amendment, yet the two clauses are by no means of significance only for the colored people of the former slave states. Some of the most important law-suits in which these clauses have been involved have been fought out in the northern states, and principles of public law of the broadest kind, but with no relation whatever to the race-question, have been involved in them. However unnecessary it may seem at first glance, both clauses need, therefore, a somewhat more detailed discussion.

It is generally admitted that the words "due process of law" are to be understood as a technical expression and as equivalent to the "law of the land" of *magna charta*. It is therefore said that this provision imposes a limitation not only on the courts and the executive, but also on the legislative power,[1] because at the foundation of the law of the land are certain principles; the due process of law is forsaken whenever these principles are violated; and the fact that the violation occurs under the form of a legislative act will not give it legal force. But the law-giving power is simply forbidden to make arbitrary injustice into justice under the form of law, for those principles comprehend only the most general doctrines of the law, viz.: that no one shall be convicted

[1] *Den, Murray and Kayser vs. The Hoboken, etc., Company*, Howard, XVIII., 276.

unheard; that the facts alleged must be examined into; and that a decision shall be made only after a legal trial of the facts in a court of competent jurisdiction.[1] This leaves, therefore, the broadest scope to the legislative will. The words "due process of law," in the fifth and fourteenth amendments, are in full accord with this fundamental doctrine, but they do not say that the procedure must be the same under the federal constitution and the federal laws as under the state constitutions and state laws. As far as the fourteenth amendment is concerned, the states are perfectly free to give the "due process of law" whatever shape they please, as long as they do not violate these fundamental principles. Their own constitutions or laws have made binding upon them in substance the obligations laid upon the federal government by the five amendments already mentioned, but they were not compelled to do this by the federal constitution, and can, so far as it is concerned, change this condition of affairs at any moment. The controversies in constitutional law that may arise out of this provision of the fourteenth amendment would probably never present any considerable difficulties, if it were always easy to define with certainty the meaning of the words, "deprive of property." It was long since decided that the corresponding provision of the fifth amendment, and consequently that the fourteenth, does not forbid every compulsory taking of property without the intervention of a court. The right of taxation absolutely excludes such an interpretation. Moreover, it has not been so much the direct as the indirect taking of property which has given rise to the chief differences of opinion. When, in what manner, and to what extent may a state regulate the management of private property? These are ques-

[1] Webster's *Works*, V., 487, 488.

tions which, partly in connection with the great question of the obligation of legislative contracts, and partly in connection with the question of the guaranty of equal legal protection, have repeatedly of late years occupied the courts, and have justly excited the utmost public interest.

In the case already cited, *Munn vs. Illinois*, 94 U. S., 113, the supreme court laid down the principle that "private property which is affected with a public interest ceases entirely to be *juris privati*." If any person dedicates his property to a use in which the public has an interest, he grants the public an interest in this use, and must himself be subject thereto, so that he must be controlled, so far as this interest so created by him is concerned, by the common good of the public. As to certain kinds of property, this principle has for a long time had a restricted meaning in American jurisprudence. It has never been disputed, for instance, that common carriers had certain duties to the public, and that these could be regulated by law. The question is, however, whether the principle in its broad generality, as laid down in this case by the supreme court, can be admitted, and whether the control by the public — that is, by the state — can always assume the shape of the state's deciding entirely by itself what an owner shall be paid for the use of his property? The principles are elastic enough to involve manifest absurdities, such as the regulation of the rent of dwelling-houses by the state; and it is certain that the state, if it can establish the price to be asked for the use of private property affected with a public interest, could establish that price at such a figure that the owner would be deprived of his property within the meaning of the constitution. In such a case the regulation of the price by law would be manifestly unconstitutional, for the owner would not have been deprived of his property by due process of law. If, for instance, it costs a railroad two cents to carry a passenger a mile, and the state permits it to ask only one cent a mile, the stockholders are deprived of part of their property, because they are thus prevented from getting any income from it. But if the state compels them, as common carriers, to continue business, they are directly deprived, every day, for the benefit of the public using the trains, of a part of their capital, because the operating expenses eat up the capital. Experience has already shown that this kind of oppression does not belong merely to the realm of empty speculation. Public opinion has indulged in highly exaggerated ideas of the profits of railroads, and under the pressure of this public opinion some most dubious experiments have been tried. On the other hand, railroads, elevator companies, and similar corporations, often have a practical monopoly, by which they can oppress, and have in fact oppressed, the public in a way most hurtful to the common weal. The state is therefore warranted in interfering by law to prevent this. A reasonable legal protection for the public against improper profits, when free competition provides no, or at least no sufficient, protection, will not be regarded as a taking of property in the sense of the constitution. As to railroad companies, it has already become very evident that, from other points of view as well, a more thorough state control than formerly may rightly be demanded. Free competition has caused far greater evils than monopoly. The so-called railroad wars not only injure the stockholders, but often lead to catastrophes for the bondholders (who are practically unprotected), and throw the whole business system of the country out of gear. These continually increasing evils have reached such a point that, in my judgment, public opinion will declare with growing emphasis in favor of the doctrine laid down by the supreme court, in spite of the no small danger that its application will be marked with mistakes and misuse at the outset. Ways and means of preventing and curing mistakes and abuses can certainly be found. Many of them will be prevented by the steady growth in public favor of civil service reform, which deprives the public offices of the character of "spoils," of party rewards for party services, and so exerts a strong influence in giving the better elements of the people once more the preponderance in legislative bodies. This will bring about a deep-seated change in the legal systems of the individual states. On certain points, in reference to which the principles of *laisser aller* have hitherto had absolute sway, these principles will be gradually narrowed down. Nevertheless, the fundamental character of all the institutions of the country, the customs and ways, the entire body of thought and feeling of the people, still give ample assurance that state-interference, even if carried too far in this or that particular, will not degenerate into its opposite, that is, into state-control of society.

Other decisions of the federal supreme court, such, for instance, as the Slaughter House cases, already mentioned, show the same tendency in another direction. They do not involve so much the establishment of a new principle as the creation of a check upon the attempts to restrict, unfairly, an already recognized principle on the ground of the fourteenth amendment. The attempt was made to interpret the guarantee of equal protection by the laws in a way which sought on the one hand to make out of this guarantee a strait-jacket for the law-giving power at the expense of the common weal, and on the other hand to subject certain sides of social life to a pressure opposed to the prevailing condition of affairs and simply intolerable. In the name of legal equality efforts were made to limit the police power of the states in a way which would have made a proper care of the public good impossible in many cases. So, too, in the name of legal equality efforts were made to enforce social equality for the negroes. Both views were based on radical tendencies. The states retained the freedom of action they need. On the latter point, it is certain that even to the negroes themselves and even in the former slave states this result was of great value. The whites are not constantly excited against them by having their society forced upon them daily and hourly in railroads, steamboats, hotels, schools, etc.; and still the principle of republican equality is preserved, because the colored people are not treated as inferiors; they get what they pay for; but the law does not require the fact to be ignored, that they are another race, whose complete social amalgamation with the whites would run counter to nature, and therefore in the interest of both races should not be sought.

§ 85. ARRESTS, SEARCH WARRANTS AND SEIZURES. The fourth amendment corresponds to the principle of English law which has found its popular formula in the proud phrase: "My house is my castle." Every man is to be protected against arbitrary acts of the public powers. These must be entrusted with sufficient authority to arrest criminals and to remand them; but they cannot use force to find out whether there is good cause for a judicial inquiry. "The right of the people to be secure in their persons, houses, papers and effects against unreasonable searches and seizures shall not be violated." The second clause (connected with the first by an "and") sets forth what conditions must be fulfilled in order to justify searches, seizures and arrests. It is not expressly stated that these can take place only under a warrant, but this is evident because this clause is simply explanatory of the former. Such an invasion of individual rights without a warrant is not permissible; and, too, quite a number of conditions must be fulfilled in order to give a warrant legal force. These conditions are that probable cause must be shown by oath or affirmation for its issuance and that the warrant itself must clearly describe the place to be searched, the person to be arrested, or the objects to be seized. This latter provision was directed against the so-called general warrants (since abolished) of England, which without such specifications authorized the making of arrests, searches and seizures. The police may of course, without a warrant, in the legitimate discharge of their duties, demand and force admission into a house and make arrests. When a crime has just been committed, this power to arrest without a warrant belongs to every man. The person so arrested must, however, be brought at once before a competent court or magistrate. If any search or seizure has been made without a full compliance with the conditions of this amendment, the person making it is always required to prove that the case is one in which the public interest required this to be done.[1]

§ 86. CRIMINAL JUSTICE. The fifth, sixth and eighth amendments treat especially of the legal safeguards and benefits which must be given a person accused of crime. The sixth amendment is simply an amplification of the third paragraph of the second section of the third article of the constitution. The provision that the trial of all

---

[1] A law which authorized revenue officers to require a merchant to produce his books and papers in order that they might satisfy themselves that the tax-laws had not been evaded has been held constitutional by the courts. This decision may be all right, but the law has led to the grossest abuses.

crimes shall be by jury is enlarged by the guarantee of a speedy and public trial. Inasmuch as some of the states had been divided into two judicial districts, it is moreover provided that the trial shall take place, not only in the state, but also in the judicial district, in which the crime has been committed. Besides this, the accused must be informed of the nature and cause of the charge; must be confronted with the witnesses against him; is entitled to compulsory process for witnesses for the defense and also to the assistance of counsel.[1] The word "jury" means the common-law jury of twelve men, who must give a unanimous verdict. If they cannot agree a new jury must be drawn. According to the act of June 8, 1872, when a jury is being impaneled, in cases of treason and other capital crimes, the accused is entitled to twenty peremptory challenges (that is, may reject twenty jurors without giving any reason) and the United States to five; in other felonies the corresponding figures are ten and three; and in all other cases three jurors may be set aside by each party. The fifth amendment provides that no person shall be held to answer for a capital or "otherwise infamous crime" except "on a presentment or indictment of a grand jury." In a presentment the grand jury acts upon its own knowledge without any indictment having been presented to it, and the indictment must afterwards be supplied by the court. In indictments the grand jury does not act on its own initiative, but on an indictment submitted to it for its decision. It is admitted that the expression "infamous crime" is a technical one, but the definitions are neither sufficiently clear nor entirely harmonious.[2] This is, however, to a certain extent,

[1] In England, persons accused of crime were not entitled to the assistance of counsel until the passage of the act of 1836.
[2] Brunner, in the supplement to the second edition of Desty's *Con-*

of no importance, because in all crimes which come within the judicial power of the United States, the complaint is made either by presentment or indictment. A grand jury, according to the law of March 3, 1865, must consist of not less than sixteen nor more than twenty-three jurors.¹ This provision of the fifth amendment does not apply to the federal army or to the militia when the latter, in time of public peril or of war, is in the service of the United States; in other words, they may be subjected by law to courts-martial. No one can be compelled in any criminal case to be a witness against himself. No one can be twice put in jeopardy of life or limb for the same offense. A man is put into jeopardy (in the sense of this clause) only when the jury has given a verdict. If the trial has to be stopped for any legal reason, it does not count as a trial under this provision. So, too, of course, when the person tried is granted a new trial; because the law gives him this for his own benefit. A new trial is granted when the court considers the finding contrary to law or to the evidence produced. In capital cases the court can, even without the consent of the accused, discharge the jury if it thinks there is good ground for doing so. If the jury bring in a verdict which covers only some points of the complaint, the accused is protected against a new trial as to these, but not as to the others. If the jury is dismissed without the consent of the accused, and it was not a case in which the law recognizes this as necessary, such, for instance, as a mistrial, he cannot again be tried for the same offense

stitution of the United States, p. 320, says: "Infamous crimes, in the meaning of this clause, are only those made infamous or declared a felony by express act of congress:" and cites in proof of this *United States vs. Wynn*, McCrary, III., 266.

¹ See J. Proffatt, *Law of Jury Trial*, San Francisco, 1877; H. Hirsh, *Law relating to Juries*, N. Y., 1879.

although he has not been acquitted.[1] The eighth amendment forbids the requirement of excessive bail, the imposition of excessive fines and the infliction of cruel and unusual punishments. Bail is always admitted, except when the crime charged is punishable by death or lifelong imprisonment. Even in these cases it may be taken.

§ 87. JURY TRIALS IN CIVIL CASES. The seventh amendment provides "that in suits at common law, where the value in controversy shall exceed twenty dollars, the right of trial by jury shall be preserved; and no fact tried by a jury shall be otherwise re-examined in any court of the United States than according to the rules of the common law." As only the preservation of a right is here concerned, this evidently refers to the English common law at the time of the adoption of the constitution, and the intention is to extend the right, so far as constitutional law permits, to cases in which it did not exist before. Moreover, since it is only a right, the parties can waive it.[2] So, too, the right is sufficiently preserved when, in case of appeal from the first decision, a trial by jury may be demanded. It is to be noticed, again, that the right is restricted to suits

[1] To the provisions of the fifth amendment as to criminal procedure, there is coupled-on the prohibition against taking private property for public uses without just compensation. It goes without saying that the right of expropriation belongs to the federal government only when public uses within its jurisdiction are concerned. It relates back to the "right of eminent domain" and this belongs to the states, except as to those rights deduced from this, which the constitutional purposes of the federal government require to be vested in it. In the territories the United States have the right of eminent domain. If a territory be transformed into a state, the right passes over to the latter. As to the right of eminent domain see Cooley, *Constitutional Limitations*, ch. XV.

[2] This is not true of criminal cases. In them the jury is a necessary part of the court, and the accused cannot waive it.

at common law; in equity and in admiralty and maritime courts, it does not exist. If in a common-law suit the question of fact has been decided by a jury and an appeal is taken, the appellate court has nothing to do with the question of fact; it has simply to decide whether the law was properly applied. It is only when a new trial is granted that questions of fact are retried, but even then they must be decided again by a jury. The seventh amendment also applies in common-law suits, which have first been tried with a jury in a state court and are then brought by appeal before the United States supreme court.

AMENDMENT OF THE CONSTITUTION.

§ 88. For Amending the Constitution, different methods are provided by the fifth article. The initiatory step may be taken either by congress or by the state legislatures. The latter cannot propose any amendments, but congress must call a convention for this purpose if the legislatures of two-thirds of the states demand it. This has never yet happened. All amendments have been proposed by congress, in which body two-thirds of each house must favor the proposition. The states decide whether its proposals shall be ratified, but congress determines whether the vote of the states is to be cast by their legislatures or by conventions called for that particular purpose. In either case, a ratification requires the assent of three-fourths of the states. The constitution says nothing as to an obligation on the part of the states to come to any conclusion about a proposed amendment. In practice it has been decided that there is no such obligation. I have already discussed the question whether and how far a state is bound by its assent once given. This has never been properly settled, and it is by no means impossible that it may yet give rise to serious difficulties.

PART THIRD.

THE CONSTITUTIONAL AND GENERAL LAW OF THE SEPARATE STATES.

§ 89. PRELIMINARY REMARKS. I cannot attempt to treat the general law of each of the thirty-eight states separately. Regard for space would make this impossible, even if the sketch were confined to the most superficial outline. Yet a superficial sketch would present an endless array of repetitions. But, on the other hand, the most cursory perusal of the different state constitutions suffices to convince any one that it would be just as inadmissible to select a certain state and to analyze its general law as a type of the whole. The selection would be entirely arbitrary; for there are so many and such important differences in details that no state can be used as a pattern or type of the rest. It must suffice, therefore, to give a general characterization in broad outlines, laying especial stress upon what is common to all or nearly all, and briefly noting the most important differences. In order to lessen the repetition which is unavoidable, and not to heap up a mass of useless details, I shall not always note to how many or to which states what I say applies. If the matters concerned are peculiar to one or to a few states, this will be pointed out. The omission to point it out must nevertheless not be construed as meaning always that the statement is one of quite general application. In the more important questions in which this is the case I shall say so expressly.

§ 90. ORIGIN OF THE CONSTITUTIONS. The constitutions of the states are without exception the work of constitutional conventions.[1] But many constitutions contain provisions that became constituent parts of them without the meeting of any constitutional convention. Conventions are instruments which the people use for reasons of expediency in constitution-making; but their task should always be limited to drafting a plan of a constitution. The people — as all the constitutions say, in a more or less precise formula — are the sole possessor of political power, and they alone, therefore, can give the state its fundamental law. These are fundamental principles. It is not only theoretically that they are of the highest importance. It has repeatedly become of the greatest political significance, that conventions — partly by appealing to precedents in the struggle of the colonies with the mother country, and partly in imitation of the convention of the first French revolution — have claimed to be the bearers of the people's sovereignty,— a claim that in its final logical results tends to a complete overturning of the fundamental principle of American popular government, that is, transforms popular sovereignty into its very opposite.[2] This doctrine, which rests on the logical ab-

[1] Americans distinguish between revolutionary and constitutional conventions, and many conventions are held in the United States which have nothing to do with adopting or amending a constitution.

[2] It suffices to recall those conventions which decreed their respective states out of the Union after the presidential election of 1860. The Lecompton convention in Kansas, in 1857, was theoretically of peculiar interest and practically of great importance. It proposed to the people to vote, not whether or no they would adopt the whole constitution as drafted, but simply whether they would have "the constitution with slavery" or "the constitution without slavery." The majority of the people did not want the constitution at all. At the election ordered by the convention "the constitution with slavery" was adopted by 6,266 against 567 votes. The territorial legislature had already fixed a later day for voting on the general question, and at this election 10,266 votes were cast against the constitution

surdity of a transfer of sovereignty, which is identical with its entire alienation, is constantly losing ground, especially as far as the drafting of an entire constitution is concerned. Some of the constitutions provide, not only that the people shall decide whether a general revision of the constitution is to be made by a convention, but also that the revised or new constitution shall be submitted to the people and be voted upon by them. Hundreds of thousands of citizens can act, of course, only through representatives, as far as the drafting of the constitution is concerned, but in these cases the people have reserved to themselves, expressly and unconditionally, the initiative as well as the final decision.[1]

Here, therefore, no argument can be found in support of the other erroneous, and at least equally dangerous, doctrine that "the people"— meaning by this the majority of the persons with full political rights — can, by virtue of their sovereignty, amend a constitution in any form or manner other than that prescribed in the constitution. The idea of popular sovereignty has entirely lost in the United States that vague and demagogic character which in the first French revolution made it the cause as well as the cloak of all imaginable horrors.

and only 162 in favor of it. The result was a bitter and protracted parliamentary struggle, which finally ended with the victory of the free-soil party and of the principle of popular sovereignty, but only after the slave states had seceded. The number of conventions which have not submitted their work to the people is not small. Jameson (p. 446) reckons forty of them up to 1866. Twenty-nine of these revised the existing constitutions. During the same time there were seventy-eight conventions which followed the correct principle. Some constitutions contain no provisions at all about revision by convention.

[1] This applies only to the revision of a constitution by a convention. I shall refer hereafter to the initiative of legislatures as to separate amendments.

Popular sovereignty is the sole basis, not only in theory but in practice, of the entire legal system of the Union as well as of the several states; but according to the American theory and practice, popular sovereignty is not identical with a boundless arbitrariness. The people cannot be bound, but they can bind themselves; and precisely because they have bound themselves they have less right to place themselves above the law established by their own sovereign will. Although this perverted conception of the substance of sovereignty has already had its history in the United States,[1] these principles nevertheless, from generation to generation, have more and more mingled with the flesh and blood of Americans; and this explains the fact, often so surprising to Europeans, that we see displayed upon the broadest democratic basis a political system which, in general, is characterized by an eminently conservative spirit. Demagogy has often found in this system a wide field, but experiments and innovations have so far shown themselves only as exceptions which prove the rule, and the agitation in these exceptional cases, except as to the doctrines of the radical abolitionists, has never passed beyond legal bounds. Not despite, but in a great measure because of, the carrying out of the principle of popular sovereignty, the United States have hitherto been a less favorable field for revolutionary tendencies than most European states. We must not conclude from this, as Americans are wont to do, that this would self-evidently and always be the case, under other relations and with other nations.

§ 91. CONSTITUENT PARTS OF THE CONSTITUTIONS. The constitutions usually consist of three parts: the bill of

[1] See, especially, the history of "Dorr's rebellion" in Rhode Island in 1841. The essential facts of it are concisely stated by Jameson, p. 216 *et seq.*

rights, the constitution proper, or frame of government, and the so-called schedule. The last, strictly construed, is no constituent part of the constitution at all, but only an appendix of temporary importance. Some constitutions do not have it at all. It contains mainly provisions as to how the people shall manifest their acceptance or rejection of the proposed constitution, and as to the arrangements necessary (in case of acceptance) in passing from the old to the new condition.

The bill of rights contains the "fundamental rights." As a rule it is thus entitled, and is put at the beginning of the constitution. The discussion of bills of rights in detail does not seem necessary, for not only do they agree in their essential contents, but they merely set forth at large and in detail the principles which have already been stated as arising from the so-called bill of rights of the federal constitution. It must be emphasized that here, too, the fundamental rights are not first granted by the constitution; they are regarded as existing rights, and are enumerated in the constitution only in order to protect them in the most effective way against any violation by the organs of public power. And for this reason, the bill of rights often ends with the declaration that the enumeration of certain fundamental rights must not be construed as meaning that the people have waived others.

ORGANIZATION OF THE GOVERNMENT. The separation of the legislative, executive and judicial powers is as thoroughly carried out in all the states as in the federal government. Many of the state constitutions expressly declare that no one of the three shall trespass upon the spheres of the others, so far as the constitution does not otherwise provide.

§ 92. THE LEGISLATIVE POWER. As a rule the official name of a state legislature is "the general assembly," but in ordinary speech it is called simply the legislature. In all the states the legislatures consist of two chambers; the more numerous is styled the assembly or house of representatives, and the smaller the senate. Neither the franchise nor the right to seek office were originally controlled by radical democratic principles. In the course of time these have become more and more victorious everywhere. Although certain restrictions still exist here and there, yet all in all I am justified in saying that since the adoption of the fifteenth amendment so-called universal suffrage has become the rule everywhere. So, too, the restrictions on the right to seek office relate only to the age and to the domicile. The provisions as to the latter are much more strict than in the constitutional states of Europe. In the latter the principle prevails that the voters may seek their representatives where they please, but in the United States it is thought necessary to lay great stress upon local representation. In some of the states the regulation of this question is not even left to legislation; the constitutions provide that the transfer of the domicile from the election district involves absolutely the loss of the office and excludes — of course — re-election. As generally recognized is the principle that paid officials cannot be members of the legislature. This applies, indeed, to state as well as federal officials.[1] On the other hand, no member of the legislature can be appointed to a state office which was created or had its emoluments increased during his term of membership. In a few of the states clergymen are also excluded from the legislature. If different qualifications are required for membership in the two chambers, it is only as to age.

[1] Some officeholders, such as justices of the peace, are usually excepted, because they cannot be regarded as officials in the ordinary sense of the word, although they occupy a public office.

A difference in principle, such as that which applies to the two houses of congress has no existence in the case of the two chambers of a legislature. The senators as well as the members of the assembly are directly voted for at the polls, and the sole difference is in the size of the election district.[1]

The term of office is, with few exceptions, a different one, and that of the senators is generally twice that of the assemblymen. The rule is four and two years, respectively. These figures are never exceeded. In the assembly the members' terms all end at the same time. In the senate, as a rule, half the members hold over. This increases the possibility (as it does in the case of congress) that the two chambers will be controlled by different parties; but, on the other hand, the continuity in the upper chamber serves to strengthen conservative tendencies. More stress may be laid upon this because — as we shall see when we discuss the executive power — in the separate states even more than in the federal government, parliamentary government, in the European sense of the word, is something entirely foreign to American constitutional and general law.

The regular meetings of the legislatures take place, some annually and some every second year. Of late, the drift of public opinion has been such that probably in the

[1] In Illinois the constitution of 1870 introduced minority representation for the house of representatives. The section reads: "The house of representatives shall consist of three times the number of the members of the senate, and the term of office shall be two years. Three representatives shall be elected in each senatorial district. . . . In all elections of representatives aforesaid, each qualified voter may cast as many votes for one candidate as there are representatives to be elected, or may distribute the same, or equal parts thereof, among the candidates, as he shall see fit, and the candidates highest in votes shall be declared elected."

course of time annual sessions will disappear. Experience, it is said, has proven in many states, that the legislatures, having naught to do with higher politics, can very well, in ordinary times, attend in one session to all real wants in the way of legislation for two years, and extraordinary circumstances are sufficiently cared for by the fact that the governor can call special sessions of the legislature. The experience of the states which have annual legislative sessions has also shown that the legislatures, when they do not find enough to do, always know how to make something to do. Once assembled, they seem to feel in duty bound to sit for a certain time and to pass a certain number of laws. The legislative statistics of the states which have tried both plans show that with annual sessions just as many laws are passed each year as with biennial sessions are passed every second year. In the former case it is evident that many laws which were at least unnecessary have been enacted; and unnecessary laws, simply because they are unnecessary, always do harm. The stability of relations so essential to the welfare of the state and of society is thus quite uselessly destroyed and a highly dangerous craving for experiment fostered. That there is much truth in this argument cannot be disputed by any one who examines the facts without prejudice. The opinion that it might be wise to bridle the legislative zeal for law-making is too old a one, in the United States, to be suppressed by declaring it to be a heresy affecting the fundamental principles of democracy. Several constitutions limit the length of the session. Indeed, they measure out the time in quite a niggardly way — forty and forty-five (but also sixty and ninety) days. Of course, the established time can be exceeded, but it needs so large a majority to do this that it cannot be done easily or on any but really valid grounds. The constitution of Nebraska (adopted 1867) tried an odd remedy. It did not limit the duration of the sessions, but while, like the constitutions of all the other states, it adopted the principle of paying the members of the legislature a *per diem*, it provided that they should not be paid this for more than forty days. As far as the desired effect can be expected from this sort of pressure, it could also be brought about by paying a proper annual salary instead of a *per diem*. This has also been tried (in Wisconsin, by an amendment adopted by the people in 1867), but except in the case of these states public opinion has either not yet been warmed up to these experiments, or has busied itself only with the question whether changes in this direction are desirable.

The question of the powers of the legislatures is essentially different in constitutional law from the question of the powers of congress. Congress has only the powers granted it by the federal constitution. The legislative power of the state legislatures, on the contrary, is unlimited, as far as no limits are set to it by the federal or the state constitution.[1] This does not mean, however, that these restrictions must always be expressed in explicit words. As it is generally admitted that the factors of the federal government have certain "implied powers," so it has never been disputed that the state legislatures are subject to "implied restrictions," that is, restrictions which must be deduced from certain provisions of the federal or state constitution, or that arise from the polit-

---

[1] "The rule of construction of state constitutions is that they are not special grants of power to legislative bodies, like the constitution of the United States, but general grants of all the usually recognized powers of legislation not actually prohibited or expressly excepted. The exception must be construed strictly as against those who stand upon it, and liberally in favor of the government." *Southern Pacific R. R. Co. vs. Orton*, 6 Sawyer, 157; Hammond, I., 20, § 28.

ical nature of the Union, from the genius of American public institutions, etc. But in a discussion of the authority of the state legislatures, the question always is, not what can they do, but what cannot they do? Then comes the further question: how must they do what they are authorized to do? On both questions, I can here present only a few especially significant or especially characteristic results of the doctrines already developed.

The legislative initiative belongs exclusively to the legislatures and to both chambers in exactly the same way. It is true that here and there an assembly has been granted the privilege of originating all "money bills," but the idea has steadily become of more general acceptance that there is even less reason for a legislature's than for congress's taking the English constitution as a pattern in this particular. For the senates of the state legislatures are just as much popular bodies (*i. e.*, representatives of the people) as the assemblies. There is therefore no analogy of relations. This freedom of initiative does not, however, involve complete freedom in matters of form. A large number of state constitutions provide expressly that every law shall contain but one subject,— a provision that might well be brought into the federal constitution, because wrong is often done in federal legislation by the so-called "riders."[1] The "appropriation bills," especially, have been used to carry through measures which, if proposed independently, would either not have received a majority of votes in congress or else not have been approved by the president. As long as it has not been expressly declared unconstitutional, in so many words, to couple together in one law subjects foreign to each other, and, moreover, as long as the president (or, in a state, the governor) can only approve or return appropriation bills

[1] See my *Constitutional History*, III.

in toto, the majority of one or the other house will be exposed to the temptation — especially in times of great political excitement — of making their will law in this disloyal and disgraceful way.

Of scarcely less importance is the provision, found likewise in many constitutions, that each bill must be read three times loudly and distinctly, word for word. If this had to be done in congress, much mischief would be prevented. There the bills are often read only by their titles, and at the close of each session a veritable flood of bills breaks upon the house. And they are voted upon, although most members have no inkling of the contents of a large part of them. It goes without saying that this results in smuggling through, every year, many things which could not stand the light of day.

There is a striking clause in several constitutions which provides that for the adoption of a proposed bill the majority of those present, that is, of the members voting, shall not suffice, but that a majority of all the members elected is required. The essential motive for this provision may be the quite general belief that the welfare of the people is best subserved if the legislative machine moves as safely as possible, and that therefore the disadvantages resulting from the difficulty of passing good laws are more than counterbalanced by the benefits resulting from the difficulty of passing bad laws. It is, however, not improbable that this rule is more particularly directed against the danger that laws which did not correspond with the real will of the legislature might be carried through by an unscrupulous minority by deftly seizing the opportunity of voting on them at a certain moment when a bare quorum was present. It is easy to think so, because in the constitutions of more recent date manifold other provisions have been adopted that can be explained only by the conviction that enough care can scarcely be taken to guard against the tricks of unprincipled politicians who have known how to win a seat in the legislature.[1] The precautions taken go so far in some cases that the courts either cannot take cognizance of violations of the provisions in point or for other reasons cannot make them the basis of a decision,— a manifest and very dangerous anomaly; for, if unconstitutionality makes laws null and void, and courts must decide whether laws are unconstitutional, the constitutions should contain no provisions which may cause the constitutional question to be raised at any moment, but in the very nature of the thing exclude every possibility of its decision. Moreover, the abuses in the legislatures in the separate states, to which these provisions so pointedly refer, cannot possibly be prevented by such formal precautions. These apply solely to the symptoms. They leave the causes utterly untouched. When, however, it is thought necessary to provide in a most skilful way these formal precautions, it is evident that the abuses are so grave as to demand the most serious efforts to reach their roots. And this the more, because the limits of the legislative authority of the legislatures are so wide, and as a result of the principle already laid down cannot be defined with the certainty and clearness that might be wished. It is far easier to prevent an abuse of power if what may be done can be defined than it is when the only statement is as to what may not be done, and yet the necessary freedom of action is to be preserved. But if in the prac-

[1] See in the *Nation* of July 15, 1875, the article entitled "A New Kind of Veto." It says that "provisions like these . . . proceed not upon the theory that certain subjects have been proved by experience improper for legislation, but on the much simpler theory that the legislature is a body which cannot be trusted to act honestly."

tical workings of legislation evils have come to light and have developed in such a threatening manner that it has been deemed necessary to provide such formal precautions, this is scarcely at all due to the fact that the choice of means to prevent such evils, when the constitutions were drafted, was not quite happy. The appearance and development of these evils is much more due to quite special causes, chief among which is the fact that offices are treated as party booty (spoils) for the payment of party services, and thereby politics is made a business which is the more profitable the more unclean it is, and which promises a man a surer chance to climb the political ladder the more he subordinates statesmanship to the political machine. Apart from this question of office, the regulation of which, moreover, is mainly left to the law-giving power, the constitutions have found very correctly the points which are the most essential for assuring pure legislation intended for the true welfare of the people. Moreover, the correct fundamental principles are as a rule applied to details in a proper and effective way with no small skill. Many of the constitutions put each individual member of the legislature, as far as possible, under the steady and immediate control of public opinion, by providing that in passing bills and in all elections by the legislature the vote must be by roll-call and *viva voce*, while, on the contrary, in popular elections the secret vote by ballot is the unbroken rule of all the states. The more recent constitutions are especially careful to keep the legislatures as far as possible from all temptations to abuse their power. Experience has taught that these temptations are most potent in cases of "special legislation," and therefore the tendency has become stronger to bind the hands of the legislatures as firmly as possible in relation to this; to allow them to enact only general laws in order not to give advantages of one kind or another to individuals at the expense of all. Special attention is therefore given in the constitutions to the chapter on "corporations." In relation to these the course of legislation is as precisely defined as the nature of the subject will permit. For inasmuch as this involves moneyed interests, often of vast proportions, the most powerful levers may be applied to break a wide gap for corruption. The power to pledge the means or credit of a state in any wise whatsoever for a corporation is either strictly limited or entirely denied. Some constitutions go still further. They seek generally to keep the state aloof from all matters in which considerable sums are to be spent in a manner which might offer people with easy consciences and dexterous as well as covetous hands a good opportunity to fill their own pockets out of the public purse. Several constitutions absolutely prohibit the state's undertaking such works of general utility as are called in the United States "internal improvements." Others refuse the power to contract debts in this behalf,— a policy that certainly has two sides to it. To show this I need only refer to the history of the Erie canal, which New York must in a large measure thank for her dominant position in the economic life of the Union. This example points to the second motive, that, besides the reasons assigned, lies at the foundation of these provisions. The American people is almost unanimous in the opinion that the state should undertake no tasks which private efforts can compass. This opinion has been strengthened of late by the history of the land grants to railroads, since the completion of the great transcontinental railroads, which without such assistance could not have been built.[1]

[1] These roads, however, are not the only ones which have received land grants from congress. The first grants were made September 20, 1850, for the benefit of the Illinois Central, Mobile & Chicago,

Among the most intelligent and cultured Americans the admission is, however, not infrequently made that the state's sphere of activity at present cannot be extended beyond what is barely necessary, because the government is in such hands that increased activity by it in the direction indicated might be expected to add new and greater evils to the evils now due to private control of large public interests, such as the greater part of the public channels of commerce. It is evident not only from the formal precautions already mentioned, but also from many other constitutional provisions, that the idea prevails that a legislature must be approached with a certain amount of distrust. In this respect, the constitutions are a faithful expression of public opinion. This is, indeed, one of the most characteristic differences between the constitutions of the separate states of the Union on the one hand, and on the other hand the constitutions of European states, and also that of the United States. On an important question this distrust sometimes assumes a shape which lets it appear more in the light of a guardianship, but it is none the less overwhelming.[1] As a rule, so

---

and Mobile & Ohio River roads. From the date mentioned until March 3, 1873,— since then, so far as I know, no grants have been made,— there were one hundred grants to seventy-two railroads, making a total of about one hundred and ninety million acres. The last figure is calculated from those given in the report of the commissioner of the general land office, but the government itself declares that these figures are unreliable. The Union and Central Pacific received, besides the land grants, a subsidy of about $55,000,000 in the form of a government guarantee of their bonds. The government has as security a second mortgage on the railroads. The land grants are so made that a certain number of sections on both sides of the line of road is granted for each mile built. The number of sections varies.

[1] The following utterances of the *Nation* of January 29, 1885, are very noteworthy: "The assembling of the legislatures of the various

far as financial legislation is concerned, the legislatures are subject to very precise rules. These are intended to prevent a disordered and lax management of the finances, and as they attain their aim as far as constitutional provisions can do so, they present no occasion for unfavorable criticism. The unconditional obligation, when a public debt is contracted, to make arrangements at the same time for its redemption — sometimes the redemption must take place within a very limited time — unquestionably deserves all praise. A very peculiar impression is made, however, by the fact that the constitutions fix the maximum of the permissible state debt, and in fact fix it so low that even a small city could bear the burden without peril. The extraordinary instances of a war, of sedition or of an invasion are always excepted, indeed, and

states for their winter's work has attracted fresh attention to the machinery of legislation and produced many suggestions on the subject. All of these rest generally on the idea that most legislative work in the United States is defective and slipshod; that the laws are badly drawn; that they are passed without proper reference to and comparison with statutes already in force; that they are frequently jobs disguised as statutes. Governor Hill, of this state [New York], in his first message, recommended that a lawyer be appointed as permanent legislative counsel, to draft bills, to advise the members and committees with reference to proposed legislation, and to inspect the various bills before their final passage, so as to detect errors and imperfections and to suggest neccessary amendments. The necessity of taking some such step, he thinks, is shown very clearly by the fact that, during the session of 1883, in this state, some forty-five bills were recalled from the executive chamber after their final passage for necessary amendment and correction, while during the session of 1884 there were fifty such instances(!). The critics of the governor's recommendation can only say in reply to this that such work ought to be done by the legislative committees themselves; but the evil to be cured is the fact that the committees will not do it. The only machinery for preventing bad legislation at Albany is the veto of the governor, and the governor now has to do the work of legal adviser to the legislature, through the veto power, in a very clumsy way; *i. e.*, the American states are rich enough to make their ordinary taxes meet their ordinary wants by honest and half-way reasonable economy without difficulty. But a refusal, except in the cases when the very existence of the state is more or less threatened, of the right to negotiate a loan,— for the right of borrowing a few hundred thousand dollars is but a nominal one,— such a refusal can be justified only on the supposition that certain tasks which are ordinarily performed by the civilized states of the old world ought not to be undertaken by the American states, if these tasks require the expenditure of more money than the current revenue can supply. In such matters, the states cannot go to work in a far-sighted way for future benefits. They must limit themselves to a policy of to-day and to-morrow. It is evident from the

he has in most cases to correct defects by killing the bills, when, if the legislature could have been properly advised at the outset, amendments might have been made which would have enabled him to sign them." These circumstances are the more significant because in all legislatures lawyers form the most prominent element. These evils appear in their worst form in the so-called "private bills." Of these the article quoted says: "As soon as business begins, a great crop of bills is introduced, most of which are designed to give some person or corporation a special privilege under, or exemption from, the operation of laws binding on the community. These bills are drawn up, not by the legislators who introduce them, but by lawyers privately retained and paid by the special interests behind the bills, and who, naturally enough, as long as they get what their clients want, care very little what the effect on the general body of the law may be. When the bills, thus prepared, get into committee, there are no rules of any value governing the procedure with regard to them. Those interested adversely have not necessarily any notice to appear; there is no attempt to take proof judicially, but 'counsel' are permitted to make any statements they please." As a remedy the procedure is proposed, the introduction of which, more than half a century ago, put such an effective end to similar confusion in England. In Massachusetts this approved method has already been introduced to a certain extent.

provisions cited as to internal improvements that this was more or less consciously the intention of the framers of the state constitutions. In this they have found themselves on the whole in accord with the character of the actual development of the relations of life in the United States up to the present time. Americans — viewed from the stand-point of the most highly civilized states of Europe — are still obliged to apply the greatest part of their strength in working out of the rough and in laying broad and deep the foundations of a civilized state of the highest order. They have not the surplus of time, of intellect and of capital needed to extend the state's activity as far and place it on as sure a footing as in the oldest civilized states of Europe. Hitherto, too, they have had no occasion to give up the fundamental idea of their policy, for the result has proved that the peculiar problems of civilization, with which they have been brought face to face, will be soonest and best solved by the state's retiring into the back-ground. In that event, the organization of society and its organic work result in the freest possible action; and in society the initiative and power of the individual is given the widest scope. The duties of the state are much more limited, and therefore general law has not only a different but a much smaller field; but the (strictly speaking) constitutional-law side of general law is far more developed than in any nation on the European continent. Even the language shows this. It contains no word that fully corresponds to our German idea of general law. It is therefore scarcely surprising, that — at least as far as my knowledge extends — there is no work which treats of general law as we would understand this in Europe. All the books worth consideration treat only of constitutional law or particular parts of it. They simply touch here and there upon those points of general law which are not in the narrower sense of the word constitutional. This and also the great scarcity of monographs on this part of general law indicate, in fact, that there is no proper interest in such questions. But this is partly explained by the fact that from lack of material many chapters must be written in as many lines as pages would be required in which to treat the subject in a European state.

The United States have immense, and some of the states have very considerable, expanses of public lands. But they do not cultivate them. They simply sell them. These public lands hide mineral treasures of every kind. But the state does not mine them. It simply passes laws as to how private persons can acquire the right of mining. As to how the mining is carried on, it concerns itself little or not at all. There are no mining-officials just as there is no administration of the public domain. Legislation on mining is practically restricted to the point named. The products of agriculture are so enormous that they have become one of the most important factors in the world's economy, but agriculture is so far outside the domain of the federal government that it can do little more than gather statistics about it.[1] The separate states on the whole adhere to the principle that the farmer, like the shoe-maker and tailor, must find out for himself what is good for him.[2] There is a series of

[1] It seems, therefore, foolish to try at the present time (January, 1885) to create an agricultural department at Washington.

[2] Some attempts have been made to promote the improvement and development of natural resources by state aid. Thus, for instance, the constitution of Maryland provides that a "superintendent of labor and agriculture" shall be elected by the people to serve for four years and leaves it to the legislature to determine whether the office shall continue to exist. His chief duties are to be to "supervise all the state inspectors of agricultural products and fertilizers" and to

questions in which the general good imperiously and urgently demands the interference of the state (for instance in the management of forests) to lead public opinion to such a point that it will allow or demand the setting aside of the doctrine of *laisser faire*. With absolutely criminal laxness all energetic measures to prevent the forest fires caused by carelessness, which annually destroy millions of property, are still neglected. And although de-foresting has already become a public calamity and danger of terrible magnitude, nothing has yet been done to prevent it except offering rewards of different kinds for tree planting.[1] Neither the United States nor the states, therefore, have taken any especial care about natural products. As far as trade is concerned, the federal govern-

"enquire into the undeveloped resources of wealth of the state of Maryland, more especially concerning those within the limits of the Chesapeake Bay and its tributaries, which belong to the state, and suggest such plans as may be calculated to render them available as sources of revenue." His duties, moreover, embrace those of the former commissioner of immigration and the immigration agent. (Many states have officials who are charged with the advancement of immigration and everything connected therewith.) In Alabama, the constitution of 1868 created a bureau of industrial resources with similar but still more comprehensive duties. Even where the constitutions provide nothing of this kind, something has sometimes been done by legislation here and there. The federal government does a great deal for the discovery and improvement of natural resources by its very exact geological surveys. These show in detail all other particulars about the districts examined. Even the preservation of the wealth of fish in the ocean and in the lakes has been the care of the federal government. The act of February 9, 1871, created a commissioner of fish and fisheries for the study of the questions involved.

[1] In this respect the federal government does more than the individual states. If a man plants trees in a certain way for eight years upon ten out of one hundred and sixty acres, and at the end of the eight years has at least six hundred and seventy-five vigorous trees on each of the ten acres, he becomes the owner of the entire tract.

ment comes to the front, for it has to regulate foreign and inter-state commerce. Since it has not hitherto deemed it necessary to have a special minister of commerce, the states, of course, have felt much less need of entrusting special officers with the care of commercial interests. Industry is very greatly influenced by federal tariff legislation, but industries as such lie outside the jurisdiction of the federal government. Factory-laws and business legislation are matters for the separate states, which, so far as I know, have given them so little attention that they can scarcely be called the care and province of the state.[1] Of the many-sided social-political problems so vigorously agitated in Germany at present, the only one, so far as I am informed, which has played any part in state or federal legislation, is the question of the legal or normal day of labor. In what states and in what way the question of child-labor in factories has been regulated by law, I am unable to say; for the laws of all the thirty-eight states are not at my disposal. At least some of the states have put certain limits on individual freedom in this respect. This is evident from the general laws relating to attendance at school. The school system and ecclesiastical affairs will, however, be discussed later in special paragraphs. Here it need only be said that the state's interference with these, in comparison with what all the European states do, is also very slight. The bureau of education at Washington must confine itself, on grounds of constitutional law, to collecting statistical and other materials, elaborating them in a useful way, and bringing them to the knowledge of the people; and even in the individual states a "minister of public in-

[1] This may not be entirely true of all the states, especially the North Atlantic states.

struction" would be a luxury. A "Kultus-minister"—a minister of worship—is simply a non-existent thing for the United States and for the separate states. There is no field in the separate states even for a minister in charge of the channels of public intercourse. The post is controlled by the nation, and railroads and telegraphs with few exceptions are purely private undertakings. "Public works" these certainly are, but in general they play such a subordinate part that even where there is a board of public works, its duties are often assigned to other higher public officials as secondary work. Public benevolent institutions, hospitals, blind asylums, deaf-and-dumb asylums, houses of correction for neglected children and juvenile offenders, poor-houses, etc., are supported by all the states. In the new and sparsely settled states, of course everything desirable in this direction is not, and cannot, be done at once. But even in most of the older states the public care for these interests does not go as far and is not as systematic as in the most highly developed nations of Europe. This is partly because even these older states are still in process of development, but in a great measure also because private charity relieves the state of these as well as of many other burdens to an extent which would be strange in Europe. The fact that the states are almost all still in the process of formation, as well as the more intense and comprehensive independent action of various organizations for public purposes within the states, bring about the result that the entire state administrative apparatus, in organization and in efficiency, has crystallized, far less than in Europe, into fixed, systematic and thoroughly constituted forms. The administrative *personnel* is much more changeful and therefore the administration does not possess the same stability. Although this is fraught with manifold evils, yet these evils are far less numerous and important than an European observer would suppose. This is partly because the administration has much more limited tasks, and partly because the people have for generations undergone a schooling in self-administration and self-government which the people of continental Europe have never had. If the general law of America has much less extent than that of Europe, on the other hand the chapter on self-government in the public relations of the United States is far more extensive.

§ 93. THE EXECUTIVE. At the head of the executive power of all the states is a governor, elected directly by the people. All male inhabitants are eligible as governor, provided they are of full age, have the franchise, and have been for a certain time citizens of the United States and inhabitants of the state. This time is very different in different states. The right of re-election is unlimited in most states. Where this is not the case the same person can occupy the office, at most, only a certain number of years within a fixed period, or else an immediate re-election is prohibited. If the popular elections result in no choice, the legislature elects one of the two candidates who received the highest number of votes. The particular provisions for this event vary greatly. The term of office is from one to four years. In about half the states it is four, and in the majority of the remainder two years. If by death, removal from office or sickness a vacancy occurs in the gubernatorial chair, the lieutenant-governor, elected by the people at the same time as the governor and for the same period, exercises the functions of governor.[1] After the lieutenant-governor, the president of the senate and then the speaker

[1] Impeachment is common to all the states. In all essential matters, the procedure follows the prototype of impeachment under the

of the assembly replaces the governor. A minority of the states have no lieutenant-governor. In these, the president of the senate generally takes the place first, but sometimes the secretary of state does so.

The duties and rights of the governor correspond on the whole to those of the president of the United States, but in sundry respects his authority is much less. His first and most general duty is to take care that the laws are executed. He represents, further, the state externally, especially in relation to the other states. He influences legislation in the same way as the president does. In his messages, in which he makes a report to the legislature of the condition of the state, he also suggests the enactment of such laws as seem necessary or expedient, but he can make no formal proposal of a law. All bills require his assent. If he does not approve them, they must be adopted by a very large majority in both houses in order to become laws nevertheless. As a rule, a two-thirds majority is required, sometimes two-thirds not only of those present, but of the whole membership.[1]

federal constitution. The assembly is prosecutor, the senate judge. A two-thirds majority is required for conviction. Its consequence is the loss of office. It is noteworthy that some of the constitutions expressly forbid the impeached official's acting in his official capacity during the trial. In others this provision is restricted to the judges.

The lieutenant-governor, as long as he does not exercise the functions of governor, is *ex officio* president of the senate. He can vote only in case of a tie.

[1] The "system of checks and balances," in which Americans rightly see one of the most substantial guaranties of the preservation of a rational rule of liberty, has found application, in some few constitutions, in relation to this question, either not at all or only to a very limited extent. Either the governor has no veto at all or else a simple majority of the members-elect of both houses suffices to make a bill law over the veto. It is, however, significant that these provisions are found as a rule in some of the older constitutions. The dom-

Moreover, the governors of some states have this great advantage over the president, that they can refuse to approve separate parts of an appropriation bill, and yet approve it as a whole.[1] If the governor considers it necessary, he can call an extraordinary session of the legislature. He is commander-in-chief of the militia, when they are not employed in the service of the United States. The constitutions of several states, however, expressly provide that he must get the consent of the legislature before personally taking command of them and assuming the immediate leadership. Besides this, his right to appoint the militia officers is more or less restricted. Not only do his appointments usually require confirmation by the senate, but the right of appointment is limited in many cases to the higher ranks, sometimes indeed to the highest. In some states the highest officers are elected by the legislature, and these appoint the others, while the non-commissioned officers are elected by the men.[2] The right of pardon possessed by the governor is also, as a rule, a very limited one. Sometimes he can use it only with the co-operation of other high officials,[3] and more often he must give the legislature an exact report and state the rea-

---

inant tendency is undoubtedly the conservative one. For example, the West Virginia constitution of 1861 gave the governor no veto, but it was granted him by the constitution of 1872.

[1] This important provision is rapidly finding place in an increasing number of constitutions.

[2] All able-bodied citizens from eighteen (or twenty-one) years of age to forty-five are usually liable to serve in the militia. Many constitutions permit persons conscientiously opposed to carrying arms to escape by paying a fixed sum. These moneys are often assigned to the school fund. In the Oregon constitution of 1857, the absolution is restricted to times of peace.

[3] For example, the so-called "council," an institution that has proved itself of so little worth that it is found in none of the younger states, and older ones in which it formerly existed have abolished it.

sons for the exercise of his power. The greatest distinction between the authority of a governor and that of the president is in regard to the right of appointment. Even comparatively speaking, the number of offices to be filled by executive appointment is much less in a state than in the Union. The highest state officials, who take the place, more or less, of ministers, are not appointed at all. This is of the greatest significance. They are the advisers of the governor, for he is expressly authorized to demand written opinions from them on all questions involved in their duties. They are, however, as a rule, not only deliberative organs of the executive power committed to the governor, but they have, under the constitution, an independent share in the supreme executive power. Some constitutions expressly declare that a "governor and" such and such officials shall constitute "the executive department." This is why, at the beginning of this paragraph, I could only say that *at the head* of the executive power of all the states there is a governor. And even where it is not expressly stated that other officials have an independent share of the executive power, it is nevertheless the case in fact, because the other higher officials — sometimes all, and sometimes at least some of them — are given their offices without any co-operation by the governor, direct or indirect. As a rule they are elected by the people, but sometimes by the legislature. When some are appointed and some elected, the attorney-general is usually among those appointed. In the separate states, therefore, much less than in the federal administration, is there a cabinet in the European sense of the word. And in the states, in ordinary speech, a cabinet is never heard of.[1] The executive in most of the

[1] The Florida constitution of 1868, under which all the officers in question are appointed by the governor with the consent of the sen-

states is not a unit. This bars parliamentary government in them to even a greater extent than in the Union. The governor of Virginia, according to the constitution of 1850, was more dependent upon the legislature in this respect than the governor of any other state. For his term of office was four years, and the higher state officials were elected by the legislature for only two years. The observation just made applies to Virginia, however, in spite of this, just as unconditionally as it does to all other states. The occasional majority of the legislature can confide a very considerable part of the executive power to persons in full political accord with it, but the greater portion is still vested in the governor. So far as the constitution makes him the bearer of the executive power, it gives him the position of a factor of the government co-ordinate with the legislature, such as the federal constitution gives the president. It is still more evident from the Indiana constitution of 1851, that the high-

ate, is an exception, for it expressly designates them as "a cabinet of administrative officers." A quite peculiar organism was created by the North Carolina constitution of 1868. Although the particular officers are elected by the people, art. III., § 14 (executive department), provides: "The secretary of state, auditor, treasurer, superintendent of public works and superintendent of public instruction, shall constitute *ex officio* the council of the state, who shall advise the governor in the execution of his office, and three of whom shall constitute a quorum; their advice and proceedings in this capacity shall be entered in a journal to be kept for this purpose exclusively, and signed by the members present, from any part of which any member may enter his dissent; and such journal shall be placed before the general assembly when called for by either house." A council of state, elected by the people, whose individual members are party organs of the highest executive officer, and which is, as a whole, partly a pseudo-cabinet and partly an agent of the legislature, by which the political acts and omissions of the governor, as well as of the pseudo-cabinet itself, are in a way subjected to permanent police supervision, is a political bastard, that ought indeed to be the only one of its kind.

19

est state officials are not ministers, much less as a whole a cabinet, with which the governor is to rule in a parliamentary way. Under it the secretary of state, auditor and treasurer are elected by the people for two years, while the governor is elected for four years. Other constitutions, too, fix different terms for the treasurer and for the governor. If the treasurer were a minister, this would be an inexplicable anomaly. But not only as to the treasurer, but as to all the others who with and under the governor constitute the executive department, the political side of the office is relegated to the back-ground. This is true even of the secretary of state, for in spite of his high-sounding title, he is simply chief clerk and custodian of the state seal. But if these officials are sometimes not simply, and often not even chiefly, organs of the governor, they are fundamentally officials only in the more limited sense of the word. It is only the governorship which bears a sharply defined political character. This is the natural result of the fact that the executive is granted only such an indirect and restricted share in legislation, and of the fact that legislation itself has only a relatively narrow field of operations, and this practically outside of politics. The jurisdiction of the federal government is so wide, and the state legislature is (within the sphere of action left to the central powers of the states by the high development of self-government) in the very nature of things so much the dominant factor in a democratic republic,[1] that the separate states have wisely

[1] This is sharply emphasized by the provision in several constitutions, that officials — even judges — on demand of a two-thirds majority of the legislature shall be removed from office by the governor. As a rule, certain definite grievances must form the basis for such a demand. At this point, I may mention that the principles of civil service reform are daily gaining ground, that is, that offices without political significance are filled by appointment, are gradually losing

renounced the complex apparatus of ministers and ministries. The number of the officials who with the governor constitute the executive department, viz., *i. e.*, advisers of the executive and executive organs, is different in the different states. Even in their names there is variety. Besides, or in place of, those already mentioned, some states have a comptroller-general, a solicitor-general and a surveyor-general.

§ 94. THE COURTS. The organization of the judicial system presents so many differences, and even where these are slight, the names of the courts are often so different, that a general characterization in a few sentences is impossible, unless the discussion is restricted to that which is common to the judicial systems of all civilized states in modern times. Two points must, however, be presented, because in them the judicial system of the several states is substantially different from that of the United States. Although it has never yet been thought that the provision of the federal constitution, for the appointment of all federal judges "during good behavior," should be complained of as unwise, yet nearly all the states have wholly abandoned this principle. The judicial term is only for a fixed number of years, and often by no means for many years. The term of office varies very much in the different states. The general rule,

---

their former character of party booty — spoils. Whether the United States will ever have as firm an official tenure as prevails in Europe is nevertheless, to say the least, very doubtful. They are still very far from it. How deep the roots of the conviction that "rotation in office" is a democratic principle, or, indeed, a necessary requirement of a free state, have penetrated, can be inferred from, for example, the facts that the Mississippi constitution of 1868 provided that no official should be elected or appointed to serve "during good behavior," and that the Oregon constitution of 1857 actually forbade the creation by law of an office with a term of more than four years.

however, is, that it is longer as the court is higher. When several judges sit in a court, as a rule no integral renewal of the court takes place. In addition to the limitation last noted, the principle of irremovability is generally recognized. But the judges, like other officials, are subject to impeachment. But it is evident that Americans have not been blind to the dangers involved in yielding too much, on this very point, to the democratic tendency to make everything fluid and nothing fixed. In another direction, in turn, the "democratic principle" has made a wide breach in the old traditions and steadily widened it. True, the judges are still appointed, in several states, by the governor, but election has become the rule. In some states the legislature elects, but in a much greater number, the people. The constitutions place no express restrictions upon eligibility to the judicial office, and in spite of some unfortunate experiences the states in which judges are elected by the people believe that they have no less capable or less pure judges than the others. There are no signs of a reaction. The attacks of the opposition have become, moreover, much less frequent and much less fierce.

§ 95. CONSTITUTIONAL AMENDMENTS. With the unexampled external development of the United States, there has gone hand in hand a progressive democratization of their institutions. Nevertheless, the conservative basis of the character of the American people, derived from England, has remained in force; — how much so appears clearly in the provisions which, in a certain sense, must be designated as the most important of every constitution,— the provisions for amending the constitution. Amendments are not made easily in any state. And in some states they are rendered so difficult, that it may be said that it is almost absolutely certain that a constitution can be amended only when the people, after mature reflection, have become convinced that they wish the change and why they wish it. But this is noticeably true only when isolated amendments are in question. The guaranties provided are much weaker when a general revision is undertaken. The reason for this is that such a general revision is always made by a convention elected *ad hoc*, and such a convention, as has been already shown, represents in a much greater degree than the legislature, according to the prevalent opinion, the sovereign will of the people, and — thus the unspoken argument proceeds — consequently also reflects much more the wisdom of the people. And this opinion is not entirely incorrect, indeed, even on the latter point, for the people are wont to lay much more stress on the election of a convention than on the frequent and ever recurring legislative elections, so that men of fitting character, ability and judgment obtain decisive influence and not persons who have won a position in politics simply by their dexterity in guiding and using the party machine. Moreover, a general revision of the constitution is such an important undertaking, that it will not be attempted if there are not actually urgent decisive reasons for it. And if this be the case, then all the important questions have long beforehand been thoroughly discussed, so that on the one hand the convention knows what public opinion is, and on the other the people cannot come to vote upon the propositions of the convention without a full consideration of their nature and extent. In the constitutions of some of the states, indeed, the democratic fundamental principle, that the constitution must correspond to the will of the people, reaches rather a drastic expression in the provision that at fixed periods (every twenty years) the question must be submitted to the people, whether or no there shall be a convention. As a rule the people must always decide this, although it is left to the legislature to determine whether and when the question shall be submitted. The certainty, indeed, of a decision by the people, after the expiration of a fixed space of time, and quite independent of the will of the legislature, as to whether a general revision of the fundamental law shall take place, may also tend to make the people more inclined to give the constitution an "honest trial" for a sufficient time, and to turn coldly from demagogic agitation for constant criticism and change. The provisions of all the constitutions as to general revisions [1] admit of the expectation that, if no extraordinary state of affairs exists, no convention will be called without urgent occasion, in a lightsome spirit of innovation; that a convention will undertake its work in the full consciousness of its exalted responsibilities with great carefulness, cool reflection and sound judgment; and, finally, that the people in its decision upon the results of this work will be guided, not by momentary impulse, but by calm consideration of facts. Experience has sufficiently proven this, but it has also sometimes shown that, under certain circumstances, passion and demagogic agitation can triumph over sober thought and justice.[2] Without

---

[1] It has already been mentioned that all the constitutions do not contain detailed provisions as to the holding of conventions.

[2] I recall the California constitution of 1879, sometimes called the "sand-lot constitution." This name was given it, because it was formed and adopted under the influence of an agitation which an ignorant demagogue of very ordinary kind brought about by his popular assemblages on the sand lots of San Francisco. It was a campaign of the lower classes of society, in the first place against the Chinese, and to a certain degree also against capital. And even though the programme of the more radical leaders was not carried out, they nevertheless bore away no insignificant victory.

wishing to decide whether the holding of conventions for a general revision of the constitution or the adoption of their propositions by the people should be made more difficult and how this can best be brought about, I must note with praise the fact that many constitutions in their provisions about single amendments take double and treble precautions against all dangers of this kind. On the other hand, it is unquestionably a disadvantage if — as, for example, the constitutions of Kentucky of 1850, and of Nebraska of 1867, provide — an amendment can be made only by a convention.[1]

The initiative as to isolated changes and additional articles belongs to the legislature. The proposed amendment must, however, not only be agreed to by both houses, but in nearly half the states, a simple majority of the members-elect is not sufficient; a majority of three-fifths or two-thirds is required. In a minority of the states the proposal is then at once submitted to the people by its publication for a certain time in a fixed number of papers, and at the next general election the people vote for or against it. In most of the states, however, an opportunity is given to the people to express an indirect opinion, because they can let the proposal influence, so far as they see fit, their choice of members of the next legislature. The latter must also vote on the proposition, and only when it has adopted it by the required majority is the matter submitted to the people. In popular votes, almost without exception, a simple majority suffices for adoption. Exceedingly odd are the

[1] Of the obligation of submitting to the people the conclusions of the convention, nothing is said in these constitutions. The new Nebraska constitution of 1875 allows an amendment by a three-fifths vote in each house of the legislature and a majority of the popular vote. It also requires a constitutional convention to submit its work to the people.

provisions of the South Carolina and Alabama constitutions of 1868, and the Texas constitution of 1869, which put the popular vote between the decisions of the two legislatures.[1] Of course, the question comes before the second legislature only when the propositions of the former have been adopted by the people. However this method is to be regarded on political grounds, it is nevertheless difficult to make it accord with the principle of popular sovereignty. Several constitutions leave to legislation the task of providing for the details as to when and how the proposed amendments are to be submitted to the decision of the people. A defeated proposal, according to several constitutions, cannot be renewed for a certain time. An amendment of the Vermont constitution, adopted in 1870, grants exclusively to the senate the initiative as to proposed amendments; even the senate can use the privilege only every tenth year; two-thirds of its members must be in favor of the proposal, while in the house of representatives a simple majority suffices; in the next legislature, which must vote upon the proposal, only a majority in each house is required. The constitution of Delaware is entirely isolated in requiring, after the proposal of amendments by the legislature, their approval by the governor.

§ 96. THE TAX SYSTEM. (A) *General direct property taxes.* Numerous and self-evident as the differences in the tax-systems of the states are in detail, there is nevertheless a sufficient agreement in principle to make a general characterization of them possible. In the discussion of the like provisions of the federal constitution, it was shown that the right of taxation of the federal govern-

---

[1] Alabama in 1875, and Texas in 1876, each adopted a new constitution. Both of these constitutions allow amendments by the vote of one legislature and ratification at the polls.

ment and of the several states was concurrent, that is, they can levy taxes upon the same objects. Independent of particulars already cited and of no substantial material importance, such as the public property, the administration of justice, the salaries of officials, etc., the only exception to this rule, unfavorable to the states, is imported goods. As the federal government alone regulates foreign commerce, so it alone can collect duties on imports. This one exception, however, marks a distinction of taxation between the Union and the separate states which may almost be designated as a radical one. The federal government has always met its financial needs mainly by duties. In comparison with them, the only important taxes in ordinary times are those on tobacco and intoxicating liquors (whisky). Land sales, indeed, in the course of years, have brought in considerable sums, and also in the domain of internal revenue the Union has opened many more sources of income. But its financial system is characterized as to revenue by these three factors and particularly in fact by the duties. Direct taxes have been levied by the federal government only in exceptional cases. The backbone of the financial administration of the separate states, on the other hand, is direct taxation, to which personal and real property is liable. The general taxes are based on assessments made by assessors or appraisers. Some constitutions fix a time after which all personal property must be newly assessed, but this, as a rule, is left to legislation. Several constitutions also contain the provision that the valuation or assessment must correspond with the selling-price. As a rule, however, it is, as a matter of fact, lower. The assessment returns therefore do not present an entirely correct portraiture of the actual prosperity of the people. If the entire Union is taken into view, this is manifestly impossible, because by law or custom the valuations in the different states are made according to a more or less varying standard, quite independent of the fact that in spite of the express command of the constitutions, even with the best intentions, a perfectly uniform assessment cannot be made. The rates at which the different sorts of property are taxed as well as the methods of taxation vary in manifold ways, and change even in the same state. The constitutions generally limit themselves to the establishment of the principle that taxation shall be equal. It is, however, expressly stated that all property is taxable, or that all property shall be taxed according to its actual value, or that no kind of property shall be burdened with a higher tax-rate than any other kind, etc. Sometimes it is especially provided that all corporations for purposes of gain, as well as all investments of capital in paper securities of every kind, shall be taxed. Some constitutions, however, make property taxable only when it exceeds a certain minimum. This minimum is rather small. On the contrary, no state extends the "homestead" privilege so as to bar the collection of taxes due the state.[1] There

[1] The view is still continually met that there is an American homestead law. But in fact the federal law bearing this name relates, as already shown, only to the granting of a homestead of one hundred and sixty acres or less of the federal lands for a small entrance or patent fee. The homestead privilege, on the contrary, is based on state law or on the provisions of the state constitutions. It is therefore very different in the different states and it never has the scope often ascribed to it in Europe. The privilege is, in brief, this: That property, real and personal, up to a certain value is exempt from seizure or execution for *certain* debts, but *only* for certain debts. Taxes, purchase-money mortgages, debts for buildings erected on the homestead or other work done on it, are excepted. What a complicated matter this is may be inferred from the fact that the work of S. D. Thompson, *A Treatise on Homestead and Exemption Laws*, 1878, contains over eight hundred pages. See, also, J. H. Smith, *Law of Homesteads and Exemptions*, San Francisco, 1875.

are, however, further and more significant exceptions to the general taxation of property. They are obligatory according to some constitutions; others only permit the legislatures to make them. Cemeteries, public school buildings, charitable institutions, buildings exclusively devoted to divine services, and public property exclusively subserving public purposes, are most frequently exempt from taxation. Some constitutions go much further. The exemption is extended to all literary and scientific institutions, to all property serving religious purposes, to all public property, even that of the counties and municipalities, to clothing, furniture, tools, instruments and books up to a certain value, etc.

(B) *Capitation tax.* The ideal of tax legislation, in all modern civilized states, must be to have each individual bear the public burdens in the exact proportion that his ability to pay taxes bears to the tax-paying ability of the entire population. The realization of this ideal is impossible. It can be approached only by combining different taxes in such a way as to make their defects balance each other. An equal tax, judged from the stand-point of absolute justice, can never be proportionate, because equally valuable property of the same kind is by no means necessarily owned by persons equally able to pay taxes. Legislation, however, cannot from the nature of things take into consideration the particular incidence of taxation on a single piece of property, and the equal taxation of equally valuable property of the same kind is always less inequitable than the levying of an equal direct tax upon all individuals merely as parts of the population. It is only here and there that this point has been given such attention that the levying of such a tax has been unconditionally prohibited. Some constitutions — but a very small number — direct its levy. About half the constitutions do not touch the question at all and give the legislatures full and free play. The rest occupy a middle ground, corresponding with the public opinion or the actual situation of affairs in those states the constitutions of which are silent on the subject. The legislatures are permitted to levy a poll or capitation tax, but it is admitted that in general such a tax is grievous and oppressive, and therefore the right is given very narrow limits. The maximum rate allowable is almost always fixed; and this — considering American monetary conditions — is always a small one, usually $1 or $1.50. The tax is further restricted to male inhabitants or citizens of at least twenty-one years of age. And, finally, the revenue is generally made applicable to prescribed purposes,— in fact, as a rule, exclusively to the public schools, but occasionally also to charitable institutions. This prescription of purposes shows why the tax is regarded as admissible, although its principle is generally condemned. The poorer classes are most interested in a general free common school system, and the less they have to pay direct property taxes, the more equitable, yes, the more desirable, it is that they shall contribute something to the maintenance of these common schools. For it is even more important in democratic free states than in any other to keep alive in the consciousness of every citizen with full political rights, by making him pay some tax, that rights become privileges if not counterpoised by corresponding duties. The weight of these considerations in causing the levy of capitation taxes appears quite clearly where the right of voting is made dependent on the payment of a poll tax.

(C) *Other taxes.* Income taxes are mentioned only in a very few constitutions. It does not follow that they are not allowable in other states, but as the constitutions for the most part contain rather exhaustive provisions for tax legislation, this indicates that this method of taxation does not enjoy in the United States the favor it is more and more receiving among European statesmen and landlords. Indeed, it will not be entirely unjustifiable if the question is decided the other way in America. When the economic and all other relations have not yet attained a certain stability a general income tax causes many sorts of difficulties and inconveniences, which exist either not at all or in a very much more limited degree in relation to other taxes. Americans are aware that in many respects incomes are the best measures of taxation. They know, too, how the revenues are increased if taxation falls not only upon property, but also income. Both reasons will probably bring about the introduction of the income tax, sooner or later, in all the states of the Union; but many a state will consent to this only when the public needs cannot be met without a considerable increase of the ordinary taxes. However this may be, in fact, the different kinds of "specific taxes," next to the general direct property tax, play at present the most important part in the financial system of the several states. Among these specific taxes, the business or occupation taxes deserve the first mention. The Louisiana constitution of 1868 directly states that these are intended as income taxes.[1] Even where this is not expressly stated, the constitutions sometimes take care that the taxes shall not be the same for all the different trades, but shall bear a certain proportion to the extent or proceeds of the business

---

[1] After the general authorization to levy such taxes, this clause follows: "All tax on income shall be *pro rata* on the amount of income or business done." The authority to levy an income tax is not unbounded. It is granted, but only as to "all persons pursuing any occupation, trade or calling." Title VI., art. 118.

carried on. When, for instance, the Alabama constitution of 1868 obliges the legislature to impose a special tax upon all railroads, insurance and banking companies, etc., for the benefit of the school fund, it is difficult to assume that it intends to tax a little local railroad a few miles long as much as railroads which might be regarded as the arteries of trade. And this is true even if laws based upon another interpretation of the paragraph cannot be declared certainly unconstitutional. The Illinois constitution of 1870, however, enumerates, in immediate connection with businesses of the kind just mentioned, hawkers, hucksters, jugglers, grocers, hotel and saloon keepers, etc. This is difficult to harmonize with the views stated if it be not assumed that the framers of the constitution intended to leave it to the discretion of the legislature in what cases the specific tax shall be a fixed one, and in what cases the tax shall be determined by the extent of the business. The latter is never the case in a license tax. The Virginia constitution of 1870 calls the specific taxes which are to be levied licenses. There is, therefore, no doubt that under it only the particularly enumerated occupations can be burdened with a specific tax.[1] In turn the question might be raised whether this is also true in cases where only the expression "to tax" is used. For it may be disputed whether licenses can be regarded as taxes in the strict sense of the word. As, however, in the cases of hawkers, peddlers, jugglers, etc., only licenses can be intended, this argument would be somewhat forced. But, although it is regarded as inadmissible, naturally the importance of specific taxes as a source of revenue is always more or less impaired by such an enu-

[1] The list, indeed, contains a clause giving to the legislature the widest scope. It says, in conclusion: "And all other business which cannot be reached by the *ad valorem* system."

meration.[1] In order to avoid this, other constitutions, such, for instance, as that of North Carolina of 1868, have empowered the legislature to tax all trades, professions and franchises. This power, to my knowledge, has hitherto never been carried out in its full extent in any state. I do not believe that any state has ever overstepped or even reached the limits which the Texas constitution of 1879 fixed by adding to the general formula of authorization the clause that, by "occupation," agriculture and "mechanical pursuits" should not be understood. On the other hand, no constitution which mentions specific taxes has drawn such narrow limits to them as the Arkansas constitution of 1868, which commands the legislature " to tax all privileges, pursuits and occupations that are of no real use to society," and forbids the taxation of all others. How the laws of Arkansas have illustrated this remarkable provision in detail I am unable to say. I have treated this whole question in connection with the constitutions, partly because it seemed to possess not a little interest *per se*, partly because it sufficiently appears from the constitutional provisions cited how different the conditions of the states are in this respect, while the

---

[1] The constitution of Illinois further sets forth: "The specification of the objects and subjects of taxation shall not deprive the general assembly of the power to require other subjects or objects to be taxed, in such manner as may be consistent with the principles of taxation fixed in this constitution." Even if the states, in applying the doctrine that constitutions should establish only the principles of tax-legislation, have not kept within the same limits, yet this doctrine, as a matter of fact, forms the foundation of the provisions in question in all the constitutions. So the principle already stated applies here, that the legislatures may do whatever they are not forbidden to do. It cannot be concluded, for example, because many constitutions contain no special provisions relating to specific taxes, that the actual systems under them must be substantially different from those in the states with constitutions which do contain such provisions.

fundamental character of their tax systems is one and the same.

§ 97. SCHOOL SYSTEM.[1] *Advancement thereof by the Federal Government.* The democratic federal republic's capacity for existence has not diminished, but has rather greatly increased, although in three generations the narrow settlements along the coast of the thirteen Atlantic states have developed into the giant nation extending from ocean to ocean, and the population has increased more than fourteen-fold. This is in great part due to the fact that close upon the heel of the irrepressible pioneer, penetrating the western wilderness, came the school. The federal government was no slight contributor to the possibility of this. Neither the articles of confederation nor the constitution of 1789 granted the central power any authority whatever in regard to a system of instruction in the states, but early in the day it saw that the care and development of the school system was a national interest of vital importance. And it found ways and means to aid it greatly without becoming guilty of the slightest usurpation. The old congress deserves the renown of having, at a time when the overwhelming centrifugal tendency had already practically deprived it of all real power, taken the path which the federal government has since steadily trod, to its honor and to the good of the country. Even in the act of 1785, organizing the territory lying northwest of the Ohio, the sixteenth section — a square mile — of every township was set aside for the support of common schools. In the famous "ordinance of 1787," the definitive act of organization of the Northwest Territory, this provision was renewed and the grant to each state formed out of the territory of two whole townships, "for a university,"

---

[1] F. Burke: *Law of Public Schools*, N. Y., 1880

was added.[1] A law of September 4, 1841, granted a number of states five hundred thousand acres apiece (inclusive of the grants made earlier), and provided that every new state should receive a like grant. "Internal improvements" were usually the nominal object of this gift, but as a matter of fact, a large amount of the proceeds went to the schools. With the law of August 14, 1848, for the organization of the territory of Oregon, congress began to give to the school-fund of the new territories the thirty-sixth as well as the sixteenth section of each township. In the midst of the civil war, July 2, 1862, congress passed a law giving to each state land enough to endow at least one "college," in which "such branches of learning as are related to agriculture and the mechanic arts" should be especially taught. The size of the gift was made dependent on the population. It was at least thirty thousand acres for each senator and representative of the state, under the census of 1860. Besides this, the school-funds of certain states got a share of the surplus in the federal treasury distributed in 1836 — some $15,000,000 — and also part of the proceeds of the sale of more than sixty-two million acres of "swamp and overflowed lands," donated the states by the federal government in 1849, 1850 and 1860.

General Characterization. The original states of the Union have thus shared in the land grants for schools only to a relatively small degree. However great these grants have been, of course they could not, even in the new states, be more than a contribution towards the amount needed for the system of instruction. Even in these new states, most of the money needed must be

---

[1] G. W. Knight, *History and Management of Federal Land Grants in the Northwest Territory*, N. Y., 1885; in the papers of the American Historical Association.

raised by taxes, partly state and partly local. As to both kinds of school-taxes, the regulations of the thirty-eight states differ widely in both form and substance. The system of instruction is by no means in the same stage of development in all the states, and divergent views prevail on the question as to how far the care of popular education ought to be, or can be, recognized as an immediate task of the state. And, therefore, the size of the school-budget — whether that of the state alone or that of the state and the municipalities together — varies greatly *per capita*. As a rule the former slave-states, especially the planter-states, are more or less in arrear in this respect. If we but consider that at the outbreak of the civil war part of these states had no general common school system and that the slave-children were not allowed to be educated, we must cordially recognize the progress they have made,— and made despite their complete economic ruin and despite the radical social revolution of the last twenty years. Some of them, indeed, have gone so far as to establish in their constitutions the principle of compulsory attendance at school or rather of compulsory education,— a principle not yet adopted by many northern and western states. The conclusion must not be drawn, however, from the establishment of the principle, that in these particular states all children now enjoy instruction. In the southern states, the actual condition of affairs makes it in many ways impossible to give all children the opportunity of an education, much less to compel them to take it. Compulsory education, moreover, has not succeeded hitherto even where such an opportunity has been offered every child. This is due in a great degree to the fact that public opinion has not yet declared itself in favor of compulsory education as emphatically as it has demanded for many years that the state, in connection with the local authorities, should see to it that every child had the chance of receiving a common school education, free of cost.

Common Schools. The demand of public opinion on the whole does not extend further than these, although there are everywhere public free schools of a higher grade. Some of them are supported by the municipalities; some of them by a municipality and the state together. The expression "common schools" as a rule means only the elementary or primary schools. Common schools of a higher grade are called grammar or high schools. Nevertheless there is no "*American* common school system," although Americans themselves very frequently use this expression. Not only are there different names in the different states, but the same names sometimes mean more or less different things. Each state, however, has its common school system, bearing here or there its special stamp. A general characterization, which should give a very correct picture of the organization of the school system of each state, is therefore impossible. The following statements indicate only what seems to emerge from the multiplicity of details as a general type — modified in this or that way, sometimes more and sometimes less.

Organization of the School System. The state does not support the common schools, but it contributes a considerable part of the cost of their support. The means placed by the state at the disposal of the public schools — the proceeds of taxes directly or indirectly levied for school purposes and the interest and other proceeds of the school fund — are distributed according to fixed, but not always the same, rules. In general the distribution is based either wholly or in part upon the number of school children. The rich communities, therefore, have to pay much more in taxes to the school fund of the state than they receive from it. They must not only bear the expenses of their own schools, but they must also help to support the schools of the poorer communities. All local boards, however, must raise part of the cost of their schools by local taxation. In fact, they are not always left free to decide how heavily they will burden themselves for this purpose. No maximum is set, but the law prescribes a minimum, by fixing what proportion the local contribution shall bear to that of the state. As far as spending the moneys is concerned, the local boards have a pretty free hand. As the state does not fully support the common schools, it does not claim their sole management. It takes in hand the general direction and superintendence, but does not withdraw the school system from the domain of self-government. The highest school authority in most states is a board of education. Its members are sometimes elected by the people or the legislature; sometimes appointed by the governor; sometimes they are certain officials who *ex officio* make up the board; sometimes they are chosen by a combination, in one way or another, of the different methods. The immediate head of the system of education is a single official, generally called superintendent or commissioner of public instruction. He also is elected in the one or the other way or is appointed by the governor. He is always a member of the board where a board exists. Besides this, there are commissioners. They are either state or county officials, but in either case are usually elected by the people. The immediate management of the schools is left, however, to the local school boards, school commissioners or trustees. These are generally elected by the voting population of the community. They engage and discharge the teachers. The unit in the organ-

ization of the school system is the "school district" or
the township. The district system has lost ground of
late as against the township system, because experience
has shown that decentralization has many dubious results
if it passes beyond certain limits. With the development
of the system of public instruction the tendency towards
somewhat greater centralization has gone hand in hand.
In fact, the improvement of the system and the growth
of the state's control and direction are to no small extent
exactly identical.

*Exclusion of Religious Instruction in the Common
Schools.* No state gives the churches any footing whatever in the common schools. Every church and every
congregation is left to take such care as it sees fit
of the religious instruction of the children belonging to
it. Such instruction is usually given in the Sunday
schools. These are entirely independent of the state as
well as of the community. Religious exercises in the
common schools are restricted to the reading of a chapter
in the Bible. Even this has been done away with here
and there, because the Catholics claimed that they were
wronged by the use of a Protestant translation of the
Bible; the Jews protested against the use of the New
Testament, and the Freethinkers objected to everything
which professed to be the word of God and divine revelation. These claims, protests and objections have been
recognized without reservation as just by many positive
Christians. Some famous Protestant clergymen were
among the earliest and most earnest advocates of the
doctrine that religion, so far as it took the shape of
dogma, was to be absolutely excluded from the common
schools. The most vigorous impetus given to the attack
against the former practice of beginning the school session with more or less prolonged devotional exercises was

due to the Catholic clergy. Hitherto, however, the results have been diametrically opposed to their real views. They complained of a Protestant translation of the Bible, but when Bible reading ceased they lamented still more the banishment of God from the schools, and demanded that the Catholics be given their share of the school funds so that they could care for the instruction of their children in the way demanded by their consciences and their religious convictions.[1] So far they have been unable to carry this through anywhere. Its ultimate consequences would be the distribution of the whole school fund among the different churches and the replacing of the complete secularization of the common schools with its exact opposite. But the battle over this question — a question which reaches the deepest roots of popular government in America — is by no means ended.[2]

Normal Schools. It was only in relatively recent times that the states began to make any effort to educate capable common school teachers. These efforts were incidentally caused by Dr. Julius, whom the Prussian government had sent to the United States to study the prison system. Dr. Charles Brooks, a clergyman of Massachu-

[1] For one of the most interesting and significant episodes of this struggle see my *Constitutional History*, IV., 91.

[2] President Grant, in his message of December 7, 1875, recommended that a constitutional amendment should be submitted to the states for ratification, "making it the duty of each of the several states to establish and forever maintain full public schools, adequate to the education of all the children in rudimentary branches, within their respective limits, irrespective of sex, color, birth-place or religion; forbidding the teaching in said schools of religious, atheistic or pagan tenets, and prohibiting the granting of any school fund or school taxes, or any part thereof, either by legislative, municipal or other authority, for the benefit or in aid, directly or indirectly, of any religious sect or denomination." Congress did not act upon the recommendation.

setts, was so much interested in Dr. Julius's statements about the Prussian teachers' seminaries that he forthwith made himself thoroughly acquainted with these institutes, and after his return to America began a successful agitation in Massachusetts for their imitation there. By and by other states followed the example of Massachusetts, and now every state has a greater or less number of teachers' seminaries. They are usually somewhat vaguely called normal schools. Only a very small part of them are real state institutions. Most of them depend upon the municipalities. These have displayed a splendid activity and a cheerful self-sacrifice in this respect, as well as in regard to the entire school system. Although the number of these institutes grows steadily and rapidly, yet they by no means suffice to supply the great demand for teachers of the lower grades. Under the blessed working of competitive examination, however, the average teacher has nevertheless become much more capable than formerly, when "school-keeping" was the best means poor half-grown youths had to earn money enough to enter upon whatever career their ambition dictated. The normal schools train not only male but female teachers.[1]

High Schools, etc. The extent of the support given by the states to high schools, and also to academies and colleges, is very varied. The organization as well as the work of these schools differ so much that they often have nothing in common except the name. During the seventies — possibly on account of the hard times — a current of public opinion against the expensive participation of the state in fostering the higher education seemed to

[1] The absolute as well as the relative number of female teachers is far greater in the United States than in any European nation whatever.

gain breadth and depth. The money taken from the mass of the people — so the argument ran — should be used only in such a way as to be of direct advantage to the whole people.

Universities. In most of the states a state institution bears the name of university. But it must not be inferred from the name that the institution corresponds with what is understood in Europe by a university. And even among themselves they differ so much that a general characterization is practically impossible. Only thus much may be said, that they are throughout a mixture of the German *gymnasia*, *realschule* of a high grade, industrial schools of different kinds, and university, but that the mixture and combination differ materially in the different cases. Thus, for instance, some of the southern states, which first considered the foundation of a university after the close of the war, and some of the younger western states, have contented themselves from the beginning with a very modest programme, whereas the state university of Michigan, at Ann Arbor, in the number of subjects of instruction, as well as in the work done, is among the foremost institutions of the Union. Theology is excluded from all state universities. The separate religious denominations must care for the education of the clergy, as such. The state does not concern itself in any way as to whether they do so or how they do so.[1]

[1] In 1882 there were one hundred and forty-five theological seminaries, with four thousand nine hundred and twenty-one students. The Catholic church led them all with twenty-one seminaries and one thousand one hundred and four students. Next came the Baptists, with the same number of seminaries, but only eight hundred and ninety-nine students. In all, twenty-five different religious denominations support seminaries. It is evident from this that a distribution of the school fund among the denominations is simply

Although they do not come within the theme of general law, the private institutions must be briefly mentioned, because they are in the strictest sense of the word an essential integral part of the system of instruction. The most noted institutions of learning of the highest grade are almost wholly private institutions, in this sense, that they are aided neither by the state nor by the communities. Their property comes from legacies and gifts. The foundation of their scheme of instruction is the collegiate department, in which the lower divisions correspond to the higher classes of our *gymnasia* or *realschule*, and even the highest do not go far beyond these. Where other than academic studies are pursued, it is usual to organize separate schools — medical school, law school, etc., which nevertheless form an integral part of the whole institution. If the institution is of a religious character, it occasionally has connected with it a theological seminary. The large majority of the colleges of the second and third class as well as of the academies are private institutions in the sense stated. Many of the grammar and high schools are due to private benevolence. Individuals spend year after year immense sums for educational purposes. In 1872, the legacies and gifts ran up to over $11,000,000. This has also its obverse side. The resources of education are not concentrated; the conditions of the donors often prevent the most expedient use of the money given; the arrangements are too dissimilar; and the results are too disproportionate and often very unsatisfactory.[1] Apart from the common schools, the

---

impossible. If the Catholic church ever carries through its demand, it can do so only by getting a special privilege for itself.

[1] This is evident enough from the fact that in 1882 there were no less than three hundred and sixty-five " universities " and " colleges " in the United States.

system of instruction is in some ways almost chaotic. As far as colleges and high schools are concerned, the stage of development of the central European states has not been reached.[1]

§ 98. RELATIONS OF CHURCH AND STATE.[2] "It belongs to American liberty to separate entirely the institution which has for it object the support and diffusion of religion from the political government."[3] The constitutions of all the states proclaim this principle in one form or another, and they put its chief consequences in the shape of express prohibitions. The American principle is not general toleration, but absolute religious freedom. This, according to American ideas, involves the complete withdrawal of religio-ecclesiastical relations as such from the sphere of action of the state and of political organizations of lower grade. The Americans are mistaken in their frequent assertion that this principle is carried out to its last consequences in all the states, but the differences are few and as a rule of no practical importance.

In all the states, the constitutions forbid the establishment of a state church or any distinction in favor of any religious denomination. If any advantage whatever were given one, this would be an injury to the others, and any injury suffered on account of religious convictions is op-

---

[1] Compare, besides the annual reports of the bureau of education and Barnard's *American Journal of Education;* Troschel, *Volkscharakter und Bildungsanstalten der Nordamerikaner,* 1867; Rigg, *National Education,* 1873; *A Statement of the Theory of Education in the United States of America,* 1874; F. Adams, *The Free School System of the United States,* 1875; Gilman, *Education in America, 1776–1876,* in the *North American Review,* 1876.

[2] See Cooley, *Const. Lim.,* 467–478; R. H. Tyler, *American Ecclesiastical Law,* Albany, 1866; F. Vinton, *American Canon Law,* N. Y., 1870; W. Strong, *Relations of Civil Law to Church Polity,* N. Y., 1875; S. B. Smith, *Ecclesiastical Law,* 2d ed., N. Y., 1878.

[3] Lieber, *On Civil Liberty and Self-Government,* 99.

posed to the principle of absolute religious freedom. If this is true in relation to religious organizations, it must manifestly also be true as to all individuals. States are therefore unfaithful to this principle if their constitutions make the right to hold certain or all public offices dependent upon faith in a higher being, in a future life, etc. Some state constitutions do this. This inconsequence is either not recognized or else is regarded as justifiable, for, as far as the Anglo-Americans are concerned, there is very much truth in Kapp's assertion that religious liberty is understood by the great majority to mean "that every one has indeed the liberty to profess any religion but not the right to acknowledge no religion."[1] All such provisions, however, are constantly and in an increasing ratio disappearing from the state constitutions.

TAXATION FOR RELIGIOUS PURPOSES is forbidden. Such taxes cannot be levied by the townships and counties any more than by the state.[2] Religion is an entirely private affair, and the imposition of public burdens for private affairs is inadmissible. No one can be compelled to contribute to the cost of satisfying the religious wants of somebody else. Whoever associates himself with others for such purposes and so voluntarily assumes material

---

[1] *Das Verhältniss von Staat und Kirche in der Union. Aus und über Amerika*, II., 48.

[2] For an exception, see Cooley, *Const. Limit.*, 468, note 1. I give the provision of the Illinois constitution on this point *verbatim*, because it may be regarded as typical: "Neither the general assembly, nor any county, city, town, township, school district or other public corporation, shall ever make any appropriation, or pay from any public fund whatever anything, in aid of any church or sectarian purpose, or to help support or sustain any school, academy, seminary, college, university or other literary or scientific institution controlled by any church or sectarian denomination whatever; nor shall any grant or donation of land, money or other personal property ever be made by the state or any such public corporation to any church or for any sectarian purpose." Art. VIII., sec. 1, § 3.

obligations is nevertheless, of course, bound to meet these obligations. Controversies arising from this may be decided by the ordinary courts, but they can never have a general law character.

The states are forbidden to compel participation in any religious exercises or usages whatsoever. A member of a religious congregation is so solely because he wishes to be, and he can cease to be so for whatever reason and whenever he pleases. On the other hand, the state has no right to direct religious denominations whom they shall admit to membership, why they shall exclude from membership, how they shall arrange their church rules, when and how they shall impose ecclesiastical punishments, etc. It is only when they invade the legal rights of the citizen that the person injured can seek the protection of the courts. The churches, as religious communities, have unlimited self-government, but they can never, by appealing to their articles of faith or church regulations, justify the least violation of what the state recognizes as a right. Without detriment to their absolute autonomy, they are as absolutely subject to the law as any stock company or social club.

THE FREE EXERCISE OF RELIGION cannot be hindered by the states. The Chinaman cannot be troubled in his temple of idolatry any more than the Catholic archbishop in his cathedral. No one is to be prevented from making the craziest religion his own and living up to it in accordance with the dictates of his conscience. But this holds good only so far as he does not thus come into conflict with the laws. The laws, in fact, do not affect religion, but always take care that no one, in the name of religion, shall actually oppose the requirements which the state, as a moral, civilized society, may and must make.[1] He

[1] The Illinois constitution provides: "But the liberty of conscience hereby secured shall not be construed to . . . excuse acts of

who does this encroaches upon the legal rights of others, and indeed in this case upon the legal rights of the community, whereas the constitutional guarantee of religious freedom is to him only a guarantee that on that question neither the state nor any one else shall be permitted to encroach upon his legal rights.

THE FREE EXPRESSION AND DEFENSE OF RELIGIOUS OPINIONS by word or pen cannot be restricted by the state. This right, also, is subject to the restrictions stated in the preceding section. No constitution forbids the legislature to prevent the circulation of immoral writings injurious to public morals. In some states this is made its express duty. This right and this duty cannot, however, be set aside because lasciviousness presents herself in the drapery of religious conviction. The exercise of the right is also subject to the further restriction that it shall not be so abused as to violate the legal right of others to follow their convictions.

The fundamental principles are clear, but it is easy to see that their application to concrete cases must involve many and many kinds of difficulties. Whether the great problem of the relations of church and state has been more satisfactorily solved in the United States, by complete separation, than it has been in European states, by more or less of alliance, is not a matter of enquiry here. But a presentation of American general law must point out the fact that the American solution does not, as most Americans believe and assert, absolutely exclude all misunderstandings, etc., between these two highest points of civilization. And even were that the case, yet the facts to be stated hereafter show even more clearly than those already cited that the highly complex development

licentiousness, or justify practices inconsistent with the peace or safety of the state." Art. II., sec. 1, § 3.

of the relation between church and state in Europe — a development which has gone on a thousand years or more — makes the adoption of the American theory in the old world utterly impossible.

The co-existence of absolute legal dominion over the churches, and of their complete autonomy as organized religious societies, is made possible by the fact that the state does not know them as self-contained, complex powers at all. Legislation concerns itself only with individual congregations, and even with them not as communities of one faith, but only as corporations which, under the laws, can acquire property, use it and manage it. The state does not, however, ignore the two important facts that these are corporations for religious purposes, and that every congregation belongs to a sect. Church rules, church laws, even doctrines of faith, can be enforced by the courts, and may control judicial decisions. The courts decide only questions of law, but these may depend upon a church rule, etc. Without regard to the reasonableness, the justice, the worth or the unworthiness of the articles of faith or of the ordinances of the church, they are treated by the courts as facts from which legal consequences may arise for those who have become subject to them by voluntarily becoming members of a church. The church authorities can bring no questions of a civil nature before their forum, and the state never lends them its strong arm except in questions of civil rights, such as may arise under the rules of a club as well as under the ordinances of a church.[1] In other

---

[1] The leading principles are plainly and pointedly set forth by J. P. Thompson, *Kirche und Staat in den Vereinigten Staaten von Amerika*. He says:

"Under the laws of the United States, and of the several states of the Union, each church is at liberty to organize itself according to

cases, however, the courts have recognized the right of an incorporated congregation to retain their church property, although they had changed their faith.

From the political point of view, the opposite side of the question is the more important. The state takes account of both these facts, by seeking to shape its legis-

its own model, to frame its own laws, to raise its revenue in its own way, and to administer its own discipline. The broad principle is that a church is a voluntary association; and its constitution, laws and canons are stipulations between the parties, defining their duties and obligations. The civil rights of the member are still protected by the civil tribunals; but civil courts will not interfere to prevent an investigation before an ecclesiastical tribunal of a voluntary religious association when proceeding according to its constitution, canons or rules, and when the subject-matter or person is within its jurisdiction.

"Where it appears that a local church and the rector thereof are members of, and under the supervision and control of, a general and superior church organization, to whose faith and discipline they have voluntarily attached themselves, those who continue to adhere to the faith and discipline of the general church are the beneficiaries for whose use the trustees hold the church property, although they are the minority of the local church organization.

"Where the proper ecclesiastical tribunals have obtained jurisdiction, and have tried and passed sentence of deposition upon an alleged offender, civil courts not only recognize the validity of, but give effect to, the decisions of the church courts.

"In all matters of religious faith and practice, the ecclesiastical courts, provided they have obtained jurisdiction, are as entirely independent of the civil tribunals as the latter are of the former upon all questions relating to property interests.

"Neither will the courts, in the absence of acts of incorporation which change the common law, permit a majority of the members of a church which is itself connected with and subject to the jurisdiction and government of a superior church judicatory to secede from the denomination to which they have voluntarily attached themselves, and take with them the church property. Such an act is regarded in law as a perversion of the trust; and a court of equity will reach forth its strong arm, and prevent it. The holders of the legal title are regarded in a court of equity as holding it in trust for

lation so that the churches cannot easily become a power dangerous to it. The greatest safeguard lies in this, that the whole church can never be incorporated in a state. Only a single congregation can be. It may therefore be said that in a certain sense the legal idea of the church is inseparable from that of a particular building devoted to divine worship. The mere permanent union of persons who think alike on religion does not form a church. The legal formation of a church involves the creation of a corporation, of a "congregation," which obtains legal existence by this incorporation. The congregation embraces all those who, by the acceptance of their contributions towards the common costs, have been admitted in a certain way as business partners. What a single congregation calls the "church" is the closer union of those whose lives show a livelier participation in, and fuller resignation to, the common ideal interests. The church as such legally exists only as a congregation.[1] The method and conditions of incorporation vary in the different states. The congregation is always represented in its relations to the state and the outer world by a board of trustees which must consist in part of laymen. This highly important provision may, indeed, be stripped of all significance. In New York the Catholic church has been able to arrange matters so that the trustees always

the maintenance of the faith and worship of the founders of the organization; and any diversion of it into another use is so far a breach of trust as to demand the interposition of the court. This position is sustained by many cases, English and American." See, also, *Chase et al. vs. Cheney*, 58 Ill., 509. In other cases, however, the courts have acknowledged the right of incorporated churches to retain their church property notwithstanding a change of faith. J. P. Thompson, *Kirche und Staat in den Ver. St. von Amerika*, 73 et seq.

[1] The spiritual head of the congregation is the minister. He is also the pastor of the church.

consist of the archbishop, the bishop of the diocese, the vicar-general, the pastor of the church, and two of the three laymen first elected by the church. The two laymen are simply a thin veil to hide the fact that the state has struck its flag to the church.

The ecclesiastical authorities as such have no power whatever to administer the church property. Even the trustees are subject to certain limitations in this respect. Far more important, however, is the fact that the very right of the congregation to acquire property is limited to a certain extent. These limitations affect not only the amount acquired but the method of acquisition. The right to acquire real estate is particularly limited. Yet these provisions often exist only on paper. Sometimes it is not easy to conceal a violation of them; sometimes the boards make no attempt to conceal it. Nevertheless, the principles of these laws in regulation of ecclesiastical relations provide the means for energetic public action, if a church filled with hierarchical tendencies should ever become possessed of such material power that public opinion began to perceive a danger in it.

THE ORGANS OF SELF-GOVERNMENT.[1]

§ 99. IN GENERAL. While in Europe the eighteenth century was characterized by excessive centralization, and it is only in the nineteenth that the principles of self-government have been toilsomely and very gradually brought into play against the principle of the state's universal control, the development of the United States has taken exactly the opposite course. Here the most extreme decentralization was the original basis. The history of the separate states naturally contains nothing which offers

[1] J. N. Pomeroy, *Municipal Law*, N. Y., 1864; J. F. Dillon, *Municipal Corporations*, 3d ed., 2 vols., Boston, 1881.

any analogy to the bitter experiences and hard struggles, through which the federal government bit by bit won the power imperiously demanded by the vital interests of the community, and indeed absolutely necessary for the perpetuation of the Union. The factors of the state government depend so immediately upon the people that there can scarcely be protracted and serious conflicts between government and people. At most, there may be differences between the larger cities and the legislatures; for it is not inconceivable that the former may think their special interests are systematically neglected or badly treated by the majority of the country representatives, either from ignorance or, indeed, from lack of good will. Cities like New York, Philadelphia, Boston, Chicago, St. Louis, are too populous and too powerful to allow such an opposition of opinions and interests to win a chronic character, without a struggle. In general, however, centralization can never go further in the single states than public opinion demands or at least permits. And, on the whole, public opinion has thus far held fast to the principle that all local affairs shall as far as possible be left to local authorities. The constitutional-law authority of the legislatures is great enough to cut down local government at one stroke to very modest proportions, for individual rights are never the basis of local government. Considerations of expediency lead the state to create municipal organizations of various kinds and grades; and these have only such powers as the state grants them. The powers are either expressly granted or implied in those expressly granted, because necessary in order to execute the latter. The courts also recognize to a certain extent a law of custom, because as a matter of fact certain powers are rooted so ineradicably in custom, that they are frequently not expressly granted simply because they are regarded as perfectly self-evident. On the contrary, powers deduced only by analogy are not recognized by the courts, that is, it must not be inferred because a definite right has been granted that analogous rights also exist. The grant of power is made by general law or by a special act, but there is not in the latter case, any more than in the former, a "contract" (in the sense of the federal constitution) which cannot be broken. Acts of incorporation and charters may be amended just like general laws at any moment by the legislature. They may be entirely repealed, for no vested rights pass under them with which the state thereafter cannot interfere.[1] City limits may be extended or curtailed, counties divided or combined, towns abolished, cities degraded to towns, etc., and those concerned cannot seek the protection of

[1] This is true only of the *powers* granted. "It is an unsound and even absurd proposition that political power conferred by the legislature can become a vested right, as against the government, in any individual or body of men." Judge Nelson in *People vs. Morris*, 13 Wend., 331, cited by Cooley, *Constitutional Limitations*, 269. The *property* of a municipality is of course not wholly subject to the arbitrary will of the legislature. The appropriate constitutional principles are thus stated by Cooley: "When corporate powers are conferred, there is an implied compact between the state and the corporators that the property which they are given the capacity to acquire for corporate purposes under their charter shall not be taken from them and appropriated to other uses. If the state grants property to the corporation, the grant is an executed contract which cannot be revoked. The rights acquired either by such grants, or in any other legitimate mode in which such a corporation can acquire property, are vested rights and cannot be taken away." But as the state has not only a right of general control over this kind of property, but can also change or annul "corporate powers" themselves, it may under certain circumstances be the state's right, and even its duty, to make some other disposition of the property, but always with the limitation "that the purpose for which the property was originally acquired shall be kept in view, so far as the circumstances will admit, in any disposition that may be made of it." *Ibid.*, p. 270.

the courts on the ground that their former rights were violated. On the other hand, the constitutions often set limits to the legislative power in such matters. These measures can be taken only in a prescribed way or are permitted only under prescribed conditions,— for instance, the assent of the parties in interest. Such limiting provisions especially abound in the constitutions in regard to the division or union of counties, the partition of the public property or debts when such changes are made, the removal of county seats, etc.

MUNICIPAL CORPORATIONS are divided into two main classes: municipalities in the more limited sense, which are really public legal corporations, and those often designated by American publicists as "*quasi*-corporations." The latter are created by general laws and have in every state substantially the same rights and duties.[1] Their *raison d'être* is not, as with the municipalities proper, an actual separate existence, economically and socially, but the necessity of dividing the state for administrative purposes into departments of greater or less size. They have properly no natural existence at all. They are in substance merely creatures of art. If a map of the United States which shows the chief subdivisions of the states is examined, the predominance of straight lines strikes

---

[1] The limits of the two are complex and involved. Cooley, *Const. Lim.*, p. 273, defines townships as "municipal corporations" which do "not usually possess corporate powers under special charters; but exist under general laws of the state," and to which so little "corporative existence is granted," "that they are sometimes spoken of as nondescript in character." D. B. Eaton, on the contrary, says: "Our state legislatures have tended towards becoming mere registering offices for city, village and town charters, which in their provisions are almost as diverse and hostile as were the laws and municipalities of the Middle Ages." *Municipal Government*, Journal of Social Science, 1875.

one at first glance. These lines bound these chief divisions; and these repay examination, because the institutions of the thirty-eight states show a far greater similarity as to these than as to the smaller or smallest subdivisions.

§ 100. COUNTIES. These chief divisions are now called counties in all the states except Louisiana, where they are known as parishes. Several constitutions direct the legislatures to give the counties natural boundaries, as far as practicable. As a rule this is impossible, even though the counties need not be of the same size. Many constitutions require that new counties shall be of a minimum size, varying, however, from two hundred and seventy-five to nine hundred square miles. In the newer and larger states four hundred to six hundred square miles is the normal extent. It is evident, therefore, that the counties, even in those states which exceed in size many European kingdoms, never bear the character of provinces. They are subdivisions, but subdivisions with quite extensive powers. The officials as a rule are elected, and elected, like most American officials, for a very limited time. In several states, however, they are appointed by the governor. Even then, nevertheless, they always bear the character rather of organs of self-government than of government officials in the European sense. It is one of the most important distinctions between American and European institutions — as De Tocqueville insisted — that in Europe more or less even in local government the direct or indirect control of the central government is held to be unavoidable, whereas in the United States the facts are just the other way: — the state uses the organs of local government to discharge its own tasks, for instance, levying and collecting taxes. Both the extent and the manner of this are different in the different states, for on this point as on all others the organization of self-government varies in a myriad details. But despite many differences, some of them of no slight importance, all the states offer in their county-systems a sufficiently faithful representation of the nature and form of self-government. The geographical centre of county government is called the county-seat. Here are the court-house and the jail. Every county has its own county court, with a rather limited jurisdiction, very different in the different states. Connected with the court are a sheriff, a coroner, and a prosecuting attorney. The sheriff represents the executive and administrative power of the state. He must preserve the public peace and can summon the inhabitants as a *posse comitatus* to aid him in doing so. He enforces the judgment of the courts, makes arrests, is responsible for the prisoners, and therefore has charge of the jail. The jailer is generally named by him, and is usually one of the deputies whom he has a right to appoint,— either general or special deputies. He has also certain judicial powers, which are fixed by statute and are much more limited than according to the English common law. In most of the states the constitution limits this important officer's eligibility for re-election. The coroner's chief duty is to investigate, with the aid of a coroner's jury, cases of sudden, mysterious or violent death, deaths in prison, etc. The coroner need know nothing of medicine. In Massachusetts the office was abolished in 1877, and the governor was authorized to entrust doctors with the investigation of deaths. At the head of the administration of affairs is a board of county commissioners or supervisors. As a rule they are separate officers, but the boards are sometimes made up of township commissioners or supervisors. The South Carolina constitution makes their powers extend to "roads, highways, ferries, bridges, and in all matters relating to taxes, disbursements of money for county purposes, and in every other case that may be necessary to the internal improvement and local concerns of the respective counties." The North Carolina constitution expressly gives them also "a general supervision and control of the penal and charitable institutions, schools," etc. To fulfill these duties, the board can levy and collect taxes and contract debts (in both these respects the constitution or the laws limit their actions), can acquire and dispose of property, can adopt by-laws and pass ordinances and punish any violation of them, can make contracts and bring suits (and, of course, can themselves be sued). Many constitutions expressly forbid counties, townships, etc., to lend their credit to private corporations or to take any direct interest in private enterprises. The cause of this is the misuse which has often been made of such a power. Speculators have taken advantage of the exaggerated ideas of the people about the industrial results of railroad schemes. The chancellor — so to speak — of the administration is the county clerk. Where there is no separate recorder or register of deeds, the clerk acts in that capacity. A treasurer has charge of the county funds. Taxes are often levied by separate officials, who are called assessors. The different county officers are not always elected or appointed for the same terms. Where there is a difference in the terms of office, it is especially the sheriff and treasurer who are most frequently chosen.

There is no need of going into detail about the election districts and the already-mentioned school-districts, because these are not organizations with a separate life of their own.

§ 101. TOWNS AND TOWNSHIPS. The town-system has worked so well in the New England states that it has been adopted by several of the middle and most of the western states, and has recently begun to find favor in the south. A county is divided into districts of from four to six miles square, called a town or township, and forming a body corporate. Its self-government extends to all local affairs, and rests on the broadest democratic basis. Here democratic self-government, as it existed in the city-republics of antiquity, again asserts itself against the representative system. Public affairs are discussed and decided upon in the town meeting, and every inhabitant who has a vote under the state laws is entitled to attend and to vote at the town meeting. In the announcement of a town meeting, all the questions that will be presented for discussion must be clearly set forth, so that everybody may have time to consider and form an opinion. The meetings are usually held in the largest village, or in the one nearest the centre. Populous towns, indeed, have a hall of their own for this purpose, called the town hall. Where there is none such, the church or the school-house usually serves as a meeting place. The meeting is presided over by a chairman, who is called, in the New England states, a moderator. The duties and powers of the town embrace levying and collecting taxes on the basis of assessments made by the town officials; building and maintaining roads and bridges; police; care of the poor; the school system, under the control of the state school laws; the conduct of all elections, etc. The town officials are generally elected by ballot for one year, but in some states for a longer time. The board of county commissioners finds its parallel in a board of selectmen or trustees. The fact deserves especial mention, that at the close of the year they make a general statement of accounts, and at the same time an estimate of the expenditures of the next year, which serves as a basis for the tax levy. Taxes are levied by a board of assessors, and collected by a "tax-collector." The town finances are managed by a treasurer. The selectmen are often at the same time assessors and commissioners of the poor. The town clerk often holds also the office of treasurer. The clerk is a very important officer. He not only records the proceedings and conclusions of the town meetings and of the selectmen, but also the birth, marriage and death statistics of the town. School affairs are put in charge of a committee. The officers in charge of the streets are called surveyors or road masters. The police officials are called constables.

§ 102. CITIES. In 1873, a famous and highly respected American said: "It is not only true that we have not created or adopted any municipal system, but it is also true that we have not, except in the past two years, studied the great city problem, much less gained any true conception of the principles and methods best adapted to a great city government. . . . Surely nothing else on this continent has been so badly managed, or is in a condition at once so dangerous or so disgraceful."[1] Since there is no general American municipal system, it is not possible to sketch in a few lines a correct outline of city government and management. Apart from a few facts of a general nature, the differences are so many and so essential that generalization is barred. I must content myself with a few general remarks, chiefly of a historical character, which may serve to explain and establish the assertion I have quoted. The larger cities are especially to be considered in this matter, partly because it is in them that the evils due to the system, or lack of system, have come most clearly to light, and partly because it is they which make the problem of municipal government a question of the first rank. The germs of the weeds which have sprouted up so exuberantly can also

[1] D. B. Eaton, *Municipal Government*, Journal of Social Science, 1873, p. 6.

generally be found in cities of the second and third rank. If the germs have not developed in as startling a way, this is not due to the virtue of the inhabitants. Civic virtue — outside of the mushroom mining and railroad cities of the far west — nowhere rises high above or falls far below the average level. In these smaller cities the evils are less, on account of all kinds of accidental circumstances, and especially because the capacity of development of these germs has a fixed relation to the size of the community.

The war of independence and its general political results did not change the basis of municipal affairs. The cities lived quietly along under their royal charters. It was only in the third decade of the present century that a revolution began. It was not by chance that it coincided in time with the first great aggressive movement of the slave-holders' aristocracy in the battle over Missouri. The growth of the slave-holding power and the radicalization of democracy in the free states kept equal pace. Each was one of the conditions of the other. The farther the radicalization of democracy proceeded, the more the statesman had to make room for the professional politician, able only in the little tricks of party politics, and often a demagogue of the first water. And the more the people changed the leadership of statesmen for the rule of these professional politicians and demagogues, the easier did the slavocracy find it to carry through its demands. It therefore most energetically supported the development of this tendency in the north. The infusion of radical democratic principles into municipal life was the root of all the evils under which the administration of the larger cities sickened more and more, until the condition of New York became entirely too monstrous, and with the overthrow of the city government of 1870, thinking people began to turn their serious attention to this question.

It was forgotten that the city of modern times is only an economic and social community, and not also a political one, as the city of the Middle Ages was. As there was no general system of city government, but each city had its own charter, and special laws could be passed any moment on any matter, the cities — especially the large ones — found frequent opportunity to get greater powers at the expense of the state.[1] At the same time the doctrine that the franchise is a natural right of every man became more and more the basis of municipal institutions. The mayor, the aldermen and the council (or common council) were elected directly by the people, and the vote of the lowest scamp counted just as much as that of the greatest merchant prince. Whoever knew how to cajole the masses, who contribute little or nothing to the public burdens, could take the purse of the city into his hands, — a booty great enough to allure both political parties. Instead of the common good, party interests were more and more made paramount in the city elections. The frequent recurrence of the elections, often each year, made it still easier to thrust deep into civic life the dragon-seed of partisanship, while the necessary continuity disappeared more and more from the adminis-

---

[1] "There has been no greater legislative abuse, no more prolific source of fraud, pillage and litigation, than the accumulation of special city and village laws. In New York, for example, in each of the four years succeeding 1867, the number and bulk of such laws enacted have, I think, exceeded all similar legislation in England, since the enactment of the general municipal corporations act in 1835. In 1870 the legislature of New York passed thirty-nine special laws for the city of Brooklyn alone!" Eaton, p. 12.

"We have too much surrendered the sovereignty of the states to the claims of cities and villages." *Ibid.*, p. 9.

tration of city affairs, and the business experience of the officials became steadily less. City offices, like those of the state and Union, were regarded as spoils of the victorious party, with which the faithful partisan was to be paid and a new horde of " working " and " practical " politicians was to be allured. The method of appointment was often such that no one could well be made responsible for a bad official, and the consequence of this and of the spoils system in general was that year after year a more doubtful class of persons filled the city offices. The principal official task was not the fulfillment of official duties, but the doing of political work; for whoever forfeited the favor of the local party-leaders also lost his office, and that favor depended upon how much a man was worth to the party. The washed or unwashed ward-politician, whose headquarters were usually a tap-room, drove the man of judgment and common sense entirely out of the field, and the city administration steadily developed into a real rat-pit of demagogues of all sorts and of every grade, from the man who used city politics only as a ladder by which to mount to state or national power, down to the insatiable thief whose first stolen million only inflamed his desire for the second. The better elements either really could not stem the increasing laxity, or they did not know how to take hold of matters, or they did not make a single serious effort to bring about a thorough-going reform. It is undoubtedly due in no small degree to the extreme optimism of the American people that this evil could gain such proportions. To this was added a stubborn unwillingness to give up the deep-rooted and beloved doctrine that the rights of man must be the foundation of municipal institutions as well as of national. As long as evils can become much worse than they are, Americans are not easily persuaded to consider them, and to undertake with energy and earnestness reforms which involve substantial changes. But the principal cause was unquestionably that the evil had so affected all sides of municipal life, and had reached such a point, that it had an immense power of resistance. From whatever side the attack was attempted, almost invincible obstacles presented themselves. When election day came the citizen, as a rule, had only a choice between two evils. While he had been attending to his business the thoughts and acts of the politicians had been directed during the whole year upon this decisive day. The world was shared before the citizen arrived on the ground: *i. e.*, the official list of party candidates was prepared, and it remained for him only to vote for one or the other, or else to throw away his ballot. Who had the time, the desire and the commanding position needed to assemble individuals, to organize them and to persuade them to act together, not only independently of the existing party organizations, but in direct opposition to them and the thousands and tens of thousands of mercenary voters upon whom they reckoned? The social, intellectual and moral coherence of the people was becoming less and less, because of the rapid growth of the cities under the influence of modern means of intercourse and production. The destruction of the vitalizing communal spirit, as it had existed in the conservative times of the early republic, a nation of small tradesmen and farmers, was greatly promoted by the immense influx of Europeans of different nations. Power was delivered up to the mass, and the mass was a fluctuating chaos, made up of men from all parts of America and Europe. A no small fraction of it either took not the slightest exception to the devastating rule of the demagogues, or expected to make money out of it. And if the pressure became so great that the sensible and intelgent people once assembled and won a victory at the polls, the politicians soon regained their lost ground; for they kept united and kept hold of the levers of the political machine. But the citizen went back to his business, and the method of civic administration remained unchanged. In other words, the first causes to which the evil was due were allowed to quietly continue. Public opinion, even, was systematically falsified because the leading politicians bought part of the press by the use of the official advertising. The party leaders on both sides circumvented their own parties by corrupt alliances with each other for the distribution of the offices. Finally, the crown was placed upon the whole monstrosity when an elected judge, belonging to the gang, covered up the bold knavery and the comprehensive crimes of its members.

I have intentionally sketched the situation in New York, because the evils in the communal life of great American cities come most clearly to light here. The other municipal pictures show the same general type; only the coloring and tone are not so bright, and in many cities of the third grade they darken into such a harmless grey, that in a few cases even clear eyes would no longer be able to recognize the general type.

New York seemed to be the fittest example to present, not only because here the typical lines are easiest recognized, but because in New York the bow was bent too far by the demagogues, and the catastrophe, which overthrew in 1870 the rule of the leaders of Tammany Hall, gave rise to a serious investigation of the question of city government. Already, indeed, more or less thorough reforms of every sort had been tried and brought about in many states and the initiative given in many cities, but it was only through the occurrences in New York that a general and thorough discussion of the question was caused. This has borne rich fruit, even if everything which might be desired and even everything which is absolutely necessary has not yet been done. The ends sought are to enforce personal responsibility; to make the mayor more independent; to unite the two lawmaking bodies into one; to guard the appointment of officials; to place the most important executive officers under more stringent control; to withdraw certain departments — especially the police and fire departments — wholly from party control; to give the public new and better opportunities to watch the deeds and omissions of the city office-holders; to give wider scope to the principles of civil service reform; to compress within narrower limits the evil of special legislation for cities; and gradually, in place of special charters, to bring to pass general laws for municipalities divided by law into classes.

If the condition of the great cities of America was by far the darkest picture in the public affairs of the United States, and is so still, in part, yet, on the other hand, the development of the last fifteen years on this very subject has given manifold proofs of the great political capacity and the great moral seriousness of the American people. It is very evident that American public affairs can neither be rightly understood nor fairly judged, if they are studied by themselves, that is, without regard to their historical development. This cannot be urged with too much emphasis, although the doctrine may seem, on account of its generally recognized validity, only a trite truth. Politically and socially the United States are in all essential particulars a community so like the European civilized world, that Europeans almost always fall into the error of judging about transatlantic affairs simply by comparing them with the corresponding European relations and institutions, and so, in spite of the unconditional recognition of this doctrine, they examine and criticise America from European stand-points. They can readily enumerate the essential facts which have made, and must make, the United States, politically and socially, a *sui-generis* civilized state, but they almost never take these facts into consideration in the right way and at their real worth when this theoretical knowledge is applied to concrete questions. This requires, indeed, a long life among Americans, and long work with them; for the history of the old world presents no analogies, and it is therefore only when guided by a thousand single instances of daily life, by direct personal perception and by experience, that one can fully understand the constant and all-pervading influence of those factors which are peculiar to the new world. These factors, developed to a high degree, point out the goal to be reached as well as the best way to reach it, because they form its positive basis. The more comprehensive and thorough one's knowledge is of the conditions under which the United States have attained their present social and political *status*, the more convinced will one become, despite all sharp criticism of individual instances, that a judgment of the whole phenomenon must be embodied in these words: no people of ancient or modern times has shown a greater genius for founding a state.

CONSTITUTION OF THE UNITED STATES — 1787.

NOTE: The figures after the different clauses refer to the pages of the book.

We the People of the United States, in Order to form a more perfect Union, establish Justice, insure domestic Tranquility, provide for the common defence, promote the general Welfare, and secure the Blessings of Liberty to ourselves and our Posterity, do ordain and establish this CONSTITUTION for the United States of America. 37, 47.

ARTICLE I.

SECTION 1. All legislative Powers herein granted shall be vested in a Congress of the United States, which shall consist of a Senate and House of Representatives. 112.

SECTION 2. The House of Representatives shall be composed of Members chosen every second Year by the People of the several States, and the Electors in each State shall have the Qualifications requisite for Electors of the most numerous Branch of the State Legislature. 70, 71, 72.

No Person shall be a Representative who shall not have attained to the Age of twenty-five Years, and been seven Years a Citizen of the United States, and who shall not, when elected, be an Inhabitant of that State in which he shall be chosen. 80.

Representatives and direct Taxes shall be apportioned among the several States which may be included within this Union, according to their respective Numbers, which shall be determined by adding to the whole Number of Free persons, including those bound to Service for a Term of Years, and excluding Indians not taxed, three fifths of all other Persons. The actual Enumeration shall be made within three Years after the first Meeting of the Congress of the United States, and within every subsequent Term of ten Years, in such Manner as they shall by Law direct. The Number of Representatives shall not exceed one for every thirty Thousand, but each State shall have at Least one Representative; and until such enumeration shall be made, the State of New Hampshire shall be entitled to chuse three, Massachusetts eight, Rhode Island and Providence Plantations one, Connecticut five, New York six, New Jersey four, Pennsylvania eight, Delaware one, Maryland six, Virginia ten, North Carolina five, South Carolina five, and Georgia three. 73 (note 2), 75, 118.

When vacancies happen in the Representation from any State, the Executive Authority thereof shall issue Writs of Election to fill such Vacancies. 70.

The House of Representatives shall chuse their Speaker and other Officers; and shall have the sole Power of Impeachment. 82, 158.

SECTION 3. The Senate of the United States shall be composed of two Senators from each State, chosen by the Legislature thereof, for six Years; and each Senator shall have one Vote. 70, 79.

Immediately after they shall be assembled in Consequence of the first Election, they shall be divided as equally as may be into three Classes. The seats of the Senators of the first Class shall be vacated at the Expiration of the second year, of the second Class at the Expiration of the fourth Year, and of the third Class at the Expiration of the sixth Year, so that one-third may be chosen every second Year; and if Vacancies happen by Resignation, or otherwise, during the Recess of the Legislature of any State, the Executive thereof may make temporary Appointments until the next Meeting of the Legislature, which shall then fill such Vacancies. 70.

No Person shall be a Senator who shall not have attained to the Age of thirty Years, and been nine Years a Citizen of the United States, and who shall not, when elected, be an Inhabitant of that State for which he shall be chosen. 80.

The Vice President of the United States shall be President of the Senate, but shall have no Vote, unless they be equally divided. 81.

The Senate shall chuse their other Officers and also a President pro tempore, in the Absence of the Vice President, or when he shall exercise the Office of President of the United States. 81.

The Senate shall have the sole Power to try all Impeachments. When sitting for that Purpose, they shall be on Oath or Affirmation. When the President of the United States is tried, the Chief Justice shall preside: and no Person shall be convicted without the Concurrence of two thirds of the Members present. 158, 162.

Judgment in Cases of Impeachment shall not extend further than to removal from Office, and disqualification to hold and enjoy any Office of honor, Trust or Profit under the United States: but the Party convicted shall nevertheless be liable and subject to Indictment, Trial, Judgment and Punishment, according to Law. 161.

SECTION 4. The Times, Places and manner of holding Elections for Senators and Representatives, shall be prescribed in each State by the Legislature thereof; but the Congress may at any time by Law make or alter such Regulations, except as to the Places of chusing Senators. 76.

The Congress shall assemble at least once in every Year, and such Meeting shall be on the first Monday in December, unless they shall by Law appoint a different Day. 81.

SECTION 5. Each House shall be the Judge of the Elections, Returns and Qualifications of its own Members, and a Majority of each shall constitute a Quorum to do Business; but a smaller Number may adjourn from day to day, and may be authorized to compel the Attendance of absent Members, in such Manner, and under such Penalties as each House may provide. 100.

Each House may determine the Rules of its Proceedings, punish its Members for disorderly Behaviour, and, with the Concurrence of two thirds, expel a Member. 101.

Each House shall keep a Journal of its Proceedings, and from time to time publish the same, excepting such Parts as may in their Judgment require Secrecy; and the Yeas and Nays of the Members of either House on any question shall, at the Desire of one fifth of those present, be entered on the Journal. 108.

Neither House, during the Session of Congress, shall, without the Consent of the other, adjourn for more than three days, nor to any other Place than that in which the two Houses shall be sitting. 82.

SECTION 6. The Senators and Representatives shall receive a Compensation for their services, to be ascertained by Law, and paid out of the Treasury of the United States. They shall in all Cases, except Treason, Felony and Breach of the Peace, be privileged from Arrest during their Attendance at the Session of their respective Houses, and in going to and returning from the same; and for any Speech or Debate in either House, they shall not be questioned in any other Place. 104, 104 (note).

No Senator or Representative shall, during the Time for which he was elected, be appointed to any civil Office under the Authority of the United States, which shall have been created, or the Emoluments whereof shall have been encreased during such time; and no Person holding any Office under the United States, shall be a Member of either House during his Continuance in Office. 106.

Section 7. All bills for raising Revenue shall originate in the House of Representatives; but the Senate may propose or concur with Amendments as on other Bills. 132, 133.

Every Bill which shall have passed the House of Representatives and the Senate, shall, before it become a Law, be presented to the President of the United States. If he approve he shall sign it, but if not he shall return it, with his Objections to that House in which it shall have originated, who shall enter the Objections at large on their Journal, and proceed to reconsider it. If after such Reconsideration two thirds of that House shall agree to pass the Bill, it shall be sent, together with the Objections, to the other House, by which it shall likewise be reconsidered, and if approved by two thirds of that House, it shall become a Law. But in all such Cases the Votes of both Houses shall be determined by yeas and Nays, and the Names of the Persons voting for and against the Bill shall be entered on the Journal of each House respectively. If any Bill shall not be returned by the President within ten Days (Sundays excepted) after it shall have been presented to him, the Same shall be a Law, in Like Manner as if he had signed it, unless the Congress by their Adjournment prevent its Return, in which Case it shall not be a Law. 112, 113 (note).

Every Order, Resolution, or Vote to which the Concurrence of the Senate and House of Representatives may be necessary (except on a question of Adjournment) shall be presented to the President of the United States; and before the Same shall take Effect, shall be approved by him, or being disapproved by him, shall be repassed by two thirds of the Senate and House of Representatives, according to the Rules and Limitations prescribed in the Case of a Bill. 113 (note).

SECTION 8. The Congress shall have Power to lay and collect Taxes, Duties, Imposts and Excises, to pay the Debts and provide for the common Defence and general Welfare of the United States; but all Duties, Imposts and Excises shall be uniform throughout the United States; 117, 118.

To borrow Money on the credit of the United States; 62 (note), 122.

To regulate Commerce with foreign Nations, and among the several States, and with the Indian Tribes; 136.

To establish an uniform Rule of Naturalization, and uniform Laws on the subject of Bankruptcies throughout the United States; 149.

To coin Money, regulate the Value thereof, and of foreign Coin, and fix the Standard of Weights and Measures; 124, 150.

To provide for the Punishment of counterfeiting the Securities and current Coin of the United States; 154.

To establish Post Offices and post Roads; 150.

To promote the Progress of Science and useful Arts, by securing for limited Times to Authors and Inventors the exclusive Right to their respective Writings and Discoveries; 151.

To constitute Tribunals inferior to the supreme Court; 153.

To define and punish Piracies and Felonies committed on the high Seas, and Offences against the Law of Nations; 153, 163, 200.

To declare War, grant Letters of Marque and Reprisal,

and make Rules concerning Captures on Land and Water; 46 (note), 62 (note), 164, 166, 194, 200, 205.

To raise and support Armies, but no Appropriation of Money to that Use shall be for a longer Term than two Years; 134, 167.

To provide and maintain a Navy; 167.

To make Rules for the Government and Regulation of the land and naval Forces; 171.

To provide for calling forth the Militia to execute the Laws of the Union, suppress Insurrections and repel Invasions; 170.

To provide for organizing, arming, and disciplining, the Militia, and for governing such Part of them as may be employed in the Service of the United States, reserving to the States respectively, the Appointment of the Officers, and the Authority of training the Militia according to the discipline prescribed by Congress; 169, 170.

To exercise exclusive Legislation in all Cases whatsoever, over such District (not exceeding ten Miles square) as may, by Cession of particular States, and the Acceptance of Congress, become the Seat of the Government of the United States, and to exercise like Authority over all Places purchased by the Consent of the Legislature of the State in which the Same shall be, for the Erection of Forts, Magazines, Arsenals, dock-Yards, and other needful Buildings;—And 172, 174.

To make all Laws which shall be necessary and proper for carrying into Execution the foregoing Powers, and all other Powers vested by this Constitution in the Government of the United States, or in any Department or Officer thereof. 45, 54, 158.

SECTION 9. The Migration or Importation of such Persons as any of the States now existing shall think proper to admit, shall not be prohibited by the Congress prior to the Year one thousand eight hundred and eight, but a Tax or duty may be imposed on such Importation, not exceeding ten dollars for each Person. 19.

The Privilege of the writ of Habeas Corpus shall not be suspended, unless when in Cases of Rebellion or Invasion the public Safety may require it. 196.

No Bill of Attainder or ex post facto Law shall be passed. 156, 223.

No Capitation, or other direct, tax shall be laid, unless in proportion to the Census or Enumeration herein before directed to be taken. 118.

No Tax or Duty shall be laid on Articles exported from any State. 118.

No Preference shall be given by any Regulation of Commerce or Revenue to the Ports of one State, over those of another: nor shall Vessels bound to, or from, one State, be obliged to enter, clear, or pay Duties in another. 148.

No Money shall be drawn from the Treasury, but in Consequence of Appropriations made by Law; and a regular Statement and Account of the Receipts and Expenditures of all public Money shall be published from time to time. 133.

No Title of Nobility shall be granted by the United States: And no Person holding any Office of Profit or Trust under them, shall, without the Consent of the Congress, accept of any present, Emolument, Office, or Title, of any kind whatever, from any King, Prince, or foreign State. 106, 225.

SECTION 10. No State shall enter into any Treaty, Alliance, or Confederation; grant Letters of Marque and Reprisal; coin Money; emit Bills of Credit; make any Thing but gold and silver Coin a Tender in Payment of Debts; pass any Bill of Attainder, ex post facto Law, or

Law impairing the Obligation of Contracts, or grant any Title of Nobility. 123, 164, 166, 224, 225, 231.

No State shall, without the Consent of the Congress, lay any Imposts or Duties on Imports or Exports, except what may be absolutely necessary for executing its inspection Laws; and the net Produce of all Duties and Imposts, laid by any State on Imports or Exports, shall be for the Use of the Treasury of the United States; and all such Laws shall be subject to the Revision and Controul of the Congress. 120, 149 (note).

No State shall, without the Consent of Congress, lay any Duty of Tonnage, keep Troops, or Ships of War in time of Peace, enter into any Agreement or Compact with any other State, or with a foreign Power, or engage in War, unless actually invaded, or in such imminent Danger as will not admit of delay. 120, 164, 165, 167.

ARTICLE II.

SECTION 1. The executive Power shall be vested in a President of the United States of America. 82.

He shall hold his Office during the Term of four years, and, together with the Vice President, chosen for the same Term, be elected, as follows:

Each State shall appoint, in such Manner as the Legislature thereof may direct, a Number of Electors, equal to the whole Number of Senators and Representatives to which the State may be entitled in the Congress: but no Senator or Representative, or Person holding an Office of Trust or Profit under the United States, shall be appointed an Elector. 85.

The Congress may determine the Time of chusing the Electors, and the Day on which they shall give their Votes; which day shall be the same throughout the United States. 85.

No person except a natural born Citizen, or a Citizen of the United States, at the time of the Adoption of this Constitution, shall be eligible to the Office of President; neither shall any Person be eligible to that office who shall not have attained to the Age of thirty five Years, and been fourteen Years a Resident within the United States. 84, 84 (note).

In Case of the Removal of the President from Office, or of his Death, Resignation or Inability to discharge the Powers and Duties of the said Office, the Same shall devolve on the Vice President, and the Congress may by Law provide for the Case of Removal, Death, Resignation or Inability, both of the President and Vice President, declaring what Officer shall then act as President, and such Officer shall act accordingly, until the Disability be removed, or a President shall be elected. 83.

The President shall, at stated Times, receive for his Services, a Compensation, which shall neither be encreased nor diminished during the period for which he shall have been elected, and he shall not receive within that Period any other Emolument from the United States, or any of them. 106.

Before he enter on the Execution of his Office, he shall take the following Oath or Affirmation:—" I do solemnly swear (or affirm) that I will faithfully execute the Office of President of the United States, and will to the best of my Ability, preserve, protect and defend the Constitution of the United States." 45.

SECTION 2. The President shall be Commander in Chief of the Army and Navy of the United States, and of the Militia of the several States, when called into the actual Service of the United States; he may require the Opinion, in writing, of the principal Officer in each of the executive Departments, upon any Subject relating to the

Duties of their respective Offices, and he shall have Power to grant Reprieves and Pardons for Offenses against the United States, except in Cases of Impeachment. 91, 162, 192, 210, 211 (note 4).

He shall have Power, by and with the Advice and Consent of the Senate, to make Treaties, provided two thirds of the Senators present concur; and he shall nominate, and by and with the Advice and Consent of the Senate, shall appoint Ambassadors, other public Ministers and Consuls, Judges of the supreme Court, and all other Officers of the United States, whose Appointments are not herein otherwise provided for, and which shall be established by Law: but the Congress may by Law vest the Appointment of such inferior Officers, as they think proper, in the President alone, in the Courts of Law, or in the Heads of Departments. 98, 199, 201, 207.

The President shall have Power to fill up all Vacancies that may happen during the recess of the Senate, by granting Commissions which shall expire at the End of their next Session. 209.

SECTION 3. He shall from time to time give the Congress Information of the state of the Union, and recommend to their Consideration such Measures as he shall judge necessary and expedient. 114.

He may, on extraordinary Occasions, convene both Houses, or either of them, and, in Case of Disagreement between them, with Respect to the Time of Adjournment, he may adjourn them to such Time as he shall think proper; he shall receive Ambassadors and other public Ministers; he shall take Care that the Laws be faithfully executed, and shall Commission all the Officers of the United States. 44, 81 (and note 2), 199, 209.

SECTION 4. The President, Vice President and all civil Officers of the United States, shall be removed from Office on Impeachment for, and Conviction of, Treason, Bribery. or other high Crimes and Misdemeanors. 159.

ARTICLE III.

SECTION 1. The judicial Power of the United States, shall be vested in one supreme Court, and in such inferior Courts as the Congress may from time to time ordain and establish. The Judges, both of the supreme and inferior Courts, shall hold their Offices during good Behaviour, and shall, at stated Times, receive for their Services, a Compensation, which shall not be diminished during their Continuance in Office. 60, 96, 98 (note), 106.

SECTION 2. The judicial Power shall extend to all Cases, in Law and Equity, arising under this Constitution, the Laws of the United States, and Treaties made, or which shall be made, under their Authority;—to all Cases affecting Ambassadors, other public Ministers and Consuls;—to all Cases of admiralty and maritime Jurisdiction;—to Controversies between two or more States;—to Controversies to which the United States shall be a Party;—between a State and Citizens of another State;—between Citizens of different States;—between Citizens of the same State claiming Lands under Grants of different States, and between a State, or the Citizens thereof, and foreign States, Citizens or subjects. 60, 154, 215.

In all Cases affecting Ambassadors, other public Ministers and Consuls, and those in which a State shall be Party, the supreme Court shall have original Jurisdiction. In all the other Cases before mentioned, the supreme Court shall have appellate Jurisdiction, both as to Law and Fact, with such Exceptions, and under such Regulations as the Congress shall make. 66 (note). 221, 222.

The Trial of all Crimes, except in Cases of Impeachment, shall be by Jury; and such Trial shall be held in the State where the said Crimes shall have been committed; but when not committed within any State, the Trial shall be at such Place or Places as the Congress may by Law have directed. 223.

SECTION 3. Treason against the United States, shall consist only in levying War against them, or in adhering to their Enemies, giving them Aid and Comfort. No Person shall be convicted of Treason unless on the Testimony of two Witnesses to the same overt Act, or on Confession in open Court. 154.

The Congress shall have Power to declare the Punishment of Treason, but no Attainder of Treason shall work Corruption of Blood, or Forfeiture except during the Life of the Person attainted. 154.

ARTICLE IV.

SECTION 1. Full Faith and Credit shall be given in each State to the public Acts, Records, and judicial Proceedings of every other State. And the Congress may by general Laws prescribe the Manner in which such Acts, Records and Proceedings shall be proved, and the Effect thereof. 243.

SECTION 2. The Citizens of each State shall be entitled to all Privileges and Immunities of Citizens in the several States. 247, 249.

A person charged in any State with Treason, Felony, or other Crime, who shall flee from Justice, and be found in another State, shall on Demand of the executive Authority of the State from which he fled, be delivered up to be removed to the State having Jurisdiction of the Crime. 156, 245.

No Person held to Service or Labour in one State, under the Laws thereof, escaping into another, shall, in Consequence of any Law or Regulation therein, be discharged from such Service or Labour, but shall be delivered up on Claim of the Party to whom such Service or Labour may be due. 246 (note 2).

SECTION 3. New States may be admitted by the Congress into this Union; but no new State shall be formed or erected within the Jurisdiction of any other State; nor any State be formed by the Junction of two or more States, or Parts of States, without the Consent of the Legislatures of the States concerned as well as of the Congress. 185.

The Congress shall have Power to dispose of and make all needful Rules and Regulations respecting the Territory or other Property belonging to the United States; and nothing in this Constitution shall be so construed as to Prejudice any Claims of the United States, or of any particular State. 176.

SECTION 4. The United States shall guarantee to every State in this Union a Republican Form of Government, and shall protect each of them against Invasion; and on Application of the Legislature, or of the Executive (when the Legislature cannot be convened) against domestic Violence. 165, 171, 236.

ARTICLE V.

The Congress, whenever two thirds of both Houses shall deem it necessary, shall propose Amendments to this Constitution, or, on the Application of the Legislatures of two thirds of the several States, shall call a Convention for proposing Amendments, which, in either case, shall be valid to all Intents and Purposes, as Part of this Constitution, when ratified by the Legislatures of three fourths of the several States, or by Conventions in three fourths thereof, as the one or the other Mode of Ratification may be proposed by the Congress; Provided that no Amendment which may be made prior to the Year One thousand eight hundred and eight shall in any Manner affect the first and fourth Clauses in the Ninth Section of the first Article; and that no State, without its Consent, shall be deprived of its equal Suffrage in the Senate. 52. 52 (note), 262.

ARTICLE VI.

All Debts contracted and Engagements entered into, before the Adoption of this Constitution, shall be as valid against the United States under this Constitution, as under the Confederation. 122.

This Constitution, and the Laws of the United States which shall be made in Pursuance thereof; and all Treaties made, or which shall be made, under the Authority of the United States, shall be the supreme Law of the Land; and the Judges in every State shall be bound thereby, anything in the Constitution or Laws of any State to the Contrary notwithstanding. 43, 205.

The Senators and Representatives before mentioned, and the Members of the several State Legislatures, and all executive and judicial Officers, both of the United States and of the several States, shall be bound by Oath or Affirmation, to support this Constitution; but no religious Test shall ever be required as a Qualification to any Office or public Trust under the United States. 225.

ARTICLE VII.

The ratification of the Conventions of nine States, shall be sufficient for the Establishment of this Constitution between the States so ratifying the Same. 23.

DONE in Convention by the Unanimous Consent of the States present the Seventeenth Day of September in the Year of our Lord one thousand seven hundred and

Eighty seven, and of the Independence of the United States of America the Twelfth. IN WITNESS whereof We have hereunto subscribed our Names.

Go: WASHINGTON —
Presidt. and Deputy from Virginia.

NEW HAMPSHIRE.

JOHN LANGDON, NICHOLAS GILMAN.

MASSACHUSETTS.

NATHANIEL GORHAM, RUFUS KING.

CONNECTICUT.

WM. SAM'L. JOHNSON, ROGER SHERMAN.

NEW YORK.

ALEXANDER HAMILTON.

NEW JERSEY.

WIL: LIVINGSTON, WM. PATERSON,
DAVID BREARLEY, JONA. DAYTON.

PENNSYLVANIA.

B. FRANKLIN, THOS. FITZSIMONS,
THOMAS MIFFLIN, JARED INGERSOLL,
ROBT. MORRIS, JAMES WILSON,
GEO. CLYMER, GOUV. MORRIS.

DELAWARE.

GEO. READ, RICHARD BASSETT,
GUNNING BEDFORD, Jun., JACO: BROOM,
JOHN DICKINSON.

MARYLAND.

JAMES MCHENRY, DAN. CARROLL,
DAN. JENIFER, of St. Thomas.

VIRGINIA.

JOHN BLAIR, JAMES MADISON, Jr.

NORTH CAROLINA.

WM. BLOUNT, HUGH WILLIAMSON,
RICH'D DOBBS SPEIGHT.

SOUTH CAROLINA.

J. RUTLEDGE, CHARLES PINCKNEY,
CHARLES COTESWORTH PINCKNEY, PIERCE BUTLER.

GEORGIA.

WILLIAM FEW, ABR. BALDWIN.

Attest: WILLIAM JACKSON, *Secretary*.

ARTICLES IN ADDITION TO, AND AMENDMENT OF, THE CONSTITUTION OF THE UNITED STATES OF AMERICA, PROPOSED BY CONGRESS, AND RATIFIED BY THE LEGISLATURES OF THE SEVERAL STATES PURSUANT TO THE FIFTH ARTICLE OF THE ORIGINAL CONSTITUTION. 28.

ARTICLE I.

Congress shall make no law respecting an establishment of religion, or prohibiting the free exercise thereof; or abridging the freedom of speech, or of the press; or the right of the people peaceably to assemble, and to petition the Government for a redress of grievances. 29, 50 (note), 226, 228, 229.

ARTICLE II.

A well regulated Militia, being necessary to the security of a free State, the right of the people to keep and bear Arms, shall not be infringed. 29, 50 (note), 230.

ARTICLE III.

No Soldier shall, in time of peace, be quartered in any house, without the consent of the Owner, nor in time of war, but in a manner to be prescribed by law. 29, 50 (note), 171.

ARTICLE IV.

The right of the people to be secure in their persons, houses, papers, and effects, against unreasonable searches and seizures, shall not be violated, and no Warrants shall issue, but upon probable cause, supported by Oath or affirmation, and particularly describing the place to be searched, and the persons or things to be seized. 29, 50 (note), 251, 257.

ARTICLE V.

No person shall be held to answer for a capital, or otherwise infamous crime, unless on a presentment or indictment of a Grand Jury, except in cases arising in the land or naval forces, or in the Militia, when in actual service in time of War or public danger; nor shall any person be subject for the same offense to be twice put in jeopardy of life or limb; nor shall be compelled in any Criminal Case to be a witness against himself, nor be deprived of life, liberty, or property, without due process of law; nor shall private property be taken for public use, without just compensation. 29, 50 (note), 251, 258, 261 (note).

ARTICLE VI.

In all criminal prosecutions, the accused shall enjoy the right to a speedy and public trial, by an impartial jury of the State and district wherein the crime shall have been committed, which district shall have been previously ascertained by law, and to be informed of the nature and cause of the accusation; to be confronted with the witnesses against him; to have compulsory process for obtaining witnesses in his favor, and to have the Assistance of Counsel for his defense. 29, 50 (note), 251, 258.

ARTICLE VII.

In suits at common law, where the value in controversy shall exceed twenty dollars, the right of trial by Jury shall be preserved, and no fact tried by a jury shall be otherwise re-examined in any Court of the United States, than according to the rules of the common law. 29, 50 (note), 222, 251, 261.

ARTICLE VIII.

Excessive bail shall not be required, nor excessive fines imposed, nor cruel and unusual punishments inflicted. 29, 50 (note), 251, 258, 261.

ARTICLE IX.

The enumeration in the Constitution, of certain rights, shall not be construed to deny or disparage others retained by the people. 29.

ARTICLE X.

The powers not delegated to the United States by the Constitution, nor prohibited by it to the States, are reserved to the States respectively, or to the people. 29, 51 (and note), 53, 54, 55.

ARTICLE XI.

The Judicial power of the United States shall not be construed to extend to any suit in law or equity, commenced or prosecuted against one of the United States by Citizens of another State, or by Citizens or Subjects of any Foreign State. 30, 220.

ARTICLE XII.

The Electors shall meet in their respective states, and vote by ballot for President and Vice-President, one of whom, at least, shall not be an inhabitant of the same State with themselves; they shall name in their ballots the person voted for as President, and in distinct ballots the person voted for as Vice-President, and they shall make distinct lists of all persons voted for as President, and of all persons voted for as Vice-President, and of the number of votes for each, which lists they shall sign and certify, and transmit sealed to the seat of the Government of the United States, directed to the President of the Senate; — The President of the Senate shall, in the presence of the Senate and House of Representatives, open all the certificates and the votes shall then be counted; — The person having the greatest number of votes for President, shall be the President, if such number be a majority of the whole number of Electors appointed; and if no person have such majority, then from the persons having the highest numbers not exceeding three on the list of those voted for as President, the House of Representatives shall choose immediately, by ballot, the President. But in choosing the President, the votes shall be taken by states, the representation from each state having one vote; a quorum for this purpose shall consist of a member or members from two-thirds of the states, and a majority of all the states shall be necessary to a choice. And if the House of Representatives, shall not choose a President whenever the right of choice shall devolve upon them, before the fourth day of March next following, then the Vice-President shall act as President, as in the case of the death or other constitutional disability of the President. The person having the greatest number of votes as Vice-President, shall be the Vice-President, if such number be a majority of the whole number of Electors appointed, and if no person have a majority, then from the two highest numbers on the list, the Senate shall choose the Vice-President; a quorum for the purpose shall consist of two-thirds of the whole number of Senators, and a majority of the whole number shall be necessary to a choice. But no person constitutionally ineligible to the office of President shall be eligible to that of Vice-President of the United States. 30, 84, 89.

ARTICLE XIII.

SECTION 1. Neither slavery nor involuntary servitude, except as a punishment for crime whereof the party shall have been duly convicted, shall exist within the United States, or any place subject to their jurisdiction. 30, 31 (note), 230.

SECTION 2. Congress shall have power to enforce this article by appropriate legislation.

ARTICLE XIV.

SECTION 1. All persons born or naturalized in the United States, and subject to the jurisdiction thereof, are citizens of the United States and of the State wherein they reside. No State shall make or enforce any law which shall abridge the privileges or immunities of citizens of the United States; nor shall any State deprive any person of life, liberty, or property, without due process of law; nor deny to any person within its jurisdiction the equal protection of the laws. 30, 250, 251.

SECTION 2. Representatives shall be apportioned among the several States according to their respective numbers, counting the whole number of persons in each State, excluding Indians not taxed. But when the right to vote at any election for the choice of electors for President and Vice President of the United States, Representatives in Congress, the Executive and Judicial officers of a State, or the members of the Legislature thereof, is denied to any of the male inhabitants of such State, being twenty-one years of age, and citizens of the United States, or in any way abridged, except for participation in rebellion, or other crime, the basis of representation therein shall be reduced in the proportion which the number of such male citizens shall bear to the whole number of male citizens twenty-one years of age in such State. 30, 73.

SECTION 3. No person shall be a Senator or Representative in Congress, or elector of President and Vice President, or hold any office, civil or military, under the United States, or under any State, who, having previously taken an oath, as a member of Congress, or as an officer of the United States, or as a member of any State Legislature, or as an executive or judicial officer of any State, to support the Constitution of the United States, shall have engaged in insurrection or rebellion against the same, or given aid or comfort to the enemies thereof. But Congress may by a vote of two-thirds of each House, remove such disability. 30, 80, 100 (note 2).

SECTION 4. The validity of the public debt of the United States, authorized by law, including debts incurred for payment of pensions and bounties for services in suppressing insurrection or rebellion, shall not be questioned. But neither the United States nor any State shall assume or pay any debt or obligation incurred in aid of insurrection or rebellion against the United States, or any claim for the loss or emancipation of any slave; but all such debts, obligations and claims shall be held illegal and void. 30, 122 (note 1).

SECTION 5. The Congress shall have power to enforce, by appropriate legislation, the provisions of this article.

ARTICLE XV.

SECTION 1. The right of citizens of the United States to vote shall not be denied or abridged by the United States or by any State on account of race, color, or previous condition of servitude. 30, 75.

SECTION 2. The Congress shall have power to enforce this article by appropriate legislation.

INDEX.

Adams, John, sedition law passed during his presidency, 229.
Adams, J. Q., on adoption of constitution, 26; elected president by house, 86, note 1.
Admission of new states, 33, 76, note 2, 185.
Albany congress of 1754. 4.
Alien and sedition laws, 40, note 2, 229.
Aliens, non-naturalized, may have franchise, 72.
Amendment of the constitution, 15, 28, 31 (note), 52, 262.
Amendment of state constitutions, 292.
Amendments, ratification of thirteenth, fourteenth and fifteenth, 31. note.
Annapolis convention of 1786, 15.
Appropriations, 131, and note.
Appropriations, statistics of, 135.
Articles of confederation, 3, 8.
Arthur, Chester A., becomes president, 83; negotiates commercial treaties, 204, note.
Arrests, 257.
Assembly, right of, 230.
Attainder, bills of, 223.
Attempts at federation, 4.
Bank of the United States, 126, note 2.
Bearing arms, right of, 230.
Benevolent institutions (state), 284.
Bible in public schools, 309.
Bill of rights, 29, 50, 267.
Bills of attainder, 223.
Brevet rank, 197.
Cabinet, has no executive power, 83; no constitutional existence, 90; no legal or political responsibility, 90
Cabinet in the states, 288.
Calhoun, John C., on nullification, 40.
Capitation taxes (state), 299.

Charters, 233.
Checks and balances, system of, 60.
Church and state, 225, 314.
Citizens of the separate states, 248.
City government, 329.
Civil rights, 257.
Civil service reform, 100, note, 208, note, 256, 275, 290.
Cleveland, Grover, opposes coinage of silver, 124, note.
Clinton, George, opposes ratification of the constitution, 25.
Coins and coinage, 124, note.
Colleges and universities, 313.
Common law in America, 161.
Commerce, 136.
Comity between states, 242.
Committees of congress, 109.
Committees of the whole, 111, note 1.
Compulsory education, 306.
Concurrent jurisdiction of state and federal courts, 212.
Concurrent powers in general, 56; as to taxation, 120; as to trade and commerce, 142, 147.
Condemnation, 253, 261, note 1.
Confederation, articles of, 3, 8.
Conflicts of authority, in general, 58.
Congress (Albany) of 1754, 4; (New York) of 1765, 5; (Philadelphia) of 1774, 5; (do.) of 1775, 6.
Congress, election of its members, 71; its sessions, 81; organization, 81; powers over its own members, 103; judicial functions, 103; privileges and immunities of members, 104; their salaries, 105; procedure, 108; committees, 109, note; general powers, 116; financial tasks, 130; regulates immigration, 148; naturalization, 149; postoffices, 150; its power to build post-roads, 150, note 3; regulates weights and measures, 150; patents and copyrights, 151; its criminal jurisdiction, 153; treason, 154; impeachment, 158; powers as to foreign relations, 163, 199, note 1; war powers, 164, 194; militia, 171; District of Columbia, 172; national property, 174; territories, 175; admission of new states, 185; controls suspension of *habeas corpus*, 196; decides whether state government is republican in form, 238.
Congressional elections, 71.
Conscription. 167.
Constitution, ratification of, 24; amendment of, 52, 262; rules for its interpretation and construction, 55, 116.

Constitutions (state), in general, 266; their constituent parts, 267.
Constitutional conventions (state), 264.
Contracts, 231.
Controversies between states, 219.
Conventions, constitutional (state), 264.
Conventions, national, 87.
Conventions of 1780 (Hartford), 13; of 1786 (Annapolis), 15; of 1787 (Philadelphia), 16, 43.
Copyrights, 152.
Copyrights, international, 153.
Criminal law, congressional powers concerning, 154.
Criminal procedure, 258.
Corporations, municipal, 324.
Court-martials, 197, note 3.
Courts, federal, jurisdiction of, 211; practice and pleading in, 221.
Courts, state, 291.
Courts, territorial, 98, note.
Counties, 325.
County officers, 326.
Dartmouth College case, 235.
Debt, public, 117; statistics of, 126, note 2.
Debts of states, 279.
Declaration of Independence, 7.
Demonetization of silver, 124, note.
Department of justice, organization and work of, 95, note.
Departments, the executive, 95, and note.
Direct taxes, 73, note 2.
District of Columbia, 172.
Division of powers, 67.
Divorce, national law of, suggested, 243.
Due process of law, 252.
Duties on exports, 118, and note.
Duties on imports, statistics of, 121, note 2.
Education, compulsory, 300.
Election of president and vice-president, 85.
Election, presidential, of 1876, 88.
Elections, congressional, 71, 77.
Elective judiciary (state), 292.
Electoral college, 87.
Electoral commission of 1876, 88.
Electoral votes disputed, Missouri in 1821; Michigan in 1827; Wisconsin in 1857; Louisiana in 1873; Florida, South Carolina and Louisiana in 1877, 81.

Electors, presidential, how chosen, 85.
Emancipation proclamation. 115, note 2; 195, **note 1.**
Eminent domain, 253, 261, note 1.
Enabling acts, 187.
Executive departments, 95, and note.
Executive power, belongs wholly to president, 82.
Executive power in the states, 285.
Export duties, 118 and note.
Extradition, in general, 245; cannot be compelled, 246.
Ex post facto laws, 223.
Factory laws, 283.
Federal and state authority, limits of, 56.
Federal courts, jurisdiction of, 211; practice and pleading in, 221.
Federal government, powers of, 53; organization of, 66.
Federal judges, salaries of, 106.
Federation, early attempts at, 4.
Fillmore, Millard, 83.
Finance, 117.
Forestry, 282.
Foreign relations, 163, 198.
Franchise may be given non-naturalized aliens, 72.
Freedom of conscience, 223.
Freedom of the press, 228.
Freedom of speech, 228.
Governor of a state, his functions, 286.
Granger cases, 235.
Grant, U. S., seeks third term nomination, 69, note; recommends purchase of telegraph lines by government, 145, note 2; proposes constitutional amendment providing for non-sectarian public schools, 310, note 2.
Habeas corpus, suspension of, 196.
Hamilton, Alexander, writes the *Federalist*, 24; recommends a national bank, 126, note 2.
Hartford convention of 1780, 13.
Hayes, R. B., how he became president, 90; vetoes law remonetizing silver, 124, note.
Henry, Patrick, opposes unconditional ratification of the constitution, 24.
Historical method, 2.
Homestead exemption, 298, note 2.
Houston, Samuel, 103, note 2.
Illinois, minority representation in, 269, note.
Immigration, 148.

Impeachment, 158.
Implied powers, 54, 116.
Implied restrictions on state action, 271.
Import duties, statistics of, 121, note 2.
Imports, statistics of, 121, note 2.
Income taxes (state), 301.
Independence, declaration of, 7.
Indians, 136, notes 2, 3; 248, note 4.
Individual rights, 251.
Instruction, right of, 78.
Internal improvements, 150, note 3; 276, 280.
Interior department, organization and work of, 95, note.
International copyright, 153.
Interpretation of constitution, rules for, 55, 116.
Jackson, Andrew, his farewell address, 115, note 1; his views on internal improvements, 150, note 3; demoralizes the civil service, 208.
Jefferson, Thomas, opposes the two-chamber system, 20.
Johnson, Andrew, becomes president, 83; his conflict with congress, 93, note.
Johnston, R. N., elected vice-president by senate, 86, note 2.
Judges, federal, hold office during good behavior, 98; their salaries, 100.
Judicial powers of United States, 60.
Jurisdiction, concurrent, of state and federal courts, 212.
Jury, in criminal cases, 259; in civil cases, 261.
Kentucky and Virginia resolutions, 40, note 2.
Laisser faire theory, 280.
Land grants, 178, 276, note, 305.
Lands, national, survey and sale of, 179, note.
Law, due process of, 252.
League (New England) of 1643, 4.
Lee, Robert E., opposes secession, 157.
Legal tender cases, 62, note.
Legal tenders, 122, 125, note 3.
Legislative methods (state), 272.
Legislatures (state), in general, 268; cannot instruct senators, 80.
License and business taxes (state), 302.
Lincoln, Abraham, his emancipation proclamation, 115, note 2; 195, note 1.
Madison, James, aids in writing the *Federalist* and carries ratification in Virginia, 25; his views on conditional ratification, 26;

favors use of general expressions in constitution, 53; champions state rights. 61, note; declares legal tender notes unconstitutional, 125, note 3.
Military academy, West Point, 168, note.
Military affairs, 164, 192.
Militia, 169, 230, 287, note 2.
Minority representation (in Illinois), 269, note.
Monroe, James, on internal improvements, 150, note 3.
Mormonism, 226, note 2.
Morris, Gouverneur, favors ratification of constitution, 27.
Municipal corporations, 324.
National debt, statistics of, 126, note 2.
Naturalization, 149.
National banks, 122.
National sovereignty, 50.
National lands, survey and sale of, 179, note.
National conventions, 87.
Navigation laws, 231.
Naval academy, Annapolis, 163, note.
Navy department, organization and work of, 95, note.
New England league of 1643, 4.
New states, admission of, 33, 76, note 2.
New York and Virginia delay ratifying constitution, 24.
New York congress of 1765, 5.
Nobility, titles of, 225, note 4.
Nomination of candidates for president, 87.
Non-coercion theory, 41.
Non-interference theory, 280.
Normal schools, 310.
Office, tenure of, 61.
Organization of federal government, 66.
Paper money in the United States, history of, 126, note 2.
Parliamentary government, 92, 191, note.
Parliamentary government in the states, 289.
Pardons, 210.
Patents, 151.
People vs. population, 47.
Petition, right of, 230.
Philadelphia congress of 1774, 5.
Philadelphia congress of 1775, 6.
Philadelphia convention of 1787, 16, 43.
Police powers of the states, 142.

Polk, J. K., consults senate before making treaty, 201, note.
Population and area, statistics of, 34.
Population vs. people, 47.
Powers of federal government, 53.
Postoffice department, organization and work of, 95, note.
Practice and pleading in federal courts, 221.
Preamble to the constitution, 37.
President, has all the executive power, 82; election of, 85; his salary, 106; his inaugural address, 115; his general powers, 190; military powers, 192; war-powers, 194; cannot suspend *habeas corpus*, 196; powers as to foreign relations, 199; treaty-power, 200; appointment of officials, 206; pardoning power, 210.
Presidential election of 1876, 86.
" electors, 85.
" messages, 114.
" proclamations, 115.
Private property, taking for public use, 253; dedication to public uses, 254.
Public debt, 117.
Public use of private property, 254.
Public works (state), 284.
Railroads, 145, note 2, 255.
Ratification of constitution, 24.
Re-admission of states, 31, note, 47, 188, note.
Real estate owned by United States, 174.
Reconstruction, 47, 240.
Reform, civil service, 106, note, 208, 256, 275, 290.
Regulation of commerce, 136.
Religious liberty, 225.
Removal of causes, 216, note 2.
Republican form of government, guarantee of, 236.
Resulting powers, 116.
Revenue, federal, statistics of, 121, note 2, 135.
Searches, 257.
Schools, normal, 310.
Schools, public, 304.
Schurz, Carl, his Indian policy, 136, note 3.
Secession, duty of preventing it by force, 45.
" ordinances of, null and void, 46.
" theory of, 41.
Seizures, 257.
Senators, election of, 77; legislatures cannot instruct them, 78.

Seward, W. H., his views on initiative of the house in making appropriations, 132; denies congressional jurisdiction of foreign affairs, 199; as governor of New York refuses request for extradition, 245.
Silver demonetized, 124, note.
Slavery, 18, 19, 175, 230.
Social-political legislation, 283.
Sovereignty of United States, 50.
Special legislation (state), 275.
State department, organization and work of, 95, note.
State courts, 291.
" debts, 279.
" sovereignty, 39, 157.
States, the, readmission of, 31, note, 47, 188, note; their police powers, 142; admisssion to the Union, 185; controversies between them, 219; cannot be sued, 220; their citizenship, 248; constituent parts of their constitutions, 267; their legislative powers, 268; implied restrictions upon them, 271; their legislative methods, 272; special legislation, 275; social-political legislation, 283; impeachment, 285; the executive power, 285; the governor, 286; the cabinet, 288; parliamentary government, 289; courts, 291; amendment of constitutions, 292; taxes in general, 296; capitation tax, 299; income tax, 301; license and business taxes, 302.
Statistics of population and area, 34; of imports, 121, note 2; of federal revenue, 121, note 2, 135; of the national debt, 126, note 2; of appropriations, 135; of land-grants, 276, note.
Stephens, A. H., opposes secession, 157.
Supreme court, packed to reverse legal tender cases, 62, note; its decisions on constitutional questions, 63; limits of its jurisdiction, 66, note; its stability, 69; cannot compel extradition, 246.
System of checks and balances, 60.
Taxation, 117.
" direct, 73, note 2.
" (state), 296, 299, 301, 302.
Territories, 175.
Territorial courts, 98, note.
" government, 184, note.
Test-oath cases, 224, note.
Texas, 190.
Telegraphs, 145, note 2.
Tenure of office, 69.

Tenure of office act, 93, note.
Titles of nobility, 225, note 4.
Tilden, S. J., his claims to the presidency, 90.
Town officers, 328.
Townships, 327.
Trade, regulation of, 136.
Trade-marks, 153.
Treason, 154.
Treasury department, organization and work of, 95, note.
Treaty-power, 200.
Tyler, John, 83.
Universities and colleges, 312.
Vacancies in presidential office, 83, note.
Veto, 113.
Vice-president, his functions, 82; election of, 85.
Virginia and Kentucky resolutions, 40, note 2.
Virginia and New York delay ratifying constitution, 24.
War department, organization and work of, 95, note.
War powers, 194.
Warrants, 258.
Washington, George, on convention of 1787, 16; on ratification of the constitution, 27; his farewell address, 115, note 1; consults senate before making treaty, 201, note 1.
Webster, Daniel, on the territories, 183; on commercial treaties, 204.
Weights and measures, 150.
West Point military academy, 168, note.

www.ingramcontent.com/pod-product-compliance
Lightning Source LLC
Chambersburg PA
CBHW030406230426
43664CB00007BB/766